Tort Law in France

Tort Law in France

Jonas Knetsch

This book was originally published as a monograph in the International Encyclopaedia of Laws/Tort Law.

Founding Editor: Roger Blanpain
General Editor: Frank Hendrickx
Volume Editor: Britt Weyts

Wolters Kluwer

Published by:
Kluwer Law International B.V.
PO Box 316
2400 AH Alphen aan den Rijn
The Netherlands
E-mail: international-sales@wolterskluwer.com
Website: lrus.wolterskluwer.com

Sold and distributed by:
Wolters Kluwer Legal & Regulatory U.S.
7201 McKinney Circle
Frederick, MD 21704
United States of America
E-mail: customer.service@wolterskluwer.com

ISBN 978-94-035-3574-6

e-Book: ISBN 978-94-035-3575-3
web-PDF: ISBN 978-94-035-3580-7

This title is available on www.kluwerlawonline.com

The Author

Jonas Knetsch was born in Potsdam (Germany) in 1982. Before his PhD in Comparative Tort Law, he graduated from the University Panthéon-Assas (Paris, France) and the University of Cologne (Germany).

Jonas Knetsch was a senior lecturer at the University Panthéon-Assas (2012) before being appointed full professor in 2013 following his success in the *concours d'agrégation* in private law. From 2013 to 2017, he held a professorship at the University of Reunion Island where he was largely involved in developing international relations with universities in the Comoros, Madagascar, Mauritius and Mozambique. He is currently a professor at the Jean Monnet University Saint-Étienne, a member of the *Centre de Recherches Critiques sur le Droit* (CERCRID) and visiting professor at the University of Antwerp (2019–2022). As of September 2021, he will be a professor at the Sorbonne Law School (University Paris 1 Panthéon-Sorbonne).

He has published extensively in tort and insurance law as well as in comparative law. As an elected member of the International Academy of Comparative Law, he was the French national reporter during its XXth General Congress in Fukuoka (Japan) on medical liability. He is also a fellow of the European Centre of Tort and Insurance Law (ECTIL) in Vienna. He has recently conducted research projects on tort law and insurance law issues related to self-driving cars and on the interplay of social security, private insurance and tort law compensation.

The Author

Table of Contents

List of Abbreviations

CA	Cour d'appel (*Court of Appeal*)
Cass	Cour de cassation (*French Court of Cassation*)
Civ	Chambre civile (*Civil Chamber of the Court of Cassation*, until 1947)
Civ 1/2/3	1ère / 2e / 3e chambre civile (*First, Second, Third Civil Chamber of the Court of Cassation*)
Com	Chambre commerciale (*Commercial Chamber of the Court of Cassation*)
Crim	Chambre criminelle (*Criminal Chamber of the Court of Cassation*)
CUP	Cambridge University Press
D	Recueil Dalloz
ECJ	European Court of Justice
ERPL	European Review of Private Law
ETL	European Tort Law Yearbook (2001–2009: Springer, since 2010: de Gruyter)
Gaz Pal	Gazette du Palais (LGDJ)
JCP A	La Semaine Juridique. Administration et collectivités territoriales (LexisNexis)
JCP E	La Semaine Juridique. Entreprise et affaires (LexisNexis)
JCP G	La Semaine Juridique. Edition générale (LexisNexis)
JCP N	La Semaine Juridique. Notariale et immobilière (LexisNexis)
JETL	Journal of European Tort Law
OUP	Oxford University Press
Req	Chambre des requêtes (*Chamber of Petitions of the Court of Cassation*, until 1947)
Resp civ assur	Responsabilité civile et assurances
RGAT	Revue générale des assurances terrestres (LGDJ)
RGDA	Revue générale de droit des assurances (LGDJ)

List of Abbreviations

RTD civ	Revue trimestrielle de droit civil (Dalloz)
RTD com	Revue trimestrielle de droit commercial (Dalloz)
ZEuP	Zeitschrift für Europäisches Privatrecht (C.H. Beck)

Preface

For the purpose of this monograph, primarily intended for a non-French speaking public, particular attention has been given to references in the English language. Whenever possible, footnotes and bibliography indicate relevant sources that allow anglophone readers to gain further insight. Additional sources in the French language (standard textbooks and other reference publications) are also referenced in this work.

Truinas and Saint-Étienne, February 2021

General Introduction

§1. General Background of the Country

I. Geography

1. France is a Western European country bounded by the North Sea, the English Channel and the Atlantic Ocean on the north and west, the Mediterranean Sea and the Pyrenees on the south and the Alps and the Rhine River on the east. It is considered one of the oldest and most important nations in the Western world. With a total size of 551,695 km^2 and a population of 67.15 million people (as of 2017), France is the third-largest and third-most populous country in Europe.

2. The European part of France (*France métropolitaine*) is divided into 13 *régions* (including Corsica which has a special legal status) that are subdivided into 96 *départements*. France is one of the countries with the highest number of municipalities. There are more than 36,500 *communes* varying widely in size and area, from major cities like Paris, Marseille, Lyon, Toulouse, Nice and Nantes to small villages with less than ten inhabitants.

3. The French landscape is mostly composed of low-lying plains; highlands, such as the *Massif Central* in the central part of Southern France; and mountain ranges like the Alps and Pyrenees, which form natural borders between France and its neighbouring countries of Switzerland, Italy and Spain and reach heights of 4,810 m (Mont Blanc). France has an important river system consisting of the four major rivers of the Seine, Loire, Garonne and Rhône; the European watershed divides the country into two series of basins (the Atlantic Ocean and North Sea basin and the Mediterranean Sea basin). Due to the diverse landscape, the climate in France is not uniform. Whereas the western part of France has an oceanic climate, the other parts have a semi-continental, mountain or Mediterranean climate.

4. France has overseas territories in South America (French Guiana), the Atlantic Ocean (French Antilles, Saint Pierre and Miquelon), the Pacific Ocean (French Polynesia, New Caledonia and Wallis and Futuna), the Indian Ocean and the Antarctic (Réunion Island, Mayotte and the 'French Southern and Antarctic Lands'). It possesses the second-largest exclusive economic zone in the world, covering 11,035,000 km^2, which is about 2.1% of the total surface area of Earth.

II. History[1]

A. From Gaul to the Emergence of France

5. The territory which is today known as the European part of France corresponds to the region known to the Romans as Gaul. It is inhabited by different ethnic groups, including the Gauls, a group of Celtic peoples speaking Gaulish, one of the now-extinct Continental Celtic languages. The Roman Republic annexed the southern part of Gaul as a province in the late second century BC before conquering the rest of Gaul under the leadership of Julius Caesar in the Gallic Wars (58–50 BC). The culminating moment of the Roman conquest was the Battle of Alesia which ended with a massive victory for Caesar's forces who took advantage of the internal divisions between the Gallic tribes (despite Vercingetorix's late attempt to unite the Gauls against the Roman invasion).

6. After the Roman victory, the Gauls progressively adopted the Roman language, morals and way of life, giving rise to a genuine Gallo–Roman culture characterized by the imperial cult and the emergence of early Christian communities. After the invasions of the Western Roman Empire by Germanic tribes and the Huns (known as the Migration Period), the Roman predominance over Gaul started to decline. The Germanic Franks increasingly took control, and by the end of the fifth century, the Frankish king Clovis had united most of Gaul and had established Paris as the capital of his new kingdom, laying a solid groundwork for more than five centuries of Frankish dominance. Under the reign of the Merovingians and the Carolingians, the Frankish kingdom stretched from the Pyrenees to the North Sea, encompassing large parts of what are today the Netherlands, Switzerland, Austria, Northern Italy and Germany.

7. It was under the reign of Charlemagne (also known as Charles the Great) that the mediaeval Kingdom of France arose from the western part of the Frankish kingdom, West Francia, opening a new era under the aegis of the Capetian dynasty.

B. Rise of the French Monarchy and Early Modern France

8. The decline of the Carolingians coincided with a fragmentation of political power, forcing the kings of France to seek alliances with the powerful princes. Whereas the authority of the kings was more religious than political, the princes of Normandy, Flanders and Languedoc enjoyed extensive authority. It took several centuries for the Capetians to overcome the princes' authority and establish their sovereignty over France. The orderly succession of power from 940 (Hugh Capet)

1. For a comprehensive survey of French history, *see*, for example, Hugh D. Clout (ed.), *Historical Geography of France* (Academic Press 1977); Robert Gildea, *The Past in French History* (Yale University Press 1994); Roger Price, *A Concise History of France* (CUP 3d ed. 2014); Tyler Stovall, *Transnational France: the Modern History of a Universal Nation* (Westview Press 2015); W. Scott Haine, *The History of France* (Greenwood 2d ed. 2019).

to 1328 (Charles IV the Fair) contributed to making the Capetians an eminent royal dynasty family. With the support of the church, the Capetians established a strong central government in France, laying the foundations of a political and economic centralism which is still present today.

9. The extinction of the Capetian dynasty in 1328 and the ascension of the House of Valois to the throne led to a period of great tension which climaxed in the so-called Hundred Years War when the House of Plantagenet, holding the throne of England, also claimed the throne of France. This long-lasting confrontation ended in a victory for the House of Valois and had the effect of strengthening French nationalism and increasing the political clout of the French monarchy. During the period of *Ancien Régime* (from the fifteenth century until the 1789 Revolution), France transformed into a centralized absolute monarchy. While French society opened up through the influence of Renaissance humanism and Protestant Reformation (leading to a violent religious war from 1562 to 1598), the political structures of the country and its economy continued to strengthen. In 1640, the population of Paris rose to 400,000, and France established its first colonial empire with possessions in the Americas, Africa and Asia that were administered by powerful chartered companies (*Compagnie des Indes orientales*, *Compagnie des Indes occidentales*). The political power of France peaked during the reign of Louis XIV, the 'Sun King' (*Roi Soleil*), builder of the Palace of Versailles.

C. *The French Revolution and Napoleon (1789–1815)*

10. The involvement of France in the American Revolutionary War, which ruined the royal finances, together with several years of bad harvests and the increasing isolation of the royal court, who were insensitive to the misery of the people, led to an explosive situation, even among nobles, clergy and the bourgeoisie. When the king's minister of finance asked the Assembly of Notables to approve a new land tax, the assembly instead demanded that the king (Louis XVI) call the Estates-General (*États généraux*), which represented the clergy, the nobility and the rest of France. Contesting the representativeness of the Estates-General, the members of the Third Estate declared themselves a National Assembly and agreed not to separate until they had given France a Constitution. Infuriated by the measures taken by the king against this new assembly, Parisians on 14 July 1789 stormed the Bastille prison, a symbol of royal power, which stored large amounts of weapons and ammunition.

11. While Paris was in a state of anarchy, the National Assembly (the National *Constitutional* Assembly after 9 July 1789) voted in August 1789 for the abolition of privileges and feudalism and in favour of the Declaration of the Rights of Man and of the Citizen (*Déclaration des droits de l'homme et du citoyen*), still an important constitutional source today. Under the Constitution of 3 September 1791, France became a constitutional monarchy under which Louis XVI shared power with the Legislative Assembly, soon replaced by the National Convention, but political tension between a group referred to as Jacobins and another referred to as Girondins undermined their actions.

12. Despite the political and military support given to the king by other European monarchies, the National Convention abolished the monarchy and proclaimed the French First Republic. King Louis XVI was tried, convicted and guillotined in January 1793. The rise of Maximilien Robespierre radicalized the Revolution, culminating in a dictatorship imposed by the Committee of Public Safety (*Comité du Salut Public*) during the Reign of Terror, from 1793 until 1794. After a coup directed against Robespierre (leading to his execution), an executive council known as the Directory (*Directoire*) assumed control of the French state in 1795. Accused of corruption, the Directory collapsed in 1799 in a coup led by Napoleon Bonaparte, who had become a hero of the Revolution through his popular military campaigns during the Revolutionary Wars against Prussia, Great Britain, the Dutch Republic and other monarchies.

13. Napoleon replaced the National Convention with the *Directoire* and, with the approval of a plebiscite, created an executive consisting of three consuls. Political and military power was given to the first consul, an office vested in Napoleon. In 1802, another plebiscite consolidated Napoleon's position as first consul for life; in May 1804, he was approved as Emperor. He centralized power in Paris, governing all French provinces through powerful prefects (*préfets*). In order to unify the nation and to stabilize the political and social situation, he personally supervised the creation of a new civil code drafted by a commission of four eminent jurists, thereby endowing France with modern civil legislation.

D. From the Bourbon Restauration to World War II (1815–1945)

14. The Napoleonic Wars ended with a resounding defeat. Napoleon's troops were largely defeated in the Battle of Nations in 1813, eventually leading to his abdication in April 1814 and his exile to Elba. The return of Napoleon during the Hundred Days War was short-lived, his final defeat at the Battle of Waterloo forcing him to a definitive exile on the remote island of Saint-Helena. In response to the power vacuum left by Napoleon, the monarchy was restored, and Louis XVIII, younger brother of Louis XVI, became the king.

15. Yet the Bourbon Restoration did not completely reestablish France's political influence in Europe. Although Louis XVIII and his successor Charles X passed several reactionary laws and compensated the families of the nobles who lost their propriety during the Revolution, the French parliamentary system limited royal powers so that restrictions to civil rights (such as freedom of press) resembled more or less those in other parts of Europe. The reign of Charles X was overthrown in 1830 in an uprising known as the July Revolution (*Les Trois Glorieuses*). Louis-Philippe d'Orléans, a member of the Orléans branch of the Bourbons, ascended to the throne and ruled as 'King of the French' (*Roi des Français*) and not as 'King of France' (*Roi de France*) as had his predecessors.

16. Revolutionary events ended the July Monarchy under Louis-Philippe and led to the creation of the short-lived French Second Republic (1848–1851). Napoleon's nephew was elected president but he dissolved the National Assembly in a self-coup and reclaimed his uncle's throne as Emperor of the French under the name Napoleon III. The Second Empire (1851–1871) is known for the modernization of the French economy, the rebuilding of Paris under the supervision of the prefect Georges-Eugène Haussmann and the expansion of the overseas empire. Despite his promise of a peaceful reign, Napoleon III became involved in several wars started by foreign states (Crimean War, Second Opium War) and declared war, without political need, on Prussia in 1870. After the French defeat, he was captured and deposed. France as a great power was ruined, leaving the dominant position on the European continent to the new German Empire.

17. Following France's defeat in the Franco-German War (1870–1871), the newly elected French National Assembly proclaimed the Third Republic (*Troisième République*), but the possibility of a return to monarchy remained into the 1880s. Despite the ever-present possibility of a coup, the period of 1870–1914 was one of political moderation. The moderate governments avoided state ownership of industry, provided a social safety net through a progressive income tax and supported a peaceful foreign policy while consolidating a colonial empire that was second in size to Great Britain. France was one of the Triple Entente powers in World War I, fighting alongside the United Kingdom, Russia, Italy, Japan and the United States against Germany and the Central Powers. It regained the Alsace-Lorraine province, lost to Germany in 1871, and occupied the industrial Saar Basin and the Ruhr which were of strategic importance. The Great Depression hit France later and milder than other countries.

18. Germany's invasion of Poland in 1939 caused France, alongside the United Kingdom, to declare war against Germany. After the conquest of Poland, the German army in May 1940 attacked France, carefully avoiding the Maginot Line, a state-of-the-art system of border defences designed to fight off an attack from Germany. Due to military supremacy, the German army succeeded in occupying a substantial part of France. On 22 June 1940, the French government signed an armistice, leaving the south-eastern part of France to a regime under the command of Philippe Pétain, an ageing war hero of World War I. This 'Vichy regime' sought to collaborate with Germany, keeping peace in France to avoid further occupation, albeit at the expense of personal freedom and individual safety.

E. Since 1945

19. During the German occupation, Charles de Gaulle, from his exile in London, gathered forces of French resistance, finding support in some colonies and recognition mostly from Great Britain. When the Allies landed in Normandy and in

Provence, they included 260,000 soldiers from the Free French Forces, assuring France a status as a leading player on the post-war political chessboard. In October 1946, a new Constitution established the Fourth Republic, controlled by chronically unstable governments. After a heavy defeat in the First Indochina War, France faced another anti-colonialist conflict in Algeria. The May 1958 crisis sparked by the seizure of power by French army units led to an important political shift; the National Assembly brought de Gaulle back to power in order to reshape political institutions.

20. Charles de Gaulle established the Fifth Republic with a strengthened presidency and managed to keep France together while taking steps to end the war in Algeria, much to the anger of the European settlers in Algeria (known as *Pieds-Noirs*) and the military, who had supported his return to power. In 1962, de Gaulle granted independence to Algeria and progressively to other French colonies. De Gaulle resigned in 1969 after losing a referendum in which he proposed more decentralization.

21. As a permanent member of the UN Security Council and a nuclear weapons state as well as its role in Allied-occupied Germany, France played a central role in the political unification process after 1945 that led to the European Union. Despite periods of economic recession in the 1970s and 2010s, and regardless of the internal tensions caused by the rise of resentment against immigrants (representing 5%–10% of the French population) and by massive terror attacks in 2015 and 2016, France remains a strong economic, cultural, military and political force in the twenty-first century.

III. Political System[2]

22. The Constitution of the Fifth Republic, approved by referendum on 28 September 1958, established a semi-presidential system and proclaimed that 'France shall be an indivisible, secular (*laïc*), democratic and social Republic' (Article 1). Executive power is exercised by the President of the Republic, who is elected directly by universal suffrage for a 5-year term and, as head of the state, is the pre-eminent figure in French politics. The government is led by the Prime Minister who is appointed by the President. In response to the political instability of the Fourth Republic (1946–1958), the 1958 Constitution strengthened the authority of the executive branch in relation to Parliament. In fact, the Prime Minister has a strong influence on the parliamentary agenda.

23. The French Parliament is a bicameral legislature comprised of a National Assembly (*Assemblée nationale*) and a Senate (*Sénat*). The deputies of the National Assembly represent local constituencies and are directly elected for a 5-year term.

2. *See* also David S. Bell, *Presidential Power in Fifth Republic France* (Berg 2000); Ben Clift, *The Fifth Republic at Fifty: The Changing Face of French Politics and Political Economy*, 16 Modern & Contemporary France 383 (2008); Richard Balme, *France, Europe and the World: Foreign Policy and the Political Regime of the Fifth Republic* (Palgrave Macmillan 2009).

The government can be revoked by the National Assembly through a 'censure motion' (*motion de censure*), which ensures that the Prime Minister is always supported by a majority of the National Assembly. Senators are chosen for 6-year terms by an electoral college of about 145,000 local elected officials, and half of the Senate is renewed every three years. The Senate's legislative powers are limited. On most matters of legislation, the National Assembly has the last word in case of a disagreement between the two houses. Since 1958, the Senate has always had a right-wing majority due to the over-representation of rural areas among the electoral body.

24. The French political system is also characterized by an independent judiciary which is not controlled by the executive or legislative branch. Judges, both of ordinary and administrative courts, are civil servants (*fonctionnaires*) but are vested with a special status; they have security of tenure and may not be promoted without their consent. Public prosecutors (*procureurs de la République*) are under the hierarchy of the Ministry of Justice. Although the Court of Justice of the European Union has held that prosecutors are sufficiently independent from the executive,[3] and despite a 2013 act prohibiting ministerial instructions in individual cases,[4] there is an ongoing debate on the status of the *ministère public* due to the media's suspicion regarding the prosecutors' ties to the government.

25. Until recently, French politics has been characterized by the opposition between two major political parties. The Socialist Party has, for decades, been the largest party of the French centre-left; the Republicans (formerly known as the Union for a Popular Movement) have been the most important centre-right, conservative political party. Although those parties were characterized by an important intra-party factionalism, the government of France has alternated between a centre-left coalition led by the Socialist Party with the support of minor partners (such as the Greens or the Radical Party of the Left) and a centre-right coalition led by the Republicans and its predecessors. Due to the unpopularity of incumbent President François Hollande (Socialist Party) and a series of political affairs concerning the presidential candidate of the Republicans, the 2017 presidential election gave rise to an unprecedented situation: for the first time in the history of the Fifth Republic, the candidate of a third party, Emmanuel Macron, won the presidency, and for the first time, neither of the major coalitions appeared in the second round of a presidential election. When Macron took office on 14 May 2017, he became the youngest president in French history and the youngest French head of state since Napoleon.

---

3. *See* Joint Cases C-566/19 PPU and C-626/19 PPU, *Parquet général du Grand-Duché de Luxembourg and Tours*, ECLI:EU:C:2019:1078.
4. Art. 30 Criminal Procedure Code (*Code de procédure pénale*). On this aspect, *see* in English Sara Sun Baele, *Prosecutorial Discretion in Three Systems: Balancing Conflicting Goals and Providing Mechanisms for Control*, in *Discretionary Criminal Justice in a Comparative Context* (Michele Caianello & Jacqueline Hodgson eds, CAP 2015) 27, 38–43.

IV. Economic and Social Values[5]

26. France has a mixed economy that combines extensive private enterprise with substantial state enterprise and government intervention. The government retains considerable influence over key segments of the infrastructure sectors, holding majority ownership of railway, electricity, aircraft, nuclear power and telecommunications companies. The World Trade Organization reported in 2020 that France was the world's sixth-largest exporter and the fourth-largest importer of manufactured goods.[6] Key economic sectors are the chemical industry, tourism (France is the most visited destination in the world), the fashion industry, nuclear energy and agriculture.

27. In the aftermath of World War II, two ordinances of 4 and 19 April 1945 established a comprehensive, national welfare system (*sécurité sociale*) protecting all French residents (regardless of their citizenship) against the financial consequences of illness, maternity, unemployment and disability. France spends more than 30% of its GDP on welfare, which is more than most other EU countries. Even though strongly influenced by the 1942 Beveridge Report, French lawmakers adopted a model built on the Bismarckian legislation and based on a workers' insurance system. Over the decades, the social security system has gradually been extended to civil servants, liberal professions, farmers and other non-covered persons. In 2000, universal health coverage (*couverture médicale universelle*) was established which included a right to health insurance for all French residents and a right to free coverage for the most deprived among them.[7] The great importance of public health coverage is not unrelated to the French tort law system as the interplay between civil liability, private insurance and public health insurance coverage is one of the most complex issues in contemporary civil law.[8]

28. The rise of the French welfare state also led to the concept of national solidarity (*solidarité nationale*), which is enshrined in the preamble of the 1946 Constitution[9] and has become a fundamental legal concept underpinning several layers of social politics. It is no wonder that Article L 111-1 of the French Social Security Code (*Code de la sécurité sociale*) states that 'social security is founded on the principle of national solidarity' and that the regulations on several compensation funds,

5. *See* also Henri Mendras, *Social Change in Modern France: Towards a Cultural Anthropology of the Fifth Republic* (CUP 1988); Jean-Pierre Dormois, *The French Economy in the Twentieth Century* (CUP 2004); Richard McIntyre, *The Development of Social Economy in France since 1945*, 47 Forum for Social Economics 253 (2018).
6. *World Trade Statistical Review 2020* (WTO 2020) 82.
7. For a more detailed overview, *see* Xiaoming Sun, *World Health Systems* (Wiley 2019) ch. 12.
8. *See* paras 345–351 below.
9. According to paragraph 12 of the preamble, 'the Nation proclaims the solidarity and equality of all French people in bearing the burden resulting from national calamities'. In a 1971 landmark decision, the Constitutional Council (*Conseil constitutionnel*) referred to the preamble of the 1946 Constitution and its references to the principles laid out in the 1789 Declaration of the Rights of Man and of the Citizen. Since then, the preamble of the 1946 Constitution has been considered an integral part of the body of constitutional rules (*bloc de constutionnalité*).

for example, for victims of non-tortious medical accidents, refer to *solidarité nationale*.[10] Despite the fact that the precise contours of the concept are still unclear, the term reflects the idea that the community of French residents or taxpayers (rather than the *national* community per se) is supposed to support the cost of social risks.[11]

§2. Legal System

I. Primacy of Legislation and Codification

29. The French Constitution of 1958 is based on the separation of powers and, like many other European constitutions, adheres to the idea of checks and balances with a division between the legislative, executive and judiciary branches. The legal system of France follows the logic of a civil law jurisdiction based on the primacy of legislation, even though the 1958 Constitution adopted a system of a 'rationalized parliamentarism' (*parlementarisme rationnalisé*) which gave broad powers to the executive branch and listed the relevant areas of statutory law.[12] Unlike in other jurisdictions, some fields of law, such as civil procedure or the procedural rules governing administrative courts, fall under the genuine competence of the executive branch (*pouvoir réglementaire autonome*).[13] As for the civil liability rules, Article 34 of the 1958 Constitution provides that 'the basic principles … of civil and commercial obligations … shall be laid down by statute'; tort law in France is, therefore, a matter of the parliament, at least in theory.

30. Although the principles of the law of obligations (torts, contracts) fall within the competence of statutes, 'Government may ask Parliament for authorization, for a limited period, to take measures by ordinance.'[14] The French Parliament may therefore issue 'habilitation acts' (*lois d'habilitation*) specifying the scope of the ordinance and a limited time period; after the ordinance is in effect and before the time period has elapsed, the Prime Minister has to introduce before Parliament a bill of ratification (*projet de loi de ratification*); otherwise, the ordinance shall be void. Ordinances are frequently used by the Government to adopt controversial legislation, a fact which brings criticism from the political opposition who blame the anti-democratic attitude of the executive. The 2016 reform of the law of obligations was

10. Art. L 1142-1 II Public Health Code (*Code de la santé publique*). On this aspect, *see* Florence G'sell-Macrez, *The French Rules of Medical Liability since the Patients' Rights Law of March 4, 2002*, in *Medical Malpractice and Compensation in Global Perspective* 131, 134 (Ken Oliphant & Richard W. Wright eds, De Gruyter 2013).

11. On this concept, *see* in French Jonas Knetsch, *La solidarité nationale, genèse et signification d'une notion juridique*, Revue française des affaires sociales 2014, no. 1, 32–43.

12. The separation between statutory law and regulations is enforced by the Constitutional Council (*Conseil constitutionnel*), vetting for conformity of legislative acts with the Constitution, and the State Council (*Conseil d'État*) which has the authority to annul decrees infringing on the domain of statute.

13. The Civil Procedure Code (*Code de procédure civile*) has been enacted by a governmental decree and not by a legislative act.

14. Art. 38(1) Constitution of 1958.

adopted by ordinance and not by legislative act, giving rise to a controversy between the National Assembly and the Senate.[15] The Government indicated at that time that the law of contracts was a matter of legal technique that did not raise any political issues, whereas the upcoming reform of torts should be adopted by statute after a proper Parliamentary debate.

31. The technique of ordinances is also used to transpose EU directives and to rearrange existing rules without modifying them for the sake of codification.[16] Resuming the tradition of Napoleonic codes,[17] the French government created in 1989 a High Commission for Codification (*Commission supérieure de la codification*) in order to schedule the agenda for a comprehensive recodification of French law that was then widely spread among 8,000 acts and 80,000 decrees.[18] Over the past 30 years, the executive has adopted more than 60 new codes in addition to the historic codes (Civil Code, Criminal Code, Code of Civil Procedure, Commercial Code and Code of Criminal Procedure). For example, in 2018, a new Code of Public Procurement (*Code de la commande publique*) was enacted; there are even specific codes for cinema and cartoon (*Code du cinéma et de l'image animée*), sports (*Code des sports*) and tourism (*Code du tourisme*), prompting authors to note that some aspects of the codification process reveal the strong influence that specific associations or corporations have on the administration.[19]

II. Position of the Judiciary

32. In theory, the constitutional model adopted by the 1958 Constitution does not leave any room for case law among legal sources in France. According to Montesquieu's strongly influential work *The Spirit of Law*, judges shall be no more than the 'mouth' pronouncing the words of the law (*bouche de la loi*);[20] in 1790, Robespierre addressed the Constitutional Assembly in even harsher terms.[21] Following

15. On the legislative methods used during the reform of the French law of obligations, *see* in English Guillaume Meunier, *The Reform of the Law of Obligations in France. Methods and Prospects*, in *Reforming the Law of Obligations and Company Law: Studies in French and German Law* (Walter Doralt & Olivier Deshayes eds, Société de Législation Comparée 2013) 15 and Bénédicte Fauvarque-Cosson, Juliette Gest & François Ancel, *The Process of Elaboration of the Reform of the Law of Contract*, in *The Code Napoléon Rewritten: French Contract Law after the 2016 Reforms* (John Cartwright & Simon Whittaker eds, Hart 2017) 17, 24.
16. *See* Roland Drago, *General Introduction*, in *Introduction to French Law* (George A. Bermann & Étienne Picard eds, Wolters Kluwer 2008) xxx–xxxii; Eva Steiner, *French Law: A Comparative Approach* (OUP 2d ed. 2018) 30–33.
17. On the Napoleonic codification, *see*, e.g., John Bell, Sophie Boyron & Simon Whittaker, *Principles of French Law* (OUP 2d ed. 2008) 22–24.
18. On the agenda of the High Commission of Codification, *see* Steiner, *supra* n. 16, at 40–42.
19. François Terré & Nicolas Molfessis, *Introduction générale au droit* (Dalloz 11th ed. 2019) paras 480–485.
20. Montesquieu, *The Spirit of Law* (trad Philip Stewart 2018), book XI, Ch. 6 ('the judges of the nation are, as we have said, merely the mouth that pronounces the words of the law').
21. During the session of 18 November 1790, Robespierre allegedly claimed: 'This word of "case-law" must be erased from our language. … In a state that has a constitution and a legislation, case-law of courts is nothing but the statutory law'.

the doctrine of separation of powers, courts are not allowed to interfere with the law-making function of the Parliament and the Government, which are alone vested with democratic legitimacy. The Civil Code reflects this understanding of a strict hierarchy between the statutory law and the judiciary, as Article 5 provides that 'judges are forbidden to pronounce by means of general and statutory disposition on the cases brought before them'. It follows from this that court decisions, even when pronounced by the Court of Cassation or the *Conseil d'État*, are not binding precedents; there is no 'stare decisis' rule under French law.[22]

33. In practice, however, the status of case law is very different. Although a court decision is not formally binding (with the notable exception of the decisions of the Constitutional Council),[23] judges are nowadays seen as a significant source of law and not only as 'bureaucratic implementers of rules established by the legislator'.[24] Both the Court of Cassation and the *Conseil d'État* accept their normative roles and their importance for providing a certain stabilization of case law developments in the fields of private and administrative law. Whenever a particular interpretation of the law is consistently repeated (the series of decisions is then called *jurisprudence constante*) or the Court of Cassation has issued a landmark decision (*arrêt de principe*) given by the Full Court (*Assemblée plénière*) or a Divisional Court (*Chambre mixte*),[25] no French lawyer would seriously query the normative status of the case law and its complementary role with legislation.[26]

34. However, the importance of case law in the French legal system depends heavily on the branch of law and on the impact of codification in this area. Some fields of French law are not based on statutory law or are based on only a few general provisions, having instead been created by the judiciary. For example, until recently, administrative law was basically a non-written, judge-made area of French law. For a long time, the legislature has only enacted statutes on very specific provisions, whereas the *Conseil d'État* has progressively laid out a comprehensive case law system. It was only in 2005 that the Government achieved the codification of

22. Steiner, *supra* n. 16, at 68–71. On court decisions departing from established precedents (known as *revirements de jurisprudence*, the French equivalent of overruling), *see* Michel Troper & Christophe Grzegorczyk, *Precedent in France*, in *Interpreting Precedents* (D. Neil MacCormick & Robert S. Summers eds, Ashgate 1997) 103–140 and more recently, Steiner, *supra* n. 16, at 76–79.
23. According to Art. 62 of the 1958 Constitution, 'a provision declared unconstitutional on the basis of Article 61 shall be neither promulgated nor implemented' and 'a provision declared unconstitutional on the basis of Article 61-1 shall be repealed as of the publication of the said decision of the Constitutional Council or as of a subsequent date determined by said decision'. This concerns the constitutional review of legislative acts. For a broader overview, *see* Bell, Boyron & Whittaker, *supra* n. 17, at 156–163.
24. Bell, Boyron & Whittaker, *supra* n. 17, at 26.
25. On the court institutions in France, *see* John Bell, *Judiciaries in Europe* (CUP 2006) 44–47.
26. On the distinction between *arrêts de principe* and more common *arrêts d'espèce*, *see* Steiner, *supra* n. 17, at 79–81.

the rules governing administrative conduct.[27] Other branches, such as private international law and tort law,[28] are still widely the result of case law.

III. Distinction Between Public and Private Law

35. The origins of the distinction between public and private law go back to the turbulent post-revolutionary period during which the National Constitutional Assembly adopted the Act of 16–24 August 1790, which is still in force today. According to Article 13, 'judicial functions are and shall always remain separated from administrative functions. Ordinary judges shall not interfere in any way whatsoever with administrative matters, nor hear a claim brought against a public authority on account of their official duties'. This principle of separation between the judiciary and the administrative authorities, which can be attributed to a defiance vis-à-vis the former royal courts (known as *Parlements*), resulted in preferential treatment of the executive since ordinary courts only had jurisdiction in cases related to and between individuals; that is, in private matters. Following the 1790 Act, a claimant was not allowed to bring a dispute over an administrative matter to the ordinary courts but could only apply to the head of the administration for a review (*recours gracieux*). It was not until 1872 that the *Conseil d'État*, even though created in 1799 'to resolve difficulties arising in administrative matters', became a real court, having been awarded jurisdiction to decide cases on behalf of the French people. From 1889 on, claimants could bring cases directly to the *Conseil d'État* without first addressing an application for review to the relevant minister.[29]

36. A significant consequence of the separation of ordinary courts and executive power was the emergence of a distinctive body of regulation governing administrative action. The progressive implementation of an administrative court system led to the formation of what is known today as *droit administratif*. The public law/ private law distinction has gradually become one of the specific features of French law. Judges of the administrative courts are distinct from their colleagues on the ordinary courts by virtue of their recruitment and training; it is not uncommon that administrative judges (*juges administratifs*) serve some years in an administration.[30] Even among French law professors, the distinction between *publicistes* and *privatistes* is so deeply rooted that private law professors would hardly dare

27. For a presentation of the 'Code on the relationship between the public and the administration' in English, *see* Marzia De Donno, *The French 'Code des relations entre le public et l'administration'. A New European Era for Administrative Procedure?*, Italian Journal of Public Law 2017, no. 2, 220.
28. *See* paras 39–43 below.
29. On this evolution, *see* Steiner, *supra* n. 17, at 173–174; George A. Bermann & Étienne Picard, *Administrative Law*, in *Introduction to French Law* (George A. Bermann & Étienne Picard eds, Wolters Kluwer 2008) 57, 59–60. *See* also Hugo Flavier & Charles Froger, *Administrative Justice in France. Between Singularity and Classicism*, 3 BRICS Law Journal 80 (2016); Lionel Neville Brown, John Bell & Jean-Michel Galabert, *French Administrative Law* (OUP 5th ed. 1998) 44–55, 126–128; Léon Duguit, *The French Administrative Courts*, 29 *Political Science Quarterly* 385 (1914).
30. For further details, *see* Bell, Boyron & Whittaker, *above* n. 17, at 55, 66, 69, 72.

encroach on the specialism of public law colleagues unless their area of expertise straddles the border of public and private law (e.g., in environmental law or competition law).[31]

37. In particular, in the field of tort law, the separation between public and private law has far-reaching implications. Compensation claims based on the liability of public authorities (*responsabilité administrative*) do not fall under the jurisdiction of ordinary courts and are governed by a body of specific rules. This autonomy was affirmed in 1873 by the *Tribunal des conflits*, a special court composed of judges from the Court of Cassation and the *Conseil d'État* established to resolve conflicts of jurisdiction arising in situations in which it is not clear whether a case should be decided by the administrative or the ordinary courts.[32] In the famous *Blanco* case,[33] the *Tribunal des conflits* held that 'the principles in the Civil Code which regulate the relations between individuals are inapplicable to the possible liability of the state for damage caused to individuals by persons employed in the public service (*service public*)' and that 'the responsibility of the state, being neither general nor absolute, is subject to special rules which vary depending on the exigencies of the public service and the need to reconcile the rights of the state with the rights of private persons'.[34] Although the contemporary French law of torts is characterized by a rapprochement between the rules of civil liability and those governing *responsabilité administrative*, it has been decided to address the liability of public authorities separately.[35]

IV. Sources of Private Law in General and of Tort Law in Particular

38. French private law is the product of Napoleonic codification, with the Civil Code of 1804 as its primary source. Although considerably revised in several fields of law (such as family law, contracts, the rights of creditors), the Civil Code still bears a strong resemblance to the original codification drafted in the early nineteenth century. For private lawyers, it serves as a fundamental working tool, and law students are trained to become familiar with its structure and provisions from the first year of studies onwards. The Civil Code currently in force is divided into four major 'books' (*livres*) dedicated to the legal status of persons (Book I), things and

31. Steiner, *supra* n. 17, at 170. On this issue, *see* the contributions to the collective work Baptiste Bonnet & Pascale Deumier (eds), *De l'intérêt de la summa divisio droit public-droit privé?* (Dalloz 2010).
32. On the jurisdiction of the *Tribunal des conflits, see* Steiner, *supra* n. 17, at 179–184; Brown, Bell & Galabert, *supra* n. 29, at 149–154.
33. The *Blanco* case is generally seen as the starting point of the construction of an autonomous administrative law. *See* Bermann & Picard, *supra* n. 29, at 62–63, 79. For a recent assessment of this case, *see* also Charles Bosvieux-Onyekwelu, *Revenir sur une légende en sociologue: l'arrêt Blanco et le mythe de la 'naissance' du droit administratif français*, Droit & Société 2019, 159.
34. TC, 8 February 1873. For an English translation of the case, *see* Hermann Pünder & Anika Klafki, *Liability of the Administration*, in *Cases, Materials and Text on Judicial Review of Administrative Action* (Chris Backes & Mariolina Eliantonio eds, Hart 2019) 441, para. 2.35 (FR).
35. *See* paras 104–111 below.

the modifications of ownership (Book II), the 'various ways how ownership is acquired' (Book III) and securities (Book IV).[36]

39. Surprisingly, the main source of the French law of obligations is Book III of the Civil Code, the title of which may evoke to foreign lawyers the law of property or real estate rather than a body of rules governing contracts or torts. The Third Book is also the most voluminous, covering various subjects grouped into twenty sections (*chapitres*). While it is understandable that the Civil Code drafters conceived of contracts as a means to acquire ownership of things (section 3 is dedicated to 'contracts and conventional obligations in general'), it is much more difficult to see in the rules on civil liability some kind of regulation of the acquisition of ownership. Yet even during the major reform of the law of obligations in 2016, this presentation, inherited from Roman law, has not been altered.

40. One of the most singular features of French tort law is the concise nature of the legislative framework. In the original Civil Code of 1804, the rules governing extra-contractual civil liability were only laid out in five provisions (Articles 1382 to 1386), which have remained unchanged since then, apart from some minor additions. The major legislative changes in the Civil Code provisions consisted of the enactment of specific rules on product liability that follow the original texts. While there has not been any modification to tort law provisions, the 2016 law of obligations reform did introduce a significant formal change. The famous Articles 1382 to 1386 (extra-contractual liability) and 1147 (contractual liability) have been renumbered as follows:

Civil Liability Regime	Before 1 Oct. 2016	After 1 Oct. 2016
Liability for Fault	Article 1382 Article 1383	Article 1240 Article 1241
General rule of strict liability for things Strict liability for acts of other persons	Article 1384	Article 1242
Strict liability for damage caused by animals	Article 1385	Article 1243
Strict liability for damage caused by collapsing buildings	Article 1386	Article 1244
Product liability	Articles 1386-1–1386-18	Articles 1245–1245-17
Contractual liability	Article 1147	Article 1231-1

41. To give the reader an overview of the (few) provisions on civil liability, an English translation of Articles 1231-1 and 1240 to 1245 follows:[37]

36. On the structure of the French Civil Code, *see* recently Jean-Sébastien Borghetti, *French Law*, in *The Scope and Structure of Civil Code* (Julio César Rivero ed., Springer 2013) 181–200.
37. Two semi-official English translations of the Civil Code can be found on the *Légifrance* website: a 2014 version prepared by a team of academics from law schools in Louisiana (David Gruning, Alain

Article 1231-1
A debtor shall be ordered to pay damages, in the proper circumstance, either on account of the non-performance of the obligation, or on account of the delay in performing, whenever he cannot establish that the performance has been prevented by force majeure.

Article 1240

Any act whatever of man, which causes damage to another, obliges the one by whose fault it occurred, to compensate it.

Article 1241

Everyone is liable for the damage he causes not only by his intentional act, but also by his negligent conduct or by his imprudence.

Article 1242

(1) A person is liable not only for the damages he causes by his own act, but also for that which is caused by the acts of persons for whom he is responsible, or by things which are in his custody.
(2) However, a person who possesses, regardless of the basis thereof, all or part of a building or of movable property in which a fire has originated is not liable towards third parties for damages caused by that fire unless it is proved that the fire must be attributed to his fault or to the fault of persons for whom he is responsible.
(3) This provision may not apply to the landlord and tenant relationship, which remains governed by Articles 1733 and 1734 of the Civil Code.
(4) The father and mother, in so far as they exercise parental authority, are jointly and severally liable for the damage caused by their minor children who live with them.
(5) Masters and employers, for the damage caused by their servants and employees in the functions for which they have been employed;
(6) Teachers and craftsmen, for the damage caused by their pupils and apprentices during the time when they are under their supervision.
(7) The above liability exists, unless the father and mother or the craftsmen prove that they could not prevent the act which gives rise to that liability.
(8) As to teachers, the faults, imprudence or negligent conducts invoked against them as having caused the damaging act must be proved by the claimant at the trial, in accordance with the general law.

A. Levasseur & J. Randall Trahan, www.legifrance.gouv.fr/Media/Traductions/English-en/code_civil_20130701_EN) and a 2006 version prepared by Georges Rouhette and Anne Rouhette-Berton (www.legifrance.gouv.fr/content/download/1950/13681/version/3/file/Code_22.pdf). The following excerpt has been taken from the latter, apart from Art. 1231-1 in which the wording was slightly amended by the 2016 Law of Obligations reform. *See* also the translation by Olivier Moréteau, *France*, in *European Tort Law. Basic Texts* (Ernst Karner, Ken Oliphant & Barbara Steininger eds, Jan Sramek Verlag 2d ed. 2018) 123–140.

Article 1243

The owner of an animal, or the person using it, during the period of usage, is liable for the damage the animal has caused, whether the animal was under his custody, or whether it had strayed or escaped.

Article 1244

The owner of a building is liable for the damage caused by its collapse, where it happens as a result of lack of maintenance or of a defect in its construction.

Article 1245[38]

A producer is liable for damages caused by a defect in his product, whether he was bound by a contract with the injured person or not.

42. Given the legislator's inertia in the field of civil liability, it is not surprising that the courts and above all the Court of Cassation have developed a comprehensive body of judge-made tort law rules. More so than in other fields of French law, a foreign lawyer is far from understanding the civil liability rules based only on a consultation of the relevant provisions in the Civil Code. As has been said previously, a codified legal system does not necessarily mean that legislation has an answer for any legal problem.[39] This is particularly true for the law of torts, not only in France but also in other civil law jurisdictions. However, what characterizes the French tort law system is that on several occasions, the Court of Cassation chose to override the meaning of the Civil Code provisions, going so far as to deliberately change the nature of specific liability regimes by 'deactivating' entire paragraphs or reinterpreting others. The most topical example is the liability for things (*responsabilité du fait des choses*) which was 'discovered' by the Court of Cassation in the late nineteenth century when it was confronted with new social risks arising from industrialization.[40] This emancipatory movement has increased in the second half of the twentieth century[41] and today raises the issue of the accessibility of tort law and the legitimacy of legal policy choices made by the Court of Cassation.

43. In order to recodify the French law of torts, the French Ministry of Justice launched in April 2016 a consultation on a preliminary draft of a reform to the French Civil Code provisions concerning civil liability. It had been decided earlier that the reform of the law of obligations that had been initiated more than 10 years ago would be performed in two stages: the general part of contract law first, by way

38. The provisions on product liability are more detailed, but for reasons of convenience, only Art. 1245 has been included in this excerpt. For an English translation of Arts 1245 to 1245-17 C civ, *see* Moréteau, *France*, *supra* n. 37, at 124.
39. Hein Kötz, *Taking Civil Codes Less Seriously*, 50 Modern Law Review 1 (1987). *See* also René David, *The Civil Code in France To-Day*, 34 Louisiana Law Review 907, 911 (1974).
40. *See* paras 165–168 below.
41. *See*, for example, the development of the liability of parents for the acts of their children (paras 144–148 below).

of an ordinance, and then the civil liability by way of a law. The draft proposal published in 2016 thus initiated the second step of the reform. Shortly before the presidential election in March 2017, then Minister of Justice Jean-Jacques Urvoas presented a revised version of the draft which reflected the analysis of more than 100 responses to the public consultation.[42] During the summer of 2019, the officers of the Ministry of Justice worked on a final version of the reform bill which is known to have passed the stage of inter-ministerial coordination. Even though at the time of this writing there was no clear timetable for a parliamentary vote,[43] it is likely that the tort law provisions of the Civil Code will be subject to major revision in the next few years. The objective of the announced reform is not only to codify existing case law but also to introduce substantial amendments into the current tort law system.[44] The following developments address the law as it stands in 2021 with references made to the 2017 Draft Reform to give the reader an outlook on the French tort law of the future.[45]

§3. Function of the Law of Torts

44. As in many other jurisdictions, the primary function of the French tort law is the compensation of harm caused by the tortfeasor. According to a notable formula adopted by the Court of Cassation, 'the proper function of civil liability is to re-establish as exactly as possible the balance disturbed by the harm and to replace the victim in the situation in which he would have been if the harm had not

42. An English version of the 2017 Draft can be consulted on the website of the French Ministry of Justice (http://www.textes.justice.gouv.fr/textes-soumis-a-concertation-10179/projet-de-reforme-de-la-responsabilite-civile-traduit-en-anglais-30553.html).
43. In July 2020, a group of senators presented a new bill (*proposition de loi*) on civil liability reform with the aim of bringing about a civil liability reform as quickly as possible without addressing issues that are still controversial (*see* Jonas Knetsch & Zoé Jacquemin, *France* in *ETL 2020 (2021)*, forthcoming). Considering that under French constitutional law, the government sets the pace of legislative reforms, it is highly improbable that the 2020 bill will be used as a new basis for the tort law reform. It is more likely that, after the Presidential election in 2022, the Ministry of Justice will resume the reform project on the basis of the 2017 Draft Reform, as last amended in 2019.
44. *See* also the media coverage of the press conference held to present the preliminary draft in April 2016 (http://www.textes.justice.gouv.fr/zoom-11470/zoom-sur-la-reforme-de-la-responsabilite-civile-29099.html; video interviews with Geneviève Viney, Bénédicte Fauvarque-Cosson, Mireille Bacache-Gibeili, Jean-Sébastien Borghetti and Frédéric Bibal).
45. The 2016 preliminary draft and the 2017 Draft have already been investigated by English-speaking authors. *See* Jean-Sébastien Borghetti & Simon Whittaker (eds), *French Civil Liability in Comparative Perspective* (Hart 2019). *See* also Jonas Knetsch & Zoé Jacquemin, *France* in *ETL 2016 (2017)*, 191, paras 13–21; *France* in *ETL 2017 (2018)*, 187, paras 1–8; *France* in *ETL 2019 (2020)*, 186, paras 1–5. On the academic reform proposals drafted by the Catala working group (2005) and the Terré working group (2011), *see* Paula Giliker, *Codifying Tort Law: Lessons From the Proposals for Reform of the French Civil Code*, 57 ICLQ 561 (2008); Philippe Brun & Christophe Quézel-Ambrunaz, *French Tort Law Facing Reform*, 4 JETL 78 (2013); Olivier Moréteau, *France* in *ETL 2005 (2006)*, 270, paras 1–11; *France* in *ETL 2011 (2012)*, 216, paras 1–10; *The Draft Reforms of French Tort Law in the Light of European Harmonization*, in *Festschrift für Ulrich Magnus zum 70. Geburtstag* (Peter Mankowski & Wolfgang Wurmnest eds, Sellier 2014) 77; Olivier Moréteau & Alexandru-Daniel On, *France* in *ETL 2012 (2013)*, 229, paras 1–17.

occurred'.[46] Thus, the main objective of civil liability is the restoration of the *status quo ante* and to 'make sure that the harm was only a dream', to use the words of André Tunc.[47] From this derives the principle of full compensation (*réparation intégrale*), which is one of the fundamental concepts of French tort law with only a few exceptions. As will be seen,[48] the remedies awarded to the victim shall be equivalent to the harm suffered and encompass all consequences of the harm, whether pecuniary or non-pecuniary in nature. Even though there is a common understanding of the incommensurability of distress or other non-pecuniary losses, a French tort lawyer does not hesitate to refer to the principle of *réparation intégrale* in order to claim damages for pain and suffering or the loss of enjoyment of life. The mere concept of 'reparation' in cases of personal injury or violation of personality rights may seem inconsistent, but for many scholars, it is a 'constructive utopia'.[49]

45. The importance of the compensatory function of the tort law cannot be underestimated. Whereas many other tort law systems are based on the principle that a loss should lie where it falls (also known as *casum sentit dominus*) and that it may be shifted to another person only under specific circumstances,[50] the idea behind contemporary French tort law is that a victim of a loss deserves to be compensated whatever the circumstances, especially in personal injury cases.[51] The transformation of the tort law towards a body of victim-oriented compensation rules dates back to the second half of the twentieth century in the context of the generalization of health insurance coverage and the expansion of private liability insurance. This phenomenon of 'socialization of risks', comprehensively analysed by Geneviève Viney in her famous book on the *Decline of Individual Liability*,[52] has led to a certain 'compensation ideology' with far-reaching consequences both on the grounds of liability and on the assessment of damages.[53]

46. There is debate among scholars as to other secondary functions of tort law, such as deterrence (*fonction préventive*) and sanction (*fonction punitive*). Regarding the preventive (or normative) function of tort law, it has been argued that the threat

---

46. *See*, for example, Com, 10 January 2012, no. 10-26.837. The formula is borrowed from René Savatier, *Traité de la responsabilité civile en droit français* vol 2 (LGDJ 2d ed. 1951) para. 601.
47. Jean Carbonnier, *Droit civil* vol 2 (PUF 22d ed. 2004) 2253 ('Il faut réparer le mal, faire qu'il semble n'avoir été qu'un rêve.').
48. *See* paras 277–280 below.
49. The formula is from the late Jean-Pierre Dintilhac, former president of the First Civil Chamber of the Court of Cassation and well known for having drafted a nomenclature of the head of damages in personal injury cases (*see* paras 292, 314 below).
50. *See* recently Corjo Jansen, *Accidental Harm Under (Roman) Civil Law*, in *The Challenge of Chance* (Klaas Landsmann & Ellen van Wolde eds, Springer 2016) 233.
51. Olivier Moréteau, *Basic Questions of Tort Law from a French Perspective*, in *Basic Questions from a Comparative Perspective* (Helmut Koziol ed., Jan Sramek Verlag 2015) 3, para. 1/1.
52. Geneviève Viney, *Le déclin de la responsabilité individuelle* (LGDJ 1965). *See* also in English Geneviève Viney, *Tort Liability*, in *Introduction to French Law* (George A. Bermann & Étienne Picard eds, Wolters Kluwer 2008) 237, 244–247.
53. This perspective is not, however, the view of most tort law scholars in France, since many of them consider that the extension of strict liability regimes and remedies is a form of social progress, as are, for example, social rights acquired by workers.

of civil liability 'encourages citizens to think over their conduct and to rule out, as far as possible, tortious behaviour' so that 'the anticipation of potential legal consequences the law acts on their conscience and keeps them in a state of attentiveness'.[54] It is doubtful, however, that this vision reflects the reality. The generalization of liability insurance and the rise of strict liability considerably reduce the preventive potential of civil liability.[55] In particular, in cases of accidental harm, the deterrent effect of tort law seems to be very small and other legal measures (technical standards, criminal liability, tax incentives) more effective to prevent antisocial or harmful behaviour. Nonetheless, it cannot be denied that under certain circumstances, fault-based civil liability can have a strong deterrent effect, for example, in cases of harm caused by professionals or corporations that fear for their reputations.

47. Over the past three decades, voices have been raised to criticize the inability of French tort law to adequately respond to deliberate harmful conduct, considering that the gravity of fault should have an effect on the assessment of damages. This is particularly discussed within the context of wilful violations of personality rights (e.g., through press, television or internet) and so-called *fautes lucratives*, that is, deliberately committed faults for the purpose of making a gain or saving money. For some authors, the courts or legislator should put a more punitive spin on the rules of civil liability.[56] In the case law concerning the violation of privacy rights, it can be observed that the Court of Cassation does not hesitate to assess damages for non-pecuniary harm by taking into account the deliberate character of fault and the position of the tortfeasor so that damages awarded in those cases might be described as 'disguised punitive damages'.[57] However, the legal grounds for this case law are not very strong, which has led to the proposal of a 'civil penalty' (*amende civile*) in the 2017 Draft of the civil liability reform.[58]

48. Another major topic of debate is the link between tort law and prohibitory injunctions (*actions en cessation de l'illicite*). For some scholars, the rules of civil liability should not be restricted to the compensation of a harm that has already occurred but should also address situations in which an individual is facing a risk of imminent harm.[59] In those cases, the current civil procedure rules already allow a claimant to request injunctive relief (*mesures conservatoires*) following Article 809

54. Philippe le Tourneau (ed.), *Droit de la responsabilité et des contrats* (Dalloz 12th ed. 2020) para. 0111-14.
55. Geneviève Viney, *Introduction à la responsabilité* (LGDJ 4th ed. 2019) paras 53–55.
56. For an overview *see* Viney, *Introduction*, *supra* n. 55, at paras 114–117. *See* also the reference work of Suzanne Galand-Carval, *La responsabilité civile dans sa fonction de peine privée* (LGDJ 1995).
57. *See* the examples cited by Agathe Lepage, *Droits de la personnalité* in *Répertoire de droit civil* (Dalloz 2009), paras 255–257.
58. Art. 1266-1 of the 2017 Draft. On this proposal, *see* Marco Capeletti, *Comparative Reflections on Punishment in Tort Law*, in *French Civil Liability in Comparative Perspective* (Jean-Sébastien Borghetti & Simon Whittaker eds, Hart 2019) 329, 343–349. *See* also Knetsch & Jacquemin, *ETL 2016 (2017)*, *supra* n. 45, at para. 19; *ETL 2017 (2018)*, *supra* n. 45, at para. 8. For more details, *see* also para. 360 below.
59. *See*, in particular, Cyril Bloch, *La cessation de l'illicite. Recherche sur une fonction méconnue de la responsabilité civile extracontractuelle* (Dalloz 2010).

of the Civil Procedure Code.[60] Nevertheless, the 2017 Draft suggests a transformation of this interlocutory procedure into a tort law-related procedure available to all individuals confronted with the risk of imminent harm or exposed to unlawful nuisance (*trouble illicite*), regardless of a relevant compensable loss under traditional tort law.[61] It is debatable to what extent this proposal would really make a difference and lead to greater clarity and legal certainty.

§4. Relationship Between Torts and Criminal Law[62]

49. French law distinguishes very clearly between criminal liability and torts. Civil law and criminal law are governed by different codes, enforced in distinct courts[63] and clearly different in function. Whereas the primary function of civil liability is the compensation of harm,[64] criminal law pursues the objectives of punishment and deterrence. In principle, civil and criminal liability should, therefore, be entirely separate.

50. However, unlike other legal systems, French law allows victims of a crime to initiate criminal proceedings by constituting themselves as 'civil parties' (*parties civiles*), that is, by accusing another individual of having committed a harmful criminal act and making a claim for the resulting damages.[65] They may also join a prosecution already triggered by the public prosecutor (*procureur de la République*) or an investigating magistrate (*juge d'instruction*). In both cases, victims will be

60. According to Art. 809(1) Civil Procedure Code, 'the president (of a *tribunal judiciaire*) may always, even when confronted with a serious challenge, order in a summary procedure such protective measures or measures to restore the parties to their previous state as required, either to avoid an imminent damage or to stop a manifestly unlawful nuisance'. On this provision, *see* in English George Cumming, Brad Spitz & Ruth Janal, *Civil Procedure Used for Enforcement of EC Competition Law by the English, French and German Civil Courts* (Kluwer 2007) 212–215.
61. Art. 1266 of the 2017 draft provides that 'in extra-contractual matters, independently of any reparation of loss which may have been suffered, a court may prescribe reasonable measures appropriate to prevent harm or to see that an unlawful nuisance to which a claimant is exposed is stopped'. On this proposal, *see* Paula Giliker, *Injunctions Requiring the Cessation of Unlawful Action*, in *French Civil Liability in Comparative Perspective* (Jean-Sébastien Borghetti & Simon Whittaker eds, Hart 2019) 377. *See* also Willem H. van Boom, *Comparative Notes on Injunction and Wrongful Risk-Taking*, 17 Maastricht Journal of European and Comparative Law 10, 18–21 (2010).
62. For a recent assessment of this topic in the French language, *see* Viney, *Introduction*, *supra* n. 55, at paras 102–224; Charlotte Dubois, *Responsabilité civile et responsabilité pénale. À la recherche d'une cohérence perdue* (LGDJ, 2016).
63. Bell, Boyron & Whittaker, *supra* n. 17, at 43–47.
64. *See* para. 44 above.
65. *See* Bell, Boyron & Whittaker, *supra* n. 17, at 368–373; Viney, *Tort Liability*, *supra* n. 52, at 237, 239–240; Valérie Malabat & Véronique Wester-Ouisse, *The Quest for Balance between Tort and Crime in French Law*, in *Comparing Tort and Crime: Learning from across and within Legal Systems* (Matthew Dyson ed., CUP 2015) 73, 78–81; Colin Howard, *Compensation in French Criminal Procedure*, 21 Modern Law Review 387 (1958). *See* also most recently Matthew Dyson, *Crime, Breach of Legislative Duties and Fault*, in *French Civil Liability in Comparative Perspective* (Jean-Sébastien Borghetti & Simon Whittaker eds, Hart 2019) 99, 102–104.

considered a full party to the criminal proceedings[66] and the criminal court will assess their claims for damages in accordance with ordinary tort law rules. Very common under French law, the *action civile* (in contrast to the *action publique*, i.e., the prosecution) has several advantages: the investigative powers of the public prosecutor and the investigating magistrate may give the *partie civile* increased access to evidence, especially in cases where liability is unclear; the criminal process is also considered swifter than proceedings before civil courts; and the cost of the action is borne by the state. It is therefore not at all uncommon that a specific question on civil liability is dealt with by the Criminal Chamber of the Court of Cassation.

51. In cases in which criminal proceedings have been initiated by the public prosecutor or the investigating magistrate, claimants may also bring their compensation claims before a civil court. If so, the civil court judges are bound to suspend proceedings until the criminal case is settled before the criminal court. This primacy of criminal law over tort law is commonly referred to by the French dictum '*le criminal tient le civil en l'état*', enshrined in Article 4(2) Code of Criminal Procedure.[67] However, this rule, intended to prevent contradicting judgments, was amended by an Act of 1983 which allows crime victims to bring non-compensatory claims and, in particular, claims for provisional damages (*référé-provision*) before civil courts without the need to wait for the criminal verdict.[68]

52. Closely related is the so-called theory of the 'unity of criminal and civil faults' (*unité des fautes civile et pénale*).[69] The issue is whether a criminal offence recognized as such by the criminal courts also constitutes a fault (*faute*) for the purpose of fault-based liability under Articles 1240 and 1241 Civil Code. It has traditionally been considered under French law that whenever a criminal offence has been committed, even though it does not require intention or negligence, a civil compensation claim could be made on the grounds of the wide concept of *faute*.[70] This was particularly significant as the French Criminal Code provides for very broad non-intentional offences, especially in the field of personal injury or death.[71] At the same time, the principle of 'unity of criminal and civil faults' meant that the

66. In some cases, even the civil liability insurer of the accused can join the proceedings. *See* Art. 388-1(2) Code of Criminal Procedure.
67. According to this text, 'the judgment in any action exercised before the civil court is suspended until a final decision is made on the merits of the public prosecution where such a prosecution has been initiated'.
68. *See* Malabat & Wester-Ouisse, *supra* n. 65, at 82–83; for a comparative analysis, *see* Matthew Dyson, *Tort and Crime*, in *Comparative Tort Law: Global Perspectives* (Mauro Bussani & Anthony J. Sebok eds, Elgar 2015) 93, 117–118.
69. On this issue, *see* Bell, Boyron & Whittaker, *supra* n. 17, at 369–373.
70. *See* paras 68–72 below.
71. *See*, e.g., the offences of involuntary homicide (*homicide involontaire*) and involuntary personal injuries (*violences involontaires*). *See* Catherine Elliott, *French Criminal Law* (Willan 2001) 157–173 (*see* also the English translation of the key provisions of the French Criminal Code at 208–228). From a comparative standpoint, *see* Gerhard Wagner, *Comparative Tort Law*, in *The Oxford Handbook of Comparative Law* (Mathias Reimann & Reinhard Zimmermann eds, OUP 2019) 994, 1002–1003.

acquittal of an accused by a criminal court barred the *partie civile* from claiming damages on the grounds of civil liability.

53. In 1996 and 2000, the French legislature decided to considerably loosen the ties between criminal and civil liability.[72] At that time, it was felt that the doctrine of *unité des fautes civile et pénale* had resulted in an unwanted criminal prosecution of mayors for accidents linked to their failure to implement health and safety rules (e.g., on playgrounds or sports facilities). The general idea was that in cases of 'simple negligence,' natural persons should only be liable for the consequences of their acts that are direct and immediate and that to make someone criminally liable for remoter consequences, a higher degree of fault (*faute caractérisée*) should be required.[73] Those limitations were enshrined in Articles 4-1 and 121-3 of the Criminal Code, leading to a further 'unbundling' of civil and criminal liability in the field of non-intentional crimes: whereas all criminal faults are still automatically civil faults, the opposite is not true. Criminal judges may award damages to the *partie civile* even if they decide to acquit the prosecuted person.

54. The 2017 Draft Reform does not explicitly mention the relationship between civil and criminal liability. It is thus reasonable to assume that the solutions resulting from the 1996 and 2000 legislation will continue in their current form.[74]

§5. Relationship Between Contractual and Extra-Contractual Liability

55. Another major topic of debate is the relationship between contractual and extra-contractual liability. It is often seen as one of the most complex issues of the French law of obligations, as the Civil Code does not contain any explicit rule on this issue and the Court of Cassation is still struggling to provide clear and accurate solutions.[75] One of the distinctive features of French tort law is the rule known as *non-cumul* whose implications are manifold. Given the ongoing doctrinal controversy on the distinctiveness of contractual liability, it is essential to start by presenting its specific features before delving into the meaning of the *non-cumul* rule and the scope of contractual liability.

72. J.R. Spencer & Marie-Aimée Brajeux, *Criminal Liability for Negligence – a Lesson from Across the Channel*, 59 ICLQ 1, 14–18 (2010); Dyson, *supra* n. 65, at 112. *See* also Rodolphe Mesa, *Des rapports entre infraction et faute civile et de leurs conséquences sur l'indemnisation des victimes*, D 2021, 303.
73. The rules governing criminal liability for non-intentional offences form a highly complex matter. For further details, *see* Elliott, *supra* n. 71, at Ch. 4; Catherine Elliott, *France*, in *The Handbook of Comparative Criminal Law* (Kevin J. Heller & Markus D. Dubber eds, Stanford University Press 2011) 209, 218–220; Spencer & Brajeux, *supra* n. 72, at 14–18.
74. *See* also Dyson, *supra* n. 65, at 112–113.
75. For a comprehensive survey, *see* Olivier Moréteau, *Basic Questions*, *supra* n. 51, at paras 1/73–1/89.

I. The Distinctiveness of Contractual Liability

56. Over the last decades, the consequences of non-performance of contractual obligations have been a constant subject of debate among French legal scholars. The debate started out with the fact that the Civil Code does not mention the concept of 'contractual liability', which led to a controversy on the very existence of this legal figure. In a famous paper, Philippe Rémy traced the origins of *responsabilité contractuelle*, presenting it as a 'false concept' built by authors such as Planiol and the Mazeaud brothers in the mid-twentieth century.[76] Indeed, Article 1231-1 Civil Code provides only for 'damages' in the case of non-performance of an obligation and does not refer to the concept of liability. According to Rémy, what is known as 'contractual liability' is nothing else but a monetary substitute for the benefit to which the creditor was entitled and that it should instead be called 'performance by equivalent' (*exécution par équivalent*). Yet, there is not much evidence that this doctrine has received broad support from the Court of Cassation and legal scholarship. The recent case law still refers to *responsabilité contractuelle,* and it is now acknowledged among private lawyers that, depending on the circumstances, contractual damages may not only be a substitute for the performance of contract[77] but also a form of reparation.[78] The 2017 Draft Reform is consistent with a unitary approach as both contractual and extra-contractual liability are subject to common rules and contractual liability is presented as a subcategory of the general concept of civil liability.[79]

57. Even though some scholars argue that the differences between contractual and extra-contractual liability are overestimated, it would be incorrect to see in contractual liability a mere variation of the classical 'delictual liability' and in contractual non-performance, only another *fait générateur de responsabilité*. There still are profound discrepancies between both types of liability. First of all, the non-performance of a contractual obligation does not correspond to a fault under Article 1240 since it does not necessarily imply the violation of a certain standard of conduct which is accepted by all. A contract can indeed give rise to an *obligation de résultat,* the breach of which is characterised by the mere fact that the promised outcome has not been reached; thus, the proof of non-performance is not based on an assessment of the defendant's conduct. Second, the concepts of liability for acts of

76. Philippe Rémy, *La 'responsabilité contractuelle' : histoire d'un faux concept*, RTD civ 1997, 323. *See* also Philippe le Tourneau, *La responsabilité civile* (Dalloz 3d ed. 1982) para. 160; Denis Tallon, *L'inexécution du contrat : pour une autre présentation*, RTD civ 1994, 323.

77. Bell, Boyron & Whittaker, *supra* n. 17, at 352 ('a form of "forced satisfaction"'); Yves-Marie Laithier, *The Relationship between Contractual and Extra-Contractual Liability as between Parties to a Contract*, in *French Civil Liability in Comparative Perspective* (Jean-Sébastien Borghetti & Simon Whittaker eds, Hart 2019) 37, 43–47.

78. *See* already Jérôme Huet, *Responsabilité contractuelle et responsabilité délictuelle : Essai de délimitation entre les deux ordres de responsabilité* (thesis Paris 1978, reprint LGDJ 2019). *See* also Zoé Jacquemin, *Payer, réparer, punir : Étude des fonctions de la responsabilité contractuelle en droits français, allemand et anglais* (LGDJ 2021) 85–131.

79. *See* in English Laithier, *supra* n. 77, at 42. *See* also Philippe Brun, *La distinction des deux ordres de responsabilité dans le projet de réforme*, in *Études en la mémoire de Philippe Neau-Leduc* (LGDJ 2018) 125.

others or for the acts of things cannot be easily transposed to *responsabilité contractuelle* as it is usually irrelevant whether the non-performance can be attributed to the act of another person or to the defect of a thing: the contractual partner is accountable for both.[80] Thirdly, and finally, there are major differences when it comes to the consequences of liability and to the regime applicable to compensation claims. Even though the modalities of compensation are similar (damages or *réparation en nature*),[81] Article 1231-3 Civil Code provides that 'a debtor is liable only for damages which were foreseen or which could have been foreseen at the time of the contract'. As a consequence, the assessment of contractual damages not only implies taking into account exemption or limitation clauses but also more generally the expectations of the contracting parties.[82] Regarding the regime governing compensation claims, actions under contract are subject to different limitation periods,[83] jurisdiction and conflict-of-law rules.[84] Insurance policies also tend to differentiate the coverage of extra-contractual and contractual liability.[85]

II. The Meaning of the *non-cumul* Rule

58. Widely known by comparative law scholars, the rule of *non-cumul* is not what its name suggests. There has never been any suggestion that the coexistence of contractual and extra-contractual liability could allow a claimant to 'cumulate' damages both on a contractual and a tortious basis. What is meant by the term *non-cumul* is that a contracting party is not entitled to damages from the other party in tort as long as the loss has been caused by the non-performance of a contractual obligation. Therefore, the expression *non-cumul* actually reflects a 'no-choice rule'[86] which indicates that in cases of overlap of contract and delict,[87] contract law

---

80. Some influential scholars, such as Geneviève Viney, tend, however, to emphasize the 'parallelism' between contractual and extra-contractual liability. *See* Viney, *Introduction*, *supra* n. 55, at paras 258–266 and, in English, Viney, *Tort Liability*, *supra* n. 52, at 241–242. *See* also Emmanuelle Juen, *La remise en cause de la distinction entre la responsabilité contractuelle et la responsabilité délictuelle* (LGDJ 2016) 421–520.
81. *See* para. 274 below.
82. *See* Solène Rowan, *Remedies for Breach of Contract: A Comparative Analysis of the Protection of Performance* (OUP 2012) 114–117.
83. A legislative reform in 2008 has unified the general limitation period for liability claims, regardless of the contractual or extra-contractual background. However, there are still specific limitation periods for contractual claims between merchants and for specific types of contracts. *See* Robert Wintgen, *Reforming the French Law of Prescription: A French Perspective*, in *Reforming the French Law of Obligations* (John Cartwright, Stefan Vogenauer & Simon Whittaker eds, Hart 2009) 347; Benjamin West Janke & François-Xavier Licari, *The French Revision of Prescription: A Model for Louisiana?*, 85 Tulane Law Review 1, 31–49 (2010).
84. *See* Viney, *Introduction*, *supra* n. 55, at paras 276–283, 286–293.
85. On the exclusion of the contractual liability risk in corporate liability insurance contracts, *see* Jean Bigot (ed.), *Traité de droit des assurances* vol 3 (LGDJ 2d éd. 2014) paras 1583–1585.
86. Almost every French tort lawyer insists on the mismatch between the term *non-cumul* and the actual meaning of this rule and encourages the use of alternative expressions such as *non-option*. Unfortunately, old habits die hard, especially among lawyers (as can be seen, the present monograph is no exception here).
87. Which is very likely given the broad sense of fault under Art. 1240 Civil Code. *See* paras 68–72 below.

prevails. Surprisingly, there is absolutely no legal basis for this rule in the Civil Code; it was elaborated by the Court of Cassation in the early twentieth century in order to preserve the rules governing contractual liability from the wide general liability clause based on *faute* and the absence of restrictions regarding the compensation of pure economic loss under extra-contractual liability.[88]

59. French case law, however, allows for exceptions to the *non-cumul* rule. The most important one is related to cases of a breach of contract punishable under criminal law, for example, constituting the offences of involuntary homicide (*homicide involontaire*) or involuntary personal injuries (*violences involontaires*).[89] According to the Criminal Chamber of the Court of Cassation, the compensation claim brought before a criminal court is subject to the rules governing extra-contractual liability, even though the same claim brought before a civil court would be judged in contract. Strongly criticized by several authors,[90] this case law is based on the idea that only a 'delictual fault' (*faute délictuelle*) can be the basis of an *action civile* presented to a criminal court.[91]

60. The 2017 Reform Draft enshrines the *non-cumul* rule in the Civil Code, while reversing it in cases of personal injury in which reparation is to be governed by extra-contractual liability even if the loss is caused by the non-performance of a contractual obligation.[92] This alteration of the primacy of contract is intended to put an end to an unequal treatment between claimants depending on their contractual or non-contractual status. The enactment of such a proposal would lead to the marginalization if not the elimination of implied *obligations de sécurité*.[93] In order to prevent the reform from placing claimants in a less favourable position than under the actual tort law, the Reform Draft allows them to rely on more favourable 'express stipulations' of the contract.[94]

---

88. *See,* e.g., Jean-Sébastien Borghetti & Simon Whittaker, *Introduction*, in *French Civil Liability in Comparative Perspective* (Jean-Sébastien Borghetti & Simon Whittaker eds, Hart 2019) 1, 5. For a more detailed presentation, *see* Viney, *Introduction, supra* n. 55, at paras 360–379. For a comparative study, *see* Tony Weir, *Complex Liabilities*, in *International Encyclopedia of Comparative Law* vol XI (André Tunc ed., Brill & J C B Mohr 1983) paras 47–72.
89. Laithier, *supra* n. 77, at 49.
90. For example, Viney, *Introduction, supra* n. 55, at para. 368; Michèle Muller, *L'inexécution pénalement répréhensible du contrat* (thesis Paris 2, 1976) paras 161–217.
91. From a comparative standpoint, *see* Christian von Bar & Ulrich Drobnig, *The Interaction of Contract Law and Tort and Property Law in Europe. A Comparative Study* (Sellier 2004) paras 294–304.
92. For a comment on Arts 1233 and 1233-1 of the Draft, *see* Laithier, *supra* n. 77, at 51–53.
93. On the doctrine of *obligations de sécurité*, *see* para. 61 below.
94. However, the interpretation of these words and, more generally, the acceptance of an option between contractual and extra-contractual liability give rise to difficulties. *See,* for example, Jonas Knetsch, *Faut-il décontractualiser la réparation du dommage contractuel ?*, Revue des contrats 2016, 801.

III. The Scope of Contractual Liability

61. In light of the distinctiveness of contractual liability and given the *non-cumul* rule, it is important to set out the precise scope of contractual liability. To put it simply, a liability claim between two contracting parties is subject to the law of contracts if a breach of the contract (*inexécution contractuelle*) has caused a loss to one of them. This implies not only the existence of a valid contract between the claimant and the defendant but also a loss which can be attributed to the non-performance of a contractual obligation. These two requirements may seem obvious, but especially the second one has given rise to many uncertainties since French law has always taken a very broad approach to the perimeter of contractual obligations. At the beginning of the twentieth century, the Court of Cassation introduced with respect to contracts of carriage an implied 'safety obligation' (*obligation de sécurité*), which allowed passengers who suffered personal injury during the transportation to sue the carrier for damages on the basis of contractual liability. Since then, the *obligation de sécurité* has been extended to various other contracts in which the health or safety of one of the parties is at risk.[95] It is, therefore, not uncommon for French lawyers to deal with personal injury cases that do not fall within the scope of extra-contractual liability but lie solely within the area of contracts.

62. In the same spirit, the Court of Cassation decided that in the context of 'contractual groups' (*chaînes de contrats*), a client can sue for damages in contract even though the defendant is not the other contracting party, provided that the individual contracts are 'homogeneous'.[96] In a landmark decision in 1986,[97] the Full Assembly held that a client who had instructed an architect to erect a building could claim damages in contract from the supplier of material with whom the architect had contracted. The idea was that the right to compensation on a contractual basis be attached to the defective material as an accessory (*accessoire*) running automatically with the goods to whoever becomes their owner. In 1991, the Full Assembly limited this solution to cases in which all contracts in the chain imply a transfer of ownership (*chaînes de contrats translatifs de propriété*).[98]

63. Closely related to the extension of the contractual duties and the personal scope of contractual liability is the case law on the liability of contracting parties

---

95. *See*, e.g., Steiner, *supra* n. 16, at 85 (illustration of the complex interplay between case law and legislation); Pierre Catala & Tony Weir, *Delict and Torts: A Study in Parallel Part I*, 37 Tulane Law Review 573, 576 (1963). From a comparative standpoint, *see* Hein Kötz, *European Contract Law* (OUP, 2d ed. 2017) 106–108 ('collateral duties').

96. On this case law, *see* the more detailed analysis in the English language by Kötz, *supra* n. 95, at 329–331.

97. Ass plén, 7 February 1986, no. 83-14631 (for an English translation *see* https://law.utexas.edu/transnational/foreign-law-translations/french/case.php?id=1294).

98. For a critical assessment of this solution, *see* Jean-Sébastien Borghetti, *Breach of Contract and Liability to Third Parties in French Law: How to Break the Deadlock?*, ZEuP 2010, 279, 284. *See* also Simon Whittaker, *Privity of Contract and the Law of Tort: the French Experience*, 15 Oxford Journal of Legal Studies 327, 354–357 (1995).

towards third parties, which reveals another major source of complexity.[99] Since the famous *Bootshop/Myr'Ho* case of 2006,[100] if the non-performance of a contractual obligation causes a loss to a third party, the contractual failing (*inexécution contractuelle*) may be invoked by the defendant as the legal grounds for a compensation claim in tort without further proof of fault under Article 1240 Civil Code. In this case, a commercial building had been leased to a company called Myr'Ho which then sublet it to another company named Bootshop. Arguing that the owners were not maintaining the building as they should, Bootshop filed a compensation claim against them on the grounds of extra-contractual liability. The Full Assembly of the Court of Cassation decided that a breach of contract could as such be a source of liability for the contracting party vis-à-vis a third party.[101] Yet this solution is highly controversial as it allows a third party to invoke the non-performance of a contractual obligation without proof of the violation of a general duty towards him. Moreover, it affects the legitimate expectations of the contracting parties since exemption or limitation clauses do not apply to this compensation claim. It is, therefore, likely that civil liability reform will lead to an amendment on this issue. Drawing on the German law, the 2017 Draft Reform suggests awarding an extra-contractual compensation claim on the basis of breach of contract only to 'a third party who has a legitimate interest in the proper performance of a contract' and only subject to the 'conditions and limitations' stipulated in the contract.[102]

64. In contrast, there are cases in which a defendant can only claim damages in tort, that is, on the basis of extra-contractual liability despite a context more or less related to a contractual relationship. Indeed, precontractual liability is in principle subject to fault-based liability (Article 1240 Civil Code), for example, in cases of an excessively late withdrawal from negotiations or a lack of fairness during negotiations.[103] This rule does not apply, however, in cases in which the negotiating parties had concluded a preliminary contract and had not complied with its provisions.[104] Moreover, the liability arising from a doctor-patient relationship is no longer contractual as a 2002 Act on Patients' Rights enacted a specific liability

99. *See* Philippe Stoffel-Munck, *Liability of Contracting Parties Towards Third Parties*, in *French Civil Liability in Comparative Perspective* (Jean-Sébastien Borghetti & Simon Whittaker eds, Hart 2019) 55; Borghetti, *Breach of Contract*, *supra* n. 98, at 287–292.

100. Ass plén, 6 October 2006, no. 05-13255, commented in Olivier Moréteau, *France* in *ETL 2006 (2007)*, 196, paras 32–41.

101. This is at least the interpretation approved by a majority of the commentators. For a comprehensive comment on this case in English, *see* Borghetti, *Breach of Contract*, *supra* n. 98, at 290–292.

102. For a detailed comment on Art. 1234 of the Reform Draft, *see* Philippe Stoffel-Munck, *Liability of Contracting Parties Towards Third Parties*, in *French Civil Liability in Comparative Perspective* (Jean-Sébastien Borghetti & Simon Whittaker eds, Hart 2019) 55, 62–64.

103. For an extensive study, *see* Paula Giliker, *Pre-contractual Liability in English and French Law* (Kluwer 2001) 105. *See* also by the same author *A Role for Tort in Pre-contractual Negotiations?*, 52 ICLQ 969, 979–985 (2003); *Regulating Contracting Behaviour: The Duty to Disclose in English and French Law*, 13 ERPL 621 (2005). More broadly on and with case studies, *see* John Cartwright & Martijn W. Hesselink (eds), *Precontractual Liability in European Private Law* (CUP 2009).

104. Giliker, *Pre-contractual Liability*, *supra* n. 103, at 31.

regime laid out in Article L 1142-1 Public Health Code.[105] Finally, public notaries (*notaires*) are liable on an extra-contractual basis because of their monopolistic competences, even though those professionals tend to develop their counselling activities.[106]

§6. Protected Interests

65. French tort law is eager to provide full compensation for all varieties of loss, providing, of course, that all other requirements for civil liability are fulfilled. The system of liability, built on Articles 1240 to 1245 Civil Code, does not contain any definition of what should actually be understood by 'reparable loss' (*préjudice réparable*),[107] making it particularly 'claimant-friendly';[108] no distinction is made between interests relevant under tort law and those which are not protected. As a consequence, French courts do not hesitate to compensate pure economic loss, a concept widely unknown to French tort lawyers,[109] non-pecuniary damage or loss of chance. In the words of Jean-Sébastien Borghetti, '[i]f a foreign lawyer were to look at the substantive rules of French tort law as they are outlined in the literature (both in France and abroad), or taught in France, he would be amazed, and probably also alarmed, at the breadth of tort law'.[110] This does not, however, mean that there are no limitations at all to civil liability under French law. Although the famous 'floodgates argument' is barely an issue in legal literature, the courts do not hesitate to put up barriers against undesirable compensation claims, albeit on a case-by-case logic and using other legal instruments (such as causation) besides a list of protected interests.

66. The restriction that most closely approximates an approach in terms of protected interests is the legislation regarding 'wrongful life' cases. In 2000, the Court of Cassation addressed the issue of the civil liability of a doctor who failed to detect the risk of serious congenital deformation during a medical examination on a pregnant woman. The Plenary Session held the doctor liable, ordering him to compensate not only the mother but also the child who was born with severe disabilities.

105. Simon Taylor, *Medical accident liability and redress in English and French law* (CUP 2015) 30 ('statutory liability … independent of contract'). *See* paras 90–94 below.
106. *See* Lacrima Bianca Luntraru & Liviu Pop, *Civil Liability of Public Notaries*, Fiat Iustitia 1/2017, 193 (the paper is on Romanian law, but contains numerous references to French law). *See* also in French Philippe Brun, Richard Crône, Philippe Pierre & Jeanne de Poulpiquet, *Responsabilité des notaires* (Dalloz, 3d ed. 2018) Ch. 11. For more details, *see* para. 96 below.
107. The 2017 Draft Reform suggests a definition of reparable loss: 'Any certain loss is reparable where it results from harm and consists of an injury to a lawful interest, whether patrimonial or extra-patrimonial' (Art. 1235). It is yet unclear what the drafters meant by 'lawful interest' as this concept does not refer to any list or definition. *See* also Pietro Sirena, *The Concepts of 'Harm' in the French and Italian Laws of Civil Liability*, in *French Civil Liability in Comparative Perspective* (Jean-Sébastien Borghetti & Simon Whittaker eds, Hart 2019) 205, 206.
108. Jean-Sébastien Borghetti, *The Culture of Tort Law in France*, 3 JETL 158 (2012).
109. For the vigorous plea in favour of the compensation of pure economic loss, *see* Julie Traullé, *La réparation du préjudice économique 'pur' en question*, RTD civ 2018, 285.
110. Borghetti, *Culture of Tort Law*, *supra* n. 108, at 158.

The *Perruche* case gave rise to the most commented judgement in French history, both in legal doctrine and in the national press.[111] Due to its highly ethical dimension, the *Perruche* decision divided legal academics and the general public, provoking disbelief and anger among health professionals, disability organizations, the clergy and insurance companies. One of the many criticisms was that the malformation was congenital and not caused by medical intervention so that the compensation claim should have been rejected on the grounds of causation.[112] In reaction to the doctrinal and societal upheaval, the French Parliament adopted a law to limit case law following the *Perruche* decision. According to the 2002 Patients' Rights Act, claims 'on the sole basis of being born' are prohibited, and tort law-based compensation is only permitted in cases in which the child's handicap has been directly caused by medical fault. Otherwise, the expenses for the disabled child are to be met by the state through the principle of 'national solidarity' (*solidarité nationale*).[113] The consequence of this 'shift from liability to solidarity'[114] is that the interests of a child born with congenital disabilities which remained undiagnosed due to fault of the medical corps are no longer protected by tort law. As of now, the issue of compensation for birth defects is the only explicit restriction to civil liability in terms of protected interests.

67. Even though a French lawyer would be surprised if asked about the interests that are protected by tort law and those that are not, there is a clear trend towards a prioritization of certain kinds of compensation claims and, through it, towards a priority setting among protected interests.[115] French tort law is becoming a two-tier system in which personal injury cases are subject to preferential treatment. This trend became apparent for the first time in 1985 when the so-called *loi Badinter* was enacted in order to improve the legal situation of victims of traffic accidents. This specific statutory liability regime almost automatically grants a right to compensation for non-drivers (pedestrians, cyclists, etc.) who suffer bodily harm.[116] The 2017 Draft Reform confirms that development by suggesting that the liability rules might

111. In English, *see* for example Olivier Massot, *France* in *ETL 2001 (2002)*, 191, paras 34–58; Anne Morris & Séverine Saintier, *To Be or Not to Be: Is That The Question? Wrongful Life and Misconceptions*, 11 Medical Law Review 167, 174–175 (2003); Brigitte Feuillet, *The* Perruche *Case and French Medical Liability*, 139 Drexel Law Review 139 (2011); Julia Field Costich, *The Perruche Case and the Issue of Compensation for the Consequences of Medical Error*, 78 Health Policy 8 (2005).
112. For a more detailed assessment, *see* Feuillet, *supra* n. 111, at 144–145.
113. Morris & Saintier, *supra* n. 111, at 188–191.
114. Willem H. van Boom & Andrea Pinna, *Shifts from Liability to Solidarity: The Example of Compensation of Birth Defects*, in *Shifts in Compensation between Private and Public Systems* (Willem H. van Boom & Michel Faure eds, Springer 2007) 143, 151–155.
115. The emergence of specific liability rules for personal injury forming a sort of *droit du dommage corporel* claims has been addressed only recently. *See* Stéphanie Porchy-Simon, *Réflexions sur l'autonomie du 'droit' du dommage corporel*, in *Des spécificités de l'indemnisation du dommage corporel* (Christophe Quézel-Ambrunaz, Philippe Brun & Laurence Clerc-Renaud eds, Bruylant 2017) 9; Jonas Knetsch, *Le traitement préférentiel du dommage corporel*, JCP G 2016, Suppl to nos 30–35, 9.
116. *See* paras 174–180 below.

be loosened on a number of points (causation, *non-cumul* rule, grounds of justification) for claims concerning the compensation for bodily injury (*dommage corporel*).[117] Should the reform plans be passed into law, it could be common in the future that a compensation claim would be subject to different liability regimes according to the type of loss invoked. In any case, further reflection needs to be given to the very concept of *dommage corporel,* the boundaries of which are still unclear for now.[118]

117. On the 2016 Preliminary Draft, *see* Knetsch, *Le traitement préférentiel*, *supra* n. 115. On the relaxation of causation rules, *see* also Nuno Manuel Pinto Oliveira, *Liability for Alternative Causation and for the Loss of a Chance*, in *French Civil Liability in Comparative Perspective* (Jean-Sébastien Borghetti & Simon Whittaker eds, Hart 2019) 247, 252.

118. For a recent work, *see* Stéphanie Porchy-Simon, *La victime de dommage corporel: retour sur deux concepts fondamentaux du droit de la réparation*, D 2021, 296.

Part I. Liability for One's Own Acts

Chapter 1. General Principles

§1. Concept of Fault

68. In comparative legal literature, it is a commonplace to emphasize the 'broad approach' of French tort law[119] as compared to the disparate English law of torts and to the 'law of unlawful acts' (*Recht der unerlaubten Handlungen*) of the German Civil Code. The contrast arising from the comparison is indeed striking (although sometimes overstated), especially when it comes to liability for fault, laid out in two of the most famous provisions of the French Civil Code.

> Article 1240 (former Article 1382): Any human action whatsoever which causes harm to another creates an obligation in the person by whose fault it was caused to make reparation for it.
> Article 1241 (former Article 1383): Everyone is liable for the harm which he caused not only by his action, but also by his failure to act or his lack of care.

Embodying the 'triumph of generalization from the particular actions for delicts found in Roman law',[120] those articles had a significant influence on other tort law systems. The drafters of the Civil Code deliberately chose to implement an open concept of fault based on the work of legal scholars of the *Ancien Régime*, which is similar to the concept of fault in a religious sense. In particular, the work of Domat, strongly influenced by the ideas of Canon Law, set the foundation for the provisions on civil liability. Hence, it is not surprising that they were designed in accordance with a moralistic vision focussed on the concept of *faute* as the main trigger of civil liability[121] rather than on a technical vision.

119. *See* for example Steiner, *supra* n. 16, at 250.
120. Bell, Boyron & Whittaker, *supra* n. 17, 361.
121. The reference work is Olivier Descamps, *Les origines de la responsabilité pour faute personnelle dans le Code civil de 1804* (LGDJ, 2005). *See* also Olivier Descamps, *L'esprit de l'article 1382 du Code civil*, Droits 2005, 91. In English *see* Bernadette Auzary-Schmaltz, *Liability in Tort in France before the Code Civil: The Origins of Art. 1382 ff. Code Civil*, in *Negligence. The Comparative Legal History of the Law of Torts* (Eltjo J.H. Schrage ed., Duncker & Humblot 2001) 309 and, more concise, Thomas Glyn Watkin, *An Historical Introduction to Modern Civil Law* (Routledge 2017) 307.

69. Yet this departure from the complex Roman law tradition only appeared to lead to a simplification of tort law. Since 1804, generations of civil lawyers have tried to elaborate viable definitions of the concept of fault, so far, it must be said, without great success. Even though there is agreement on the idea that *faute* reflects the breach of a duty of conduct, no matter its source, there still is much opacity on its exact outlines. In general, French lawyers seem to accommodate the malleability of the concept of 'fault' and it is widely seen as a convenient legal tool to adapt the primary liability regime to contemporary tort law problems.[122] There are only a few authors who see a problem in the generality of *faute* and do not hesitate to point out 'an increasingly abstract and disembodied idea'[123] that increasingly looks like a 'criterion for the imputation of a duty to make reparation'.[124] Even though case law proves that fault-based liability is still an important regime in practice, *la faute* has become a rather imprecise concept used by courts as a balancing item to regulate litigation, especially in personal injury cases. It is not unusual for French courts (and above all the Court of Cassation) to deduce the existence of fault from the mere proof of harm or vice-versa, blurring boundaries between the requirements of liability as conceptualized by the French legal doctrine.[125] More than 200 years after the enactment of the Code Napoléon, the apparent simplicity of liability for fault masks a highly differentiated situation. This explains why the doctrinal view on the concept of *faute* fluctuates between two extremes: whereas some authors emphasize its 'decline',[126] others prefer to speak of 'a second youth'.[127]

70. It is very likely that a foreign lawyer, unfamiliar with French tort law, is puzzled by the vague definition of *faute*. Starting from the position that fault consists in not acting as one should (that is to say, a misconduct) might not be satisfactory to a lawyer trained in another legal system who looks for additional requirements such as unlawfulness (*Rechtswidrigkeit*) or the infringement of a protected interest. The best answer that can be given is that the concept of fault is sufficiently large to absorb some of these, as the requirement of 'reparable harm' (*dommage réparable*) or the doctrine of grounds of justification (*causes d'exonération*) take over the same functions.

---

122. Geneviève Viney, *Pour ou contre un 'principe général de responsabilité civile pour faute'?*, in *Le Droit privé français à la fin du XXe siècle. Études offertes à Pierre Catala* (Litec 2001) 555. *See* also Georges Durry, *Rapport de synthèse*, Resp civ assur 2003, étude 22 ('In my opinion, it is an excellent tool we cannot do without, unless we want to cause … irreparable harm.').
123. Jean-Sébastien Borghetti, *The Definition of* la faute *in the* Avant-projet de réforme, in *Reforming the French Law of Obligations* (John Cartwright, Stefan Vogenauer & Simon Whittaker eds, Hart 2009) 271, 284.
124. Borghetti, *The Definition*, *supra* n. 123, at 286.
125. *See,* in particular, Laurène Gratton, *Le dommage déduit de la faute*, RTD civ 2013, 275.
126. Yvonne Flour, *Faute et responsabilité civile. Déclin ou renaissance?*, Droits 1987, 29. *See* also the other contributions to the special issue *Fin de la faute?*, Droits 1987.
127. Philippe le Tourneau, *La verdeur de la faute dans la responsabilité civile (ou de la relativité de son déclin)*, RTD civ 1988, 505; Christophe Radé, *L'impossible divorce de la faute et de la responsabilité civile*, D 1998, chr 301.

71. More generally, the idea of unlawfulness or wrongfulness (which could be translated as *illicéité*) is not as present in French law as in other jurisdictions.[128] Despite some doctrinal efforts to establish this concept,[129] it has never been identified as a separate requirement for civil liability. While there is a broad consensus that a behaviour can only qualify as *faute* if there is an infringement of a rule of conduct imposed by law, this qualification scheme does not operate under the banner of unlawfulness but under the more general concept of fault. Whereas in other legal systems (such as German law), the unlawfulness test is intended to balance conflicting legally protected interests,[130] those considerations are directly taken into account when determining the existence of *faute*.[131]

72. The 2017 Draft Reform does not adopt a fundamentally different approach. The famous Article 1240 of the actual Civil Code finds its counterpart in the less glamourous Article 1241 of the draft which provides that 'a person is liable for the harm caused by his fault' without giving more details. A semblance of definition is given in Article 1242 of the draft which states that 'a violation of a legislative requirement or failure in the general duty of care or diligence constitutes a fault'. Both provisions are supposed to enshrine the doctrinal consensus on civil liability for fault[132] but fail to give more information on the relevant standard of conduct and, more generally, on how to assess *faute* in practice.

§2. Duty of Care

73. Tort lawyers with a common law background might argue that the French concept of fault is similar to the notion of duty of care as laid out in the famous *Donoghue v Stevenson* case. In some ways, the assessment of *faute* does indeed imply a determination of whether the defendant had to take reasonable care to avoid acts or omissions which he could reasonably foresee would likely injure his neighbour. Nevertheless, the French approach to fault is broader than the duty of care in the tort of negligence in British law as it covers a much wider range of situations.

74. Under French law, the existence of fault is determined according to a method that can best be described as a comparison between the defendant's litigious conduct and the attitude which a 'reasonable person'[133] would have adopted in the same

---

128. Olivier Moréteau, *Basic Questions, supra* n. 51, at para. 1/141.
129. *See*, in particular, Marc Puech, *L'illicéité dans la responsabilité civile extra-contractuelle* (LGDJ 1973). For an overview of the doctrinal debate, *see* Geneviève Viney, Patrice Jourdain & Suzanne Carval, *Conditions de la responsabilité* (LGDJ 4th ed. 2013) para. 443.
130. For example, in cases of the violation of personality rights (privacy, image rights etc.).
131. *See* also Geneviève Viney, *Le 'Wrongfulness' en droit français*, in *Unification of Tort Law: Wrongfulness* (Helmut Koziol ed., Kluwer Law 1998) 57.
132. Marie Dugué, *The Definition of Civil Fault*, in *French Civil Liability in Comparative Perspective* (Jean-Sébastien Borghetti & Simon Whittaker eds, Hart 2019) 79, 83–85. *See* also Borghetti, *The Definition, supra* n. 123, at 275–282.
133. The standard of reference was traditionally referred to as the behaviour of a *bonus pater familias* or a *bon père de famille*. Used by the drafters of the 1804 Code Napoléon, this obsolete expression was replaced in 2014 by the term '*personne raisonnable*'. Some authors see this as a clear sign of

situation. If the claimant can provide evidence of a variance between this standard and the disputed conduct, then fault under Articles 1240 and 1241 Civil Code is established. This means that the central issue of the assessment of *faute* is the identification of an attitude that can be expected of a reasonable man or woman towards others, and it is on this point that the liability based on fault departs from the tort of negligence. Under French law, rules of conduct (*devoirs de comportement*) can arise from statutory law,[134] codes of professional conduct[135] and even sporting rules.[136] Yet the Court of Cassation has always preserved the lower courts' margin of appreciation and accepts that fault can be established on a case-by-case basis even in areas that are not governed by written rules. When taking a closer look at the case law of the trial courts, it appears that judges often follow their common sense as well as their understanding of morality and fairness, taking into account – without explicitly saying so – the defendant's liability insurance coverage.

75. It is often said that fault is determined by consideration of the act itself, without taking into account the defendant's particular circumstances, such as skills, intelligence, emotional state or age.[137] This abstract approach (*appréciation in abstracto*) enables French judges to apply fault-based civil liability even in cases in which the defendant has limited mental or social skills due to his age or disability; similarly, the conduct of a man usually thoughtless in his own affairs is assessed in the light of a reasonable person, irrespective of his usual clumsiness.[138] However, in practice, the case law is more complex, as trial judges do not compare the conduct of a professional (doctor, lawyer, architect etc.) to that of a lay person.[139] There are even cases in which judges do not hesitate to take into consideration the defendant's age or health condition to adapt the standard used for the purpose of assessing fault.[140] It seems that behind the statement of an *appréciation in abstracto*, the

---

the growing importance of the Common Law concept of reasonableness and, thus, as a step towards an Americanization of French civil law. *See,* for example, Jérôme Huet, *Adieu bon père de famille*, D 2014, 505; Laurent Convert, *Feu le 'bon père de famille' et l'avènement du standard 'raisonnable' : un pas vers la* 'reasonable person' *du* common law*?*, Tribonien : revue critique de législation et de jurisprudence 2018, 166.

134. E.g., duties resulting from criminal or administrative law.

135. *See* para. 87 below. For a brief comparative study, *see* Cees van Dam, *European Tort Law* (OUP, 2d ed. 2013) para. 812-2.

136. On the particularities of civil fault in a sporting context, *see* Jonas Knetsch, *France* in *ETL 2018 (2019)*, 191, paras 10–17. *See* also Patrice Jourdain, *À propos de la faute en matière sportive*, in *Le monde du droit: Écrits rédigés en l'honneur de Jacques Foyer* (Economica, 2007) 559.

137. The reference work in French doctrine is of Noël Dejean de la Bâtie, *Appréciation in abstracto et appréciation in concreto en droit civil français* (LGDJ 1965). *See* also Viney, Jourdain & Carval, *Conditions*, *supra* n. 129, at paras 462–472.

138. Dugué, *supra* n. 132, at 92.

139. Yet it is unclear whether specific skills, professional or not, may be considered if the defendant's conduct is deviant as compared to the way he would have behaved ordinarily. *See* Viney, Jourdain & Carval, *Conditions*, *supra* n. 129, at para. 471.

140. Viney, Jourdain & Carval, *Conditions*, *supra* n. 129, at paras 466–469 (with references to case law).

law is not settled. Unfortunately, the 2017 Draft Reform maintains the status quo, implying that despite their fundamental nature, those questions are a matter of case law and not subject to legislation.[141]

76. Given that the liability for fault is based on a general approach to the rules of conduct used to assess the existence of *faute*, there is hardly any room for taking into account the purpose of the infringed duties. This reasoning is known in France under the name of 'doctrine of Aquilian relativity' (*théorie de la relativité aquilienne*), which in fact corresponds to the German 'legal policy theory' (*Lehre vom Schutzzweck der Norm*).[142] Nevertheless, despite increasing interest among contemporary tort law scholars, this doctrine remains for now confined to academic debates. Neither the Court of Cassation case law nor the 2017 Draft Reform tends to relativize the general scope of the civil liability for fault.[143]

§3. Fault Classification

77. Fault can be the result of either a positive act (*faute par commission*) or an omission (*faute par omission*). In most cases, the standard of reference used to identify fault implies an obligation *not to* adopt a certain behaviour (e.g., not to kill anyone, not to hurt someone, not to deteriorate someone's belongings), the infringement of which will arise to a *faute par commission*. Sometimes, fault can also be characterized in cases of a failure to comply with an obligation to act in a certain way. The regime applicable to those *fautes par omission* (or *fautes d'abstention*) has long been restrictive, as courts have acknowledged the existence of fault only in cases in which the omission could be linked to a positive action[144] or the claimant could invoke a specific obligation to act.[145] There is broad agreement that the Court of Cassation in the famous *Branly* case abandoned this narrow approach and recognized that fault can be characterized as an intentional or non-intentional omission regardless of any specific statutory duty to act.[146] As a result, many authors think that a *faute par omission* is subject to the same regime as *faute par commission*. Yet,

141. Dugué, *supra* n. 132, at 93.
142. According to this doctrine, civil liability for fault shall be restricted to cases in which the violated norm was intended to protect the interest that was in fact harmed. From a comparative standpoint, *see* Christian von Bar, *The Common European Law of Torts* vol 2 (C H Beck 2000) paras 220–223. *See* also in French Marie Dugué, *L'intérêt protégé en droit de la responsabilité civile* (LGDJ 2019) paras 177–233.
143. Dugué, *supra* n. 132, at 90–92; Borghetti, *The Definition*, *supra* n. 123, at 284.
144. In those cases, the omission was qualified as an *abstention dans l'action*, i.e., an 'omission in action'.
145. *See*, for example, Catala & Weir, *supra* n. 95, at 614–620; F. H. Lawson, A. E. Anton & L. Neville Brown, *Amos and Walton's Introduction to French Law* (Clarendon Press 3d ed. 1967) 218–219.
146. The *Branly* case (Civ, 27 February 1951) was about an historian who omitted to mention the name of Edouard Branly in a book on the history of wireless telegraphy. For an English presentation, *see* Steiner, *supra* n. 16, at 255–256; Michel Séjean, *France*, in *Digest of European Tort Law*, vol 3 *Essential Cases on Misconduct* (Bénédict Winiger, Ernst Karner & Ken Oliphant eds, de Gruyter 2018) 1252–1253. *See* also the famous case note Jean Carbonnier, *Le silence et la gloire*, D 1951, chr 119. From a more general perspective, *see* Martin Vranken, *Duty to Rescue in Civil Law and Common Law: Les Extrêmes se Touchent?*, 47 ICLQ 934, 938–941 (1998).

once again, the actual case law gives a more nuanced picture. Pending a comprehensive assessment, one has to recognize that in some cases, courts require a specific duty to act, suggesting that there is still a certain distinctiveness to wrongful omission.[147]

78. When it comes to the distinction between intentional and non-intentional fault, Article 1241 Civil Code gives a straightforward answer. According to this provision, which has not changed since 1804, 'everyone is liable for the harm which he caused not only by his action (*fait*), but also by his failure to act (*négligence*) or his lack of care (*imprudence*)'. To understand this rule, it is important to keep in mind that the word *fait* in the sense used by the drafters of the Civil Code only refers to intentional actions, which means that the seriousness of fault is irrelevant when assessing whether there is or is not civil liability.[148] The assimilation of intentional and non-intentional fault is more clearly discerned in the 2010 *Terré* Reform Draft in which Article 5 stated that 'fault consists in committing an unlawful action, voluntarily or by negligence', which reflects the current state of French tort law.

79. However, even though intentional and non-intentional faults are not subject to separate treatment, it would be incorrect to suggest that the degree of seriousness is of no importance whatsoever in French tort law. First of all, given the importance of liability insurance in France, it is notable that insurance coverage is not available for intentional fault under French law.[149] Second, the provisions governing specific liability regimes often refer to the degree of fault with respect to contributory fault[150] or even for the purpose of establishing a right to compensation.[151] Third and last, the liability regime for fault is not as monolithic as it seems: in certain cases, the Court of Cassation has not hesitated to raise the liability threshold by adapting the required degree of fault. As will be seen, in several areas, such as compensation claims against employees,[152] managers,[153] sportsmen[154] or media organizations,[155]

147. In the same sense, Philippe Brun, *Responsabilité civile extracontractuelle* (LexisNexis, 5th ed. 2018) para. 317. Pleading for a total assimilation of *fautes par omission* and *fautes par commission*, *see* Viney, Jourdain & Carval, *Conditions*, *supra* n. 129, at para. 453. The 2017 Draft Reform remains silent, once again, on this issue. *See* the commentary Dugué, *supra* n. 132, at 94–96.

148. *See* Jean-Sébastien Borghetti, *L'ex-article 1382 du Code civil et le droit de la responsabilité civile: Requiem pour une disposition méconnue*, Revue de droit d'Assas 2020, no. 20, 153.

149. According to Art. L 113-1(2) Insurance Code (*Code des assurances*), 'the insurer does not cover losses and casualties caused by intentional or wilful (*dolosive*) fault of the insured person'. In practice, almost every insurance contract containing a liability insurance coverage provides for a contractual exclusion of casualties caused by the insured.

150. The best illustration of this is given by the liability rules applicable to motor vehicle accidents, laid out in the 1985 *loi Badinter*. According to Art. 3(1), in case of a personal injury caused to a 'non-driver', only his *faute inexcusable* or intentional fault may lead to partial or complete exoneration. *See* para. 179 below.

151. In 'wrongful life' cases, Art. L 114-5(3) Social Action and Family Code (*Code de l'action sociale et des familles*) requires proof of a health professional's 'gross negligence' (*faute caractérisée*) for the parents of the child to be awarded damages.

152. *See* para. 100 below.

153. *See* para. 101 below.

154. *See* para. 125 below.

155. *See* para. 121 below.

fault-based civil liability is confined within a restricted perimeter, with the actual case law requiring particularly severe fault.

§4. CAPACITY[156]

80. When the Civil Code came into force in 1804, it was evident to every French lawyer that civil liability for fault should be subject to a person's ability to understand the consequences of their actions (*capacité de discernement*). On the basis of this moral element (*élément moral*) of fault, young children and mentally handicapped adults could traditionally not be sued in tort and were exempt from civil liability. Yet over the past 50 years, the situation has considerably changed and today the concept of fault is generally presented as a purely objective one (*faute objective*).

81. Considering that the lack of compensation would be socially unjust in those cases and given the availability of liability insurance coverage for children and disabled adults, the French legislator introduced in 1968 a new provision in the Civil Code stating that 'a person who has caused damage to another when he was under the influence of a mental disorder is nonetheless liable to compensation'.[157] The Court of Cassation had already ruled a few years earlier that a person whose misconduct occurs during a state of dementia is nevertheless liable for the damage caused by a vehicle under his custody.[158]

82. In 1984, the Plenary Session of the Court of Cassation decided to go even further in this direction, given that the provision introduced in 1968 was understood as 'the expression of a more general idea that subjective shortcomings should not be an obstacle for liability'.[159] In a series of five landmark decisions, it addressed several issues related to children in tort law.[160] Among them, the *Lemaire* and *Derguini* cases dealt with the problem of fault applied to a young child who has not reached the age of discretion (also known as an *infans*).[161] The Court of Cassation decided that trial judges 'did not have to examine whether the minor was able to understand the consequences of his actions', implying that the very young age of

156. On this, *see* in English Nuno Ferreira, *Fundamental Rights and Private Law in Europe: The Case of Tort Law and Children* (Routledge 2011) 142–145; Laurence Francoz-Terminal, Fabien Lafay, Olivier Moréteau & Caroline Pellerin-Rugliano, *Children as Tortfeasors under French Law*, in *Children in Tort Law* vol 1 (Miquel Martín-Casals ed., Springer 2006) 169–215 and *Children as Victims under French Law* in *Children in Tort Law* vol 2 (Miquel Martín-Casals ed., Springer 2007) 89–120; Nicholas Kasirer, *The* infans *as* bon père de famille*: 'Objectively Wrongful Conduct' in the Civil Law Tradition*, 40 American Journal of Comparative Law 343, 359–377. From a comparative standpoint, *see* van Dam, *supra* n. 135, at 269–277.

157. Art. 414-3 C Civ.

158. Civ 2, 18 Decembre 1964, D 1965, jur 191.

159. Van Dam, *supra* n. 135, at 272. In French, *see* in particular Viney, Jourdain & Carval, *Conditions*, *supra* n. 129, at para. 593.

160. *See* also paras 147, 171 below.

161. Ass plén, 9 May 1984, D 1984, jur 525.

the minor was not an obstacle for *faute*. What is remarkable in the *Lemaire* and *Derguini* cases is that this solution was held not in favour of but against children as the defendants invoked their contributory fault. Apparently, for the sake of consistency, the Court of Cassation held that the concept of fault should be disconnected from capacity both for children as tortfeasors and for children as victims and, therefore, understood in a merely objective way (*faute objective*). In other words, since 1984, fault may be committed by a person who is unable to appreciate the significance of his actions, whether to grant full compensation to another person on the grounds of liability for fault or to reduce a compensation claim on the basis of contributory fault.

83. The 2017 Draft Reform maintains the idea of an objective approach to *faute*, which is defined as 'a violation of a legislative requirement or a failure in the general duty of care or diligence' (Article 1242). Even though this is not specified in this provision, it is reasonable to assume that in the absence of any requirement of capacity, the concept of fault is reduced to mere misconduct regardless of the age and illness of the defendant. However, in order to respond to criticisms, the drafters made sure that, unlike current case law, this solution would not lead to a reduction of the right to compensation on the grounds of contributory fault. According to Article 1255 of the Draft Reform, 'unless it bears the characteristics of force majeure, fault in a victim who lacks discernment has no exonerating effect'. To borrow the words of Marie Dugué, the 'idea that fault is objective … was required to protect victims, but it worked against very small children who had been partly responsible for their own harm, as their behaviour could easily be established as objectively at fault'.[162] It is obvious that from an equity perspective, the concept of *faute objective* would lose its 'bitter taste' with this amendment; nonetheless, the (re)introduction of a subjective component would make the doctrinal assessment of fault even more complex.

162. Dugué, *supra* n. 132, at 84.

Chapter 2. Specific Cases of Liability for Fault

84. The generality of the terms used in Articles 1240 and 1241 Civil Code should not mislead the foreign lawyer unfamiliar with the interplay of legislation and case law in French tort law. Even if the liability for fault may appear as a monolithic concept that is usable in all areas of human activity, an assessment of the case law of the Court of Cassation reveals a more nuanced approach to *faute* than may at first glance appear. While it is sometimes argued that the diversity of treatment in fact masks a plurality of fault-based liability regimes,[163] it may also be that the attention given to the specific context (professional duty, sports, interference with human rights) is a natural pattern of differentiation that can be observed in every jurisdiction.[164] It is true that the application of higher standards of care in some areas may blur the boundaries between fault-based and strict civil liability. Nevertheless, it seems that those grey zones inherent to contemporary tort law do not diminish the structuring and didactical value of a general ground, such as fault, for civil liability.

85. Despite the broad scope of Articles 1240 and 1241 Civil Code, separate attention needs to be given to the liability of public authorities. As has already been pointed out,[165] the law of 'administrative liability' was detached from civil law in the late nineteenth century and is today, in its essence, the preserve of the administrative courts and, above all, the *Conseil d'État.*

§1. Liability of Professionals

I. In General

86. The liability for fault also lays the foundation for the civil liability of professionals. In French law, there is no specific set of rules constituting a 'law of professional liability' (*droit de la responsabilité professionnelle*).[166] In particular, one cannot say that the actions of professionals are judged against higher standards of reference or, on the contrary, that their liability is subject to the requirement of gross negligence or wilful misconduct. To use the words of a leading textbook, the principle that 'every fault, regardless of its gravity, involves the liability of its author

163. Jean-Sébastien Borghetti & Simon Whittaker, *Principles of Liability or Law of Torts?*, in *French Civil Liability in Comparative Perspective* (Jean-Sébastien Borghetti & Simon Whittaker eds, Hart 2019) 455, 462.
164. *See,* for example, von Bar, *supra* n. 142, at paras 244–305.
165. *See* para. 37 above.
166. Although there exists a specific tort law textbook with this title, it rather exposes the application of common liability rules in a professional context. *See* Philippe le Tourneau, *Responsabilité civile professionnelle* (Dalloz 2d ed. 2005). From a comparative standpoint, *see* Ewoud Hondious, *Professional Liability*, in *Comparative Tort Law: Global Perspectives* (Mauro Bussani & Anthony J. Sebok eds, Elgar 2015) 226. *See* also the premonitory work of André Tunc, *Ébauche du droit des contrats professionnels*, in *Le droit privé français au milieu du XXe siècle. Études offertes à Georges Ripert* vol 2 (LGDJ 1950) 136.

… also applies to the liability of professionals'.[167] However, the assessment of professional misconduct from the angle of civil liability is characterised by some specific traits that cannot be ignored.

87. As mentioned before,[168] the abstract approach to *faute* does not hinder French judges from taking into account the professional context of the litigious situation and to comparing the defendant's attitude to that of the conduct that a reasonable professional would have adopted in the same circumstances. Thus, the assessment of the professional's actions or omissions is not based on a comparison with the behaviour of a lay person, which is perfectly understandable. To determine the standard of reference, professional regulations such as codes of conduct (*codes de bonne conduite*) or charters of best practices (*chartes de bonnes pratiques*) are of great importance; among those 'professional codes', also called *règles déontologiques* by French lawyers, some have been formally recognized by public authorities and are today part of official regulations.[169]

88. A second peculiarity concerns the legal basis of liability of professionals. In accordance with the *non-cumul* rule, claims in compensation related to the performance of a contractual engagement and made by contracting partners are subject to the rules governing contractual liability.[170] As a result, professional liability is seen as a part of the law of contracts rather than as a specific field of civil liability. Extra-contractual liability is only relevant in cases in which a professional's misconduct caused harm to a third person or caused it at a time when the contract was still under negotiation or not yet concluded.[171]

89. In some areas, however, the legislator has adopted specific rules of civil liability, mostly based on liability for fault, which are applicable regardless of the contractual or extra-contractual status of the claimant. This is particularly the case with respect to the liability of medical practitioners, auditors and financial institutions.

---

167. Viney, Jourdain & Carval, *Conditions*, *supra* n. 129, at para. 599.
168. *See* para. 75 above.
169. An illustration is given by the *Code de déontologie médicale*, applicable to all accredited physicians and to medical students in France. Regularly updated by the National Medical Council (*Ordre national des médecins*), the code is part of the regulatory section of the Public Health Code (Arts R 4127-1–4127-122).
170. *See* paras 58–60 above.
171. Le Tourneau, *Responsabilité*, *supra* n. 166, at 121–157 (failure to inform the future contracting partner, breach of an *obligation de sécurité* vis-à-vis a third person's goods or physical integrity).

II. Medical Practitioners and Healthcare Institutions

90. The liability of medical practitioners exercising their activity on an independent basis (mostly in a doctor's office)[172] has long been seen as a matter of contractual liability. In 1936, the Court of Cassation decided that doctors could not be sued in tort and that their liability could only be related to the breach of a contract concluded with their patient unless the patient was unable to accept the care, for instance, in cases in which the patient was unconscious. In fact, according to the famous *Mercier* case, this contract imposed on the doctor an obligation 'not to cure the patient, but to provide him in a conscientious and attentive way with the appropriate care in accordance with the current state of scientific knowledge'.[173] Despite these general terms, French jurisdictions continued to refer to the requirement of gross negligence (*faute lourde*) until the end of World War II, responding to the extreme reluctance of medical practitioners to see their practices judged by other persons than their peers. While medical liability has been seen as a specific area of civil liability ever since the 1936 *Mercier* case, it was only in the 1950s that courts began to hold doctors liable on the basis of a *faute simple*, opening the door to an extensive and nuanced case law on medical malpractice.[174]

91. In 2002, the French legislator enacted the Patients' Rights and Quality of the Health System Act (*Loi relative aux droits des malades et à la qualité du système de santé*), previously mentioned in the context of the *Perruche* case law.[175] The impact of this act was of utmost importance for the liability of medical practitioners, public hospitals and private clinics.[176] Since its enactment, all healthcare providers regardless of their legal status (natural or legal person, public or private

---

172. In France, some doctors are allowed to offer medical consultations to patients as independent medical practitioners, despite their legal status as civil servants working in public hospitals. The liability of private clinics for medical malpractice follows the regime applicable to medical practitioners. For an overview of the French healthcare system and the status of healthcare professionals, *see*, for example, Isabelle Durand-Zaleski & Johan van Manen, *Country Report: France*, in *The Law and Policy of Healthcare Financing* (Wolf Sauter, Jos Boertjens, Johan van Manen & Misja Mikkers eds, Elgar 2019) 284.

173. Civ, 20 May 1936, D 1936, 1, 88. The translation is borrowed from Simon Taylor, *The Development of Medical Liability and Accident Compensation in France*, in *The Development of Medical Liability* (Ewoud Hondious ed., CUP 2010) 70, 80. On the *Mercier* doctrine, *see* also in English Thomas E. Carbonneau, *The Principles of Medical and Psychiatric Liability in French Law*, 29 ICLQ 742, 744–748 (1980); George G. Lorinczi, *The Legal Liability of the Physician in France*, 2 American Journal of Comparative Law 226 (1953).

174. On the development of medical liability, *see* in particular Taylor, *Development*, *supra* n. 173, at 80 and by the same author, *Medical Accident Liability and Redress in English and French Law* (CUP 2015) 28–48.

175. *See* para. 66 above.

176. On this reform, *see* in English Simon Taylor, *Clinical Negligence Reform: Lessons from France?*, 52 ICLQ 737 (2003); Dominique Thouvenin, *French Medical Malpractice Compensation Since the Act of March 4, 2002: Liability Rules Combined with Indemnification Rules and Correlated with Several Kinds of Proceedings*, 4 Drexel Law Review 165 (2011); Simon Taylor, *Providing redress for medical accidents in France: conflicting aims, effective solutions?*, 2 JETL 57 (2011); Florence G'sell-Macrez *Medical Malpractice and Compensation in France: Part I: the French Rules of Medical Liability since the Patients' Rights Law of March 4, 2002*, 86 Chicago-Kent Law Review

sector) are subject to the same rules of liability, and this is now regarded as a 'statutory liability regime' (*responsabilité légale*) rather than a contractual or extra-contractual one. The unification of liability rules is one of the major achievements of the 2002 act since French courts previously applied different rules depending on whether the harm occurred in a public hospital or during treatment in a private clinic or by a private doctor. However, the legislator did not have the fortitude to put an end to the dualism of competent courts: a compensation claim against a public hospital must be brought before an administrative court whereas a private clinic or a doctor is sued before civil courts. Thus, the harmonization of substantive liability rules did not go hand in hand with a simplification of the procedural rules.

92. Despite the multiplication of cases in which health care professionals can be held liable without fault,[177] the French Public Health Code (*Code de la santé publique*) reasserts the principle of fault-based liability. According to Article L 1142-1(1), 'medical practitioners … and all establishments, services and organizations in which medical acts of prevention, diagnosis and care are given, shall only be liable for fault', without prejudice to the existing cases of strict liability.[178] In legal literature, it is now widely understood that the fault of a medical practitioner (or any other healthcare provider) may be a technical or an ethical one. As for the first category, a compensation claim may be based on an error of diagnosis (*faute de diagnostic*), inappropriate treatment, carelessness during a medical or surgical act or follow-up care, always provided that such fault has caused a reparable loss to the patient. The second category of 'medical fault' encompasses all cases in which the patient's dignity has been offended, mostly due to a lack of consent to the treatment whether related or not to inadequate disclosure, as well as in circumstances qualified as therapeutic obstinacy (*obstination déraisonnable*).

93. Unlike in other tort law systems, French courts do not follow an 'all-or-nothing' approach when there is uncertainty about the causal link between medical fault and the deterioration in the patient's health status. In particular, the use of the loss of chance concept[179] as well as strict sanctioning of inadequate disclosure often leads to a partial compensation of medical accidents.[180] The 2002 Patients' Rights Act also enacted an out-of-court settlement scheme for compensation claims against doctors or health institutions which is coupled to compulsory liability insurance coverage. Even though the functioning of the 25 Conciliation and Compensation

---

1093 (2011). *See* also Simon Taylor, Duncan Fairgrieve & Véronique Wester-Ouisse, *Medical Accidents and Pharmaceutical Product Liability*, in *Regulating Risk through Private Law* (Matthew Dyson ed., Intersentia 2018) 301, 302–313.

177. Exceptions to the fault-based liability concern, in essence, infections contracted in medical facilities (so-called *infections nosocomiales*) and damages caused by defective medical products.

178. For more details on those exceptions, *see* Taylor, *Medical Accident Liability*, *supra* n. 174, at 37–42.

179. *See* paras 302–305 below.

180. On those 'adjustment variables' in French case law, *see* in particular Taylor, *Medical Accident Liability*, *supra* n. 174, at 43–45, 137–138. *See* also Suzanne Carval & Ruth Sefton-Green, *Medical Liability in France*, in *Medical Liability in Europe: A Comparison of Selected Jurisdictions* (Bernhard A. Koch ed., de Gruyter 2011) 207 and, more recently, Michel Séjean & Jonas Knetsch, *France* in *ETL 2014 (2015)*, 195, paras 20–26.

Commissions has given rise to criticism,[181] it has to be acknowledged that the legislative reform has contributed to a reduction in blame and frustration caused by tort litigation and to the acceleration of effective redress in the field of 'medical accidents'.[182]

94. This brief survey of medical liability would be incomplete without mentioning the existence of a compensation scheme for medical accidents caused by what is commonly referred to as *aléa thérapeutique*. The concept of 'therapeutic hazard' is deemed to cover all accidents which occur in the course of medical care without any fault of a healthcare professional and which cause serious harm that does not constitute a reasonably foreseeable development of the patient's pre-existing condition. In those cases, patients or their relatives will receive full reparation from a compensation fund called ONIAM which is financed by the health insurance branch of the national social security system.[183]

III. Legal Practitioners (*avocats*, *notaires* and *huissiers de justice*)

95. There are three main non-judicial legal professions in France. The *avocat* represents clients in civil, criminal and administrative cases before courts and, more broadly, gives legal advice on a day-to-day basis to individuals and companies; the *notaire* draws up legal acts, such as contracts and wills, that are endowed with almost the same legal value as a court judgement; the *huissier de justice* has the exclusive right to notify all procedural acts related to legal proceedings and to execute those acts (such as notarial acts or judgements) which have *force exécutoire*.[184]

96. The civil liability under French law of legal practitioners in cases of professional negligence (*faute professionnelle*) follows a two-tier approach. Whereas the *notaire* is held liable on an extra-contractual basis,[185] compensation claims against an *avocat* or an *huissier de justice* have to be brought on the grounds of contractual

181. For a more thorough analysis of those commissions, *see* Taylor, *Medical Accident Liability*, *supra* n. 174, at 150–170; Thouvenin, *supra* n. 176, at 176–185.

182. *See* on all this in English the excellent analysis by Taylor, *Medical Accident Liability*, *supra* n. 174, at 150–170.

183. For more details, *see* Philippe Brun, *France* in *ETL 2002 (2003)*, 179, paras 1–61; Taylor, *Clinical Negligence Reform*, *supra* n. 176, at 742–743; Geneviève Helleringer, *Medical Malpractice and Compensation in France: Part II: Compensation Based on National Solidarity*, Chicago-Kent Law Review 86, 1125 (2011); Thouvenin, *supra* n. 176, at 172–176; Jonas Knetsch, *The French Medical Accident Compensation Scheme. A Critical Assessment of the Patients' Rights Act of 4 March 2002*, in *Compensation Schemes for Damages Caused by Healthcare and Alternatives to Court Proceedings* (Dobrochna Bach-Golecka ed., Springer 2021) 179.

184. For a comprehensive presentation of the legal professions in France, *see* e.g. Bell, Boyron & Whittaker, *supra* n. 17, at 72–77. *See* also Catherine Elliott, Éric Jeanpierre & Catherine Vernon, *French Legal System* (Longman 2d ed. 2006) 238–251; John Bell, *French Legal Cultures* (CUP 2001) 44–46.

185. *See* para. 64 above.

non-performance.[186] This distinction may seem startling to foreign lawyers, particularly as it is widely understood that lawyers of all three professions conclude a contract of agency (*contrat de mandat*) with their clients. In fact, the extra-contractual nature of the *notaire*'s liability can only be explained by the strong ties between public authorities and the profession, vested with monopolistic competences, whose certifications are legitimized by the Seal of the State (*sceau de l'État*).[187]

97. The assessment of 'professional fault' (*faute professionnelle*) in a context of litigation against legal practitioners does not call for extensive reporting. However, attention has to be drawn to the importance of the duty of advice (*devoir de conseil*) which often is the cause of action between *avocats* or *notaires* and their clients.[188] It is notable that the concept of loss of chance (*perte de chance*) was first recognized in 1889 in a case in which a client of a *huissier de justice* claimed that professional negligence deprived him of a chance to win a case before a court.[189]

IV. Builders and Architects

98. In France, the liability of builders and architects towards their clients is in principle based on breach of contract and is thus a matter of contractual liability.[190] Within this area, the non-performance by a building company or an architect is governed by a complex system of liability regimes that depends on the seriousness of the construction defect and the timing of its occurrence.[191] Whereas defects which occur before the approval (*réception*) of the work are subject to general contractual liability, a disorder which affects the building's solidity and which occurs after the acceptance gives rise under Article 1792 of the Civil Code to the builder's decennial warranty (*garantie décennale*) without any requirement of fault. It is important to note that the term 'builder' (*constructeur*) is very broadly defined in Article 1792-1 Civil Code and encompasses all contractors involved in the construction of a building; accordingly, *garantie décennale* does not apply only to general contractors but also to architects and vendors of a building that has yet to be built (*vente en l'état futur d'achèvement*). In addition to this very client-friendly liability regime,

186. On the liability of *avocats*, *see*, e.g., Yves Avril, *Responsabilité des avocats* (Dalloz 4th ed. 2021); from a comparative standpoint, Panayotis J. Zepos & Phoebus Christodoulou, *Professional Liability*, in *International Encyclopedia of Comparative Law* vol XI (André Tunc ed., Brill & J C B Mohr 1983) paras 98–133; Louis B. Buchmann, *France*, in *Professional Liability of Lawyers* (Dennis Campbell ed., LLP 1995) 97–111. On the liability of *huissiers de justice*, *see* Yannick Tylinski, *La responsabilité professionnelle des huissiers de justice* (thesis Aix-Marseille 2002).

187. On notaries' civil liability, *see* the reference work by Brun, Crône, Pierre & de Poulpiquet, *supra* n. 106.

188. Avril, *supra* n. 186, at Ch. 21; Brun, Crône, Pierre & de Poulpiquet, *supra* n. 106, at Ch. 132.

189. Req, 17 July 1889, Sirey 1891, 1, 399. *See* also para. 303 below.

190. As mentioned in paras 58–60 above, the *non-cumul* rule prevents the client from invoking an extra-contractual liability.

191. To our knowledge, there is very little academic literature in English on the French liability regimes applicable to builders and architects. *See* the (partly outdated) work by Zepos & Christodoulou, *supra* n. 186, at paras 134–161; Jean Desmadryl & François Ausseur, *France*, in *Case Studies in Post Construction Liability and Insurance* (Anthony Lavers ed., Routledge 1999) 135. *See* also the brief overview given by von Bar & Drobnig, *supra* n. 91, at para. 85.

the French Civil Code also provides for a biennial warranty (*garantie biennale*) covering elements which may be removed or replaced without deteriorating the building's structure.[192] Finally, under Article 1792-6 Civil Code, there is a one-year 'warranty of perfected completion' which is a duty to repair all shortcomings indicated by the client in the memorandum of approval or by written notice after the approval.[193]

99. One of the peculiarities of the French liability system applicable to builders and architects is the compulsory construction insurance coverage that is designed to provide the building owner effective protection against construction defects subject to a decennial warranty.[194] Since 1978, the Civil Code has imposed a statutory duty upon both contractors and their clients to carry insurance coverage (liability insurance and property damage insurance, respectively). This two-tier system allows clients to obtain immediate compensation from their own insurance companies; in a second step, these insurers will bring compensation claims against the contractors' liability insurers. The extent of this dual insurance coverage is largely determined by statutory law.[195]

V. Others

100. Employees and agents (*préposés*)[196] acting within the limits of the tasks assigned by their employers or principals (*commettant*) cannot be held liable on the grounds of Articles 1240 and 1241.[197] In the famous *Costedoat* case from 2000, the Court of Cassation sitting in Plenary Session enacted a general 'civil immunity' for the *préposés* to be preserved from the burden of liability in case of harm caused by their fault.[198] According to subsequent case law, it is only in cases in which a *préposé* deliberately commits a criminal act, albeit under the orders of the employer, that personal civil liability may be incurred.[199] The reason for such an immunity can

192. Art. 1792-3 C Civ. For more details on the interplay of the decennial and the biennial warranty, *see* e.g. Marianne Faure-Abbad, *Droit de la construction* (Gualino, 3d ed. 2016) 265–365.
193. Faure-Abbad, *supra* n. 192, at 367–384.
194. *See* the English leaflet edited by the French Insurance Federation FFA *Decennial liability insurance: a guide designed for European builders* (FFA 2015) https://www.ffa-assurance.fr/en/publications/construction-insurance-english-german-italian-spanish/decennial-liability-insurance.
195. Art. L 242-1 Insurance Code (*Code des assurances*).
196. On the concept of *préposé*, *see* paras 132–134 below.
197. *See* in English especially Paula Giliker, *Vicarious Liability in Tort: Comparative Perspectives* (CUP 2010) 35–39 and by the same author *Comparative Perspectives on Vicarious Liability: Defining the Scope of Employment*, in *Emerging Issues in Tort Law* (Jason W. Neyers, Erika Chamberlain & Stephen G.A. Pitel eds, Hart 2007) 419, 434. *See* also Suzanne Galand-Carval, *Liability for Damage Caused by Others under French Law*, in *Unification of Tort Law: Liability for Damage Caused by Others* (Jan Spier ed., Kluwer Law 2003) 85, paras 36–41.
198. Ass plén, 25 February 2000, nos 97-17378, 97-20152.
199. This results from a 2001 decision (Ass plén, 14 December 2001, no. 00-82066). Yet pending clarification by the Court of Cassation, the exact boundaries of the immunity regime still remain unclear. The 2017 Draft Reform suggests a legal enshrinement of this immunity in the following terms: 'An employee is not subject to any personal liability except in the case of intentional fault, or where without authorisation he acted for purposes alien to his attributions.' (art 1249(4)).

be found in the Court of Cassation's willingness to bring the rules regarding civil liability of employees in line with those governing the personal liability of civil servants (*agent public*) who, according to administrative law, are granted an extensive immunity for harm caused 'within their service' (*faute de service*).[200]

101. Managers can be held personally liable not only to the corporation and the shareholders on the basis of a breach of their fiduciary duties but also vis-à-vis third parties for corporate fault.[201] Even though statutory law provides for their personal liability in case of an infringement of mandatory rules or mismanagement,[202] they are granted by the French courts a specific protection regime that is similar to the one applicable to employees and other *préposés*. According to the Court of Cassation's case law, the personal liability of directors can only be recognized when their fault can be detached from their functions (*faute détachable*). This is particularly the case when 'a director intentionally committed a serious fault incompatible with the normal exercise of his corporate duties'.[203] Yet the immunity resulting from the *faute détachable* requirement remains a source of litigation, especially when it comes to determining its precise limits. According to recent case law, the immunity is limited to compensation claims initiated by third persons and cannot be extended to those made by the corporation itself or by shareholders.[204]

102. Certified accountants (*experts-comptables*) are liable towards their clients for lack of care in performing their contractual duties. In most cases, compensation for a loss will thus be subject to the demonstration of contractual fault.[205] When assuming a contractual mission as a statutory auditor (*commissaire aux comptes*) for a company, the Commercial Code provides for a specific civil liability regime based on fault. According to Article L 822-17 Commercial Code, 'statutory auditors are liable, vis-à-vis the company and any third party, for the consequences of their fault or lack of care in the performance of their duties'. While the liability towards the

200. *See* para. 109 below.

201. On this issue, *see* especially Cristina Mauro, *France*, in *Directors' Personal Liability for Corporate Fault: A Comparative Analysis* (Helen Anderson ed., Wolters Kluwer 2008) 139; Alain Pietrancosta, Paul-Henri Dubois & Romain Garçon, *Corporate Boards in France*, in *Corporate Boards in Law and Practice: A Comparative Analysis in Europe* (Paul Davies et al. eds, OUP 2013) 175, 209–232. *See* also Jacques Buhart & Nicole Lafont, *France*, in *Directors' Liability. A Worldwide Review* (Alexander Loss ed., Wolters Kluwer 3d ed. 2016) 189; Romain Schulz, Eléonora Sorribes & Sarah Xerri-Hanote, *France*, in *Directors' Liability and Indemnification* (Edward Smerdon ed., A Global Guide 3d ed. 2016) 205.

202. *See* for example Arts L 225-251 Commercial Code (*Code de commerce*) concerning public companies (*sociétés anonymes*).

203. Com, 20 May 2003, no. 99-17092. *See* on this judgment Mauro, *supra* n. 201, at 147.

204. Com, 9 March 2010, no. 08-21547. *See* in French Viney, Jourdain & Carval, *Conditions*, *supra* n. 129, at para. 857.

205. *See* for example Christian de Lauzainghein, Jean-Louis Navarro & Dominique Nechelis, *Droit comptable* (Dalloz 3d ed. 2004) para. 181.

audited company does not call for any particular comment,[206] the auditor's third-party liability raises more questions, especially from a comparative perspective,[207] and also generates complex litigation issues.[208] Although twenty years ago Lara Khoury could claim that 'the French system ... is the only legal system in which the law provides explicitly for auditors' liability towards third parties',[209] corporate collapses in 2001 (such as Enron in the US) have led to substantial changes in the legislation of other countries, thereby converging towards an explicit third-party liability regime.[210]

103. Bankers are required to comply with several obligations which arise from both the contract with their clients and from statutory law. They have to carry out different verification steps when opening a bank account and maintain confidentiality (*secret bancaire*) once the bank/client relationship has been formalised by a contract. However, the main source of litigation is the duty to inform the clients of the possible consequences, financial or economical, of major monetary transactions, such as loans. The Court of Cassation also recognizes a duty to give proper advice (*devoir de conseil*) and even to cease the provision of funds to financially troubled companies.[211] The non-performance of this duty will be sanctioned by contractual civil liability under Article 1231-1 Civil Code.

206. As the statutory auditors' missions are of general interest and based on statutory law, their civil liability towards the company is not a contractual but an extra-contractual one, even though both parties are frequently tied by a contractual agreement (*contrat de mandat*). *See* Com, 3 December 2002, no. 01-00641 and for a more detailed assessment, Jean-François Barbiéri, *Quelques observations sur le fondement, la nature et le domaine de la responsabilité civile du commissaire aux comptes*, Bulletin Joly Sociétés 2004, 617.
207. *See*, in particular, Lara Khoury, *The Liability of Auditors beyond Their Clients: A Comparative Study*, 46 McGill Law Journal 413, 454–461 (2001). *See* also Werner F. Ebke, *'Ithaca' – Or: The Long Road to a Common Understanding of the Statutory Auditor's Third Party Liability in Europe*, in *Festschrift für Rolf Stürner zum 70. Geburtstag* vol 2 (Alexander Bruns et al. eds, Mohr Siebeck 2013) 1001; Werner F. Ebke & Dirk Struckmeier, *The Civil Liability of Corporate Auditors: An International Perspective* (International Bar Association 1994).
208. Daniel Langé, *Fasc 340 Commissaire aux Comptes* in *JurisClasseur Responsabilité civile et assurances* (LexisNexis 2014) paras 137–142.
209. Khoury, *supra* n. 207, at 454.
210. *See*, e.g., Janne Chung, Jonathan Farrar, Poonam Puri & Linda Thorne, *Auditor Liability to Third Parties after Sarbanes-Oxley: An International Comparison of Regulatory and Legal Reforms*, 19 Journal of International Accounting, Auditing and Taxation 66 (2010).
211. Viney, Jourdain & Carval, *Conditions*, *supra* n. 129, at para. 507-1. *See* also more recently Mihaela Varnav, *Gestion des risques juridiques bancaires: les obligations d'information, de mise en garde et de conseil du banquier* (Larcier, 2015).

§2. Liability of Public Authorities[212]

104. The distinction between public and private law is one of the distinctive features of the French legal system.[213] In the field of tort law, this peculiarity has significant consequences as the liability of public authorities is under the jurisdiction of administrative courts which are bound, at least in theory, neither by the texts nor by the principles of civil law. The separation of administrative and civil liability results from the famous *Blanco* case in which the *Tribunal des conflits* made clear that administrative courts have jurisdiction for compensation claims against the state and that those claims would not be subject to the rules of the Civil Code.[214] Even though there is a subtle influence of civil law rules, for example, regarding the assessment of damages,[215] it is widely acknowledged that *responsabilité civile* and *responsabilité administrative* are two distinct systems 'carry(ing) on independently'[216] and almost entirely judge-made.

105. The liability of public authorities is ruled by a double-sided liability regime similar to that which exists in the field of civil liability; liability for fault (*responsabilité pour faute*) contrasts with different strict liability regimes, generally grouped under the term *responsabilité sans faute*. However, unlike what is provided for in Article 1240 Civil Code, the principle of liability for fault is not as broad as under civil law, and it is applied in a different way than in civil cases. Moreover, state liability is not considered as a specific form of vicarious liability (or 'liability

212. The liability of public authorities under French law generated much interest among English-speaking legal scholars. *See* most recently Duncan Fairgrieve & François Lichère, *France*, in *The Liability of Public Authorities in Comparative Perspective* (Ken Oliphant ed., Intersentia 2017) 155; John Bell, *The Reform of Delict in the Civil Code and Liability in Administrative Law*, in *French Civil Liability in Comparative Perspective* (Jean-Sébastien Borghetti & Simon Whittaker eds, Hart 2019) 425. *See* also Bell, Boyron & Whittaker, *supra* n. 17, at 188–195; Kathrin Maria Scherr, *Public Liability for Administrative Acts under French Law*, 14 European Public Law 213 (2008); Carol R. Harlow, *State Liability: Tort Law and Beyond* (OUP 2004) 134–141; Spyridon Flogaitis, *State Extra-Contractual Liability in France, England and Greece*, in *Tort Liability of Public Authorities in Comparative Perspective* (Duncan Fairgrieve et al. eds, BIICL 2002) 439; Louis Neville Brown, John Bell & Jean-Michel Galabert, *French Administrative Law* (OUP 5th ed. 1998) 175–212; Carol R. Harlow, *Administrative Liability: A Comparative Study of French and English Law* (thesis London, 1979); Carol R. Harlow, *Fault Liability in French and English Public Law* 39 Modern Law Review 558 (1976); Louis Trotabas, *Liability in Damages under French Administrative Law (Parts 1, 2, 3 and 4)*, 12–14 Journal of Comparative Legislation and International Law 44, 213, 56, 78 (1930–1932). *See* also from a broader comparative standpoint Duncan Fairgrieve, *State Liability in Tort: A Comparative Law Study* (OUP 2003). For an up-to-date textbook in French, *see* Hafida Belrhali, *Responsabilité administrative* (LGDJ 2d ed. 2020).
213. *See* paras 35–37 above.
214. On the *Blanco* case, *see* already para. 37 above.
215. The influence of private law on the liability of public authorities was the theme of the reference work by René Chapus, *Responsabilité publique et responsabilité privée. Les influences réciproques des jurisprudences administrative et judiciaire* (LGDJ 1954, reprint 2010). *See* also the vigorous plea in favour of a common legal framework for the liability of private and public persons by Jeremy Antippas, *Pour un droit commun de la responsabilité des personnes privées et publiques* (Dalloz 2021).
216. Bell, *Reform of Delict*, *supra* n. 212, at 425. *See* also Scherr, *supra* n. 212, at 219 ('dual concepts').

for others') since the claimant does not have to attribute the fault to a specific person who is responsible for the administrative failure. In other words, an 'anonymous fault' (*faute anonyme*), that is, a failure of an administrative unit as a whole, is an accepted ground for administrative liability.

106. Even though Article 1240 Civil Code does not apply in administrative law, the establishment of *faute* follows a similar approach, particularly since the Court of Cassation abandoned the requirement of capacity (*discernement*), thereby dismantling the moral dimension of civil fault.[217] To use the words of John Bell, the concept of *faute* under administrative law refers to the 'general failure of the administration in its duties, in a line of conduct in administrative action',[218] following the same comparative method as in civil law. The claimant has to demonstrate that there is a discrepancy between the way in which the administrative service has functioned in practice and the manner in which it should have functioned. It has been argued that the distinctiveness of state liability lies in the fact that administrative courts do not refer to the breach of a pre-existing duty owed to another person in a given situation.[219] It is not certain, however, that this circumstance is a specific feature of state liability as French civil liability is not based on the concept of 'duty to care' as known in other jurisdictions and since civil courts do not refer systematically to the breach of a duty owed to the claimant.

107. The distinguishing feature of the liability of administrative authorities under French law instead arises from the scale used to assess the requirement of fault. Until very recently, simple fault was not sufficient in numerous situations to establish the liability of public authorities. In a number of cases, especially for activities considered particularly difficult (police, prisons, hospitals), the state was only liable for *faute lourde* (gross negligence). For decades, it was even suggested that the proof of 'gross fault' was a general requirement of state liability.[220] Yet this restrictive approach has been progressively abandoned by the *Conseil d'État*, first for hospital liability, then for prison administration, emergency services and even tax authorities. At the present time, the requirement of *faute lourde* only applies to the operation of the judicial service.[221] The rule adopted for civil courts in 1972 and

217. *See* paras 80–83 above.

218. Bell, *Reform of Delict*, *supra* n. 212, at 431 (citing the reference work of Maryse Deguergue, *Jurisprudence et doctrine dans l'élaboration du droit de la responsabilité administrative* (LGDJ 1994) 148).

219. Bell, *Reform of Delict*, *supra* n. 212, at 433. The author cites in particular the thesis of Benoît Delaunay, *La faute de l'administration* (LGDJ 2007).

220. *See* René Chapus, *Droit administratif général* vol 2 (LGDJ 15th ed. 2001) para. 1462 ('According to the Civil Code, every fault, even the slightest, gives rise to liability both for one's own acts (Arts 1382 and 1383) and for acts of others (Art. 1384). Regarding to harm related to the exercise of certain administrative missions, state liability is subject to the requirement of a causal *faute lourde*.')

221. The rationale of this rule lies in the fact that in a system in which every error in judgement could become a source of liability, judicial remedies such as appeal or *pourvoi en cassation* would lose their essence. *See* also on this issue Guy Canivet, *The Responsibility of Judges in France*, 5 Cambridge Yearbook of European Legal Studies 15, 21–24 (2002–2003).

now laid out in Article L 141-1 of the Code of Judicial Organization[222] was implemented in administrative law by the *Conseil d'État* in 1978.[223]

108. Strict liability or 'no-fault liability' is often presented in textbooks on French administrative law as a series of different regimes divided into a category of 'liability for risk' (*responsabilité pour risque*) and another based on the idea of an unequal treatment before public burdens (*rupture de l'égalité devant les charges publiques*).[224] The inventory is unfortunately quite long, revealing – whatever may have been said –[225] a rather opportunistic approach: liability for the actions of dangerous things (storage of ammunition, infected blood), for third-party victims of public works, for harm to occasional or volunteer helpers of the administration, for riot damage and for potentially dangerous policy decisions (licencing prisoners, refusal to exercise public force to remove squatters, etc.). While some of those cases can be linked to the general idea of liability for risk created by the administration, others reveal that the technique of state liability is also often used to compensate harm on the basis of social solidarity, regardless of the existence or the absence of a relationship between administrative action (or omission) and the occurrence of the loss.[226]

109. Civil servants and other public sector workers are generally granted immunity from personal liability. They will not be held liable unless they commit a so-called personal fault (*faute personnelle*), often described with the words of the famous 19th century *Conseil d'État* vice-president Édouard Laferrière: a fault 'which is not linked to the "public service" (*service public*) but reveals the man with his weaknesses, his passions, his carelessness'.[227] On the other hand, if there is simply a 'service-connected fault' (*faute de service*), the public officer's immunity is preserved.[228] In order to protect the victim of harm caused by a *faute personnelle* from the risk of the public officer's insolvency, the *Conseil d'État* has developed a

222. According to this text, 'the State is obliged to repair the loss caused by the malfunctioning of the judicial service. Unless otherwise stipulated, there is liability only on proof of a denial of justice (*déni de justice*) or gross fault'.

223. CE, 29 December 1978, *Darmont*, no. 96004.

224. *See* also Heinz R. Hink, *Governmental Liability for Risk under French and German Law*, 19 Rutgers Law Review 472 (1964–1965).

225. Bell, *Reform of Delict*, *supra* n. 212, at 440 (the author claims that 'whereas public law is fairly systematic and is based on constitutional principle, private law is less coherent and seems almost ramblingly opportunistic').

226. On this idea, *see* in English Bell, Boyron & Whittaker, *supra* n. 17, at 193–195; Bell, *Reform of Delict*, *supra* n. 212, at 437–440. *See* also Roger Errera, *The Scope and Meaning of No-fault Liability in French Administrative Law*, 39 Current Legal Problems 157 (1986).

227. The formula is from Laferrière's *conclusions* under the 1877 *Tribunal des conflits* judgement in the *Laumonnier-Carriol* case.

228. Brown, Bell & Galabert, *supra* n. 212, at 186. On the concepts of *faute de service* and *faute personnelle*, *see* also Heinz R. Hink, *Service-Connected Fault Versus Personal Fault in the French Law of Government Tort Liability*, 18 Rutgers Law Review 17 (1963–1964). *See* also the major work by Bernard Schwartz, *French Administrative Law and the Common-Law World* (New York University Press 1954, reprint The Lawbook Exchange 2006) 250–304.

complex legal edifice, referred to as the *cumul de fautes* test.[229] Whenever a 'personal fault' reveals the existence of an administrative failure because the organization of the administrative unit made it possible to commit such a fault, then the administration and the public officer are liable *in solidum* so that the claimant may ask for compensation from both the state and the individual tortfeasor.[230] In practice, however, it is much more promising to bring a claim against the state before the administrative court rather than against the public officer before the ordinary courts. Even though full compensation by the state gives rise to a recourse action against the agent, reimbursement is rarely claimed by the public authorities.

110. When it comes to the consequences of the extra-contractual liability of public authorities, it is impossible to ignore the numerous similarities with civil liability. In this field, the convergence trends between private and public law are probably the most palpable, with a tendency for the administrative courts to implement techniques, concepts and solutions forged by the Court of Cassation.[231] Administrative courts have recognized a principle of full compensation (*réparation intégrale*), allowing the compensation of all types of harm, even pure economic loss,[232] while allowing the deduction of advantages and other benefits arising from the tortious situation (*compensatio lucri cum damno*).[233] Unlike under civil liability, the compensation of harm always takes the form of monetary damages; a reparation in kind (*réparation en nature*) is not officially recognized by the Conseil d'État, but lower administrative courts do not hesitate to give the administration the choice between damages and other forms of redress. Over the last years, the call for the implementation of injunctions in administrative law (currently not permitted on the grounds of separation of powers) has been getting louder.[234]

111. Finally, with regard to the contractual liability of public authorities, it is necessary to distinguish the legal nature of the contract under which the performance has given rise to a compensation claim. The French administration can conclude both government contracts (*contrats administratifs*) and private law contracts (*contrats de droit privé*), depending on whether their object is related to 'public service' (*service public*) and their stipulations reserve exceptional powers (*pouvoir exorbitant*) to the administration. Administrative courts follow the same *non-cumul* rule as the ordinary courts, except that it is more adequately called the 'primacy of

229. Jean-Pierre Dubois, *Faute des agents et responsabilité administrative* in *Répertoire de la responsabilité de la puissance publique* (Dalloz 2018) paras 66–101.
230. On the doctrine of liability *in solidum*, *see* paras 267–269 below.
231. *See* Belrhali, *supra* n. 212, at 441–462 and, in particular, Nathalie Albert-Moretti, Fabrice Leduc & Olivier Sabard, *Droits privé et public de la responsabilité extracontractuelle : étude comparée* (LexisNexis 2017) 247–275.
232. Efsthatios K. Banakas, *Public Authority Liability for Pure Economic Loss: A Comparative Study of English, German and French Law*, 45 Revue Hellénique de Droit International 39 (1992).
233. Caroline Grossholz, *Évaluation du préjudice* in *Répertoire de la responsabilité de la puissance publique* (Dalloz 2019) paras 304–332. *See* also paras 345–351 below.
234. *See,* for example, Pauline Parinet-Hodimont, *L'injonction dans la responsabilité administrative*, Revue française de droit administratif 2020, 107 (with further references).

contractual liability' rule (*primauté de la responsabilité contractuelle*).[235] Regarding the compensation claim made by the contractual partner of the administration, the same rules apply as under private law: it is sufficient to establish any contractual non-performance (*inexécution contractuelle*) that has caused harm.[236] However, during the breach of contract, the other party remains bound to the contractual obligations unless the administrative court grants a termination of the contract on the ground of 'gross fault'. As for contractual remedies, the case law of the *Conseil d'État* is not fundamentally different from the private law of contracts.[237]

§3. Abuse of Rights

112. The doctrine of abuse of rights (*abus de droit*) is one of the major achievements of a doctrinal debate at the turn of the nineteenth and the beginning of the twentieth centuries.[238] Even though its origins can be traced back to the General State Laws for the Prussian States, it was through the work of illustrious authors such as Louis Josserand, Raymond Saleilles and Georges Ripert that the question of the abusive exercise of rights was given increased attention. One of the major battlegrounds was the applicability of liability for fault as laid out in Article 1240 (then 1382) Civil Code and particularly the adequacy of the classical assessment methods for fault. It should not be forgotten, however, that the controversy on abuse of rights had a strong political, almost ideological component, because its major protagonists did not share the same vision on the social dimension of individual rights.

113. The most emblematic case related to the doctrine of *abus de droit* is probably the *Clément-Bayard* case involving two neighbouring landowners. One of them had erected a 16-metre high fence with spikes that served no real purpose other than

235. CE, 1 December 1976, *Berezowski*, no. 98946. *See* also the critical study by Michel Paillet, *Quelques réflexions sur les rapports entre responsabilité administrative contractuelle et extracontractuelle*, in *Contrats publics : Mélanges en l'honneur du professeur Michel Guibal* vol 1 (Guylain Clamour & Marion Ubaud-Bergeron eds, Presses universitaires de Montpellier 2006) 553.

236. *See* also in English Bermann & Picard, *supra* n. 29, at 85–89.

237. Marion Ubaud-Bergeron, *Droit des contrats administratifs* (LexisNexis, 3d ed. 2019) paras 814–821. *See* also on the influence of the reform of the French Law of Obligations François Llorens, *L'inexécution du contrat : une influence incertaine et au mieux marginale*, in *L'influence de la réforme du droit des obligations sur le droit des contrats administratifs* (Julien Martin ed., LexisNexis 2019) 207 and, for a more comprehensive survey, Jérémy Bousquet, *Responsabilité contractuelle et responsabilité extra-contractuelle en droit administratif* (LGDJ 2019).

238. On the French doctrine of abuse of rights, *see* in English Pierre Catala & Tony Weir, *Delict and Torts: A Study in Parallel Part II*, 38 Tulane Law Review 221, 221–236 (1964); John H. Crabb, *The French Concept of Abuse of Rights*, 6 Inter-American Law Review 1 (1964); Albert Mayrand, *Abuse of Rights in France and Quebec*, 34 Louisiana Law Review 993 (1974); Vera Bolgár, *Abuse of Rights in France, Germany, and Switzerland: A Survey of a Recent Chapter in Legal Doctrine*, 35 Louisiana Law Review 1015, 1015–1023 (1975); André Tunc, *The French Concept of* abus de droit, in *The Cambridge Lectures 1981* (Nancy E. Eastham & Boris Krivy eds, Butterworths 1981) 151; van Dam, *supra* n. 135, at para. 302-2. *See* also Philipp Janig, *The General Principle of 'Abuse of Rights': Its Roots in Domestic Law and Impact on Investment Arbitration*, in *Common Law and Civil Law Today: Convergence and Divergence* (Marko Novakovic ed., Vernon Press 2019) 221, 225–226.

to prevent airships (*dirigeables*)[239] from taking off and landing on the adjacent ground. In its landmark decision from 1915, the French Court of Cassation held that there was an abuse of property rights (*droit de propriété*), considering that the installation 'could provide no advantage to Coquerel in exploiting his land and was put there with the sole aim of damaging Clément-Bayard'.[240] Thus, the Court recognized Coquerel's civil liability under (former) Article 1382 Civil Code and ordered a compensation in kind of Clément-Bayard's harm in the form of the removal of spikes. The judgement quickly became a controversial topic among legal scholars. While some authors, such as Josserand or Saleilles, welcomed the shift of individual rights from their private domain into a more social field,[241] others like Ripert feared that the departure from the individual dimension would gradually deprive citizens of their subjective rights.[242] More than a century after the famous *Clément-Bayard* decision, the case law related to the doctrine of abuse of rights is less ideologically tainted and may be systematized using three categories of individual rights.[243]

114. Some individual rights are held to be absolute and are not subject to civil liability. The perimeter of these rights, called *droits discrétionnaires* by the French legal doctrine, is extremely limited so that one could even ask whether this category still exists. An example frequently cited in textbooks is the right of the parents to refuse their consent to the marriage of their minor child. It is argued that the exercise of the parents' *droit d'opposition* is beyond all criticism and cannot give rise to a compensation claim under civil liability. However, in 1924, the Court of Cassation ruled that a father should pay damages to his son on the grounds that he had withdrawn his consent solely for the purpose of vengeance.[244] Among absolute individual rights, there is likely to remain only the right to disinherit family members (*droit d'exhéréder*) within the limits of the legal reserve (*réserve héréditaire*). While there seems to be consensus that the category of *droits discrétionnaires* is hardly more than an empty shell, others tend to see new absolute rights in certain contractual prerogatives such as withdrawal rights for consumers.[245]

115. A second category concerns rights whose exercise is subject to immunity from civil liability except in cases of bad faith or intentional wrongdoing (*intention*

239. On the contribution of Adolphe Clément-Bayard to the development of aeronautics, *see* in English E. Charles Vivian, *A History of Aeronautics* (Champaign 1921) 349–350.

240. Req, 3 August 1915, Dalloz Périodique 1917, 1, 79. The English translation is borrowed from Catala & Weir, *supra* n. 238, at 224, n. 6.

241. On the impact in France of the idea of a 'social function of property' (*fonction sociale du droit de propriété*), developed by Léon Duguit, *see* in English Alexandre Deroche, *The Importance of the Social Function of Property: France*, in *Léon Duguit and the Social Obligation Norm of Property* (Paul Babie & Jessica Viven-Wilksch eds, Springer 2019) 65.

242. Bolgár, *supra* n. 238, at 1017. *See* also in English from a coeval perspective Maurice Amos, *Abusive Exercise of Rights According to French Law*, 2 Journal of Comparative Legislation 453 (1900).

243. The presentation is inspired by Brun, *Responsabilité*, *supra* n. 147, at paras 335–339.

244. Civ, 21 May 1924, Dalloz Périodique 1924, 1, 97.

245. Damien Roets, *Les droits discrétionnaires : une catégorie en voie de disparition*, Recueil Dalloz 1997, chr 92.

de nuire). This is generally the case for property rights or intellectual property rights. Individual liberties such as freedom of speech or artistic freedom can also be considered to fall into this category. However, there is a clear tendency to develop specific liability regimes for these situations. It is quite telling that the *Clément-Bayard* case would by now be subject to the doctrine of *troubles anormaux de voisinage*,[246] while liability cases related to freedom of speech are not governed by Article 1240 Civil Code but fall under the specific liability regime laid out in the Act of 1881.[247]

116. A third and final category encompasses individual rights which do not call for a specific treatment of civil fault. In these cases, the French courts do not hesitate to hold the holder of the right liable if the exercise of the right represents an act of negligence or carelessness, according to the *personne raisonnable* test already mentioned.[248] The recent case law provides various examples of this approach in the field of workers' rights (e.g., related to labour disputes) or, more generally, contractual prerogatives such as unilateral rights to terminate contractual agreements.[249] It would be wrong, however, to consider those three categories as rigidly defined case groups with impermeable boundaries. It is not uncommon for the Court of Cassation and even more common for the trial judges to readjust the scale of gravity of the required fault in order to take into account the specific circumstances of the case. There is indeed a lack of legal certainty when it comes to the practical application of the abuse of rights doctrine, and any attempt at systematization is contradicted to a certain extent by the volatility of the case law which fluctuates between the requirement of intentional wrongdoing and simple negligence.[250]

117. In French law, it is acknowledged that the concept of *abus de droit* can also apply to the right to sue someone in justice (*droit d'ester en justice*).[251] Abuse of legal process may be invoked throughout a counterclaim (*demande reconventionnelle*) interposed by a defendant on the ground that the claimant abused his procedural rights.[252] According to Article 32-1 of the Civil Procedure Code, a party 'who acts in justice in a dilatory or abusive manner shall be sentenced to a civil fine of EUR 15 to 1,500, without prejudice to other damages that would be claimed'. However, this explicit assertion of sanctionable abuse of legal process does not provide any practical elements on how to establish the abusive exercise of procedural rights.

---

246. *See* paras 195–199 below.
247. *See* para. 121 below.
248. *See* paras 73–76 above.
249. *See* the references cited by Brun, *Responsabilité*, *supra* n. 147, at paras 338–339.
250. Loïc Cadiet & Philippe le Tourneau, *Abus de droit* in *Répertoire de droit civil* (Dalloz 2017) paras 45–126 (for example, regarding property rights, it is said that 'case law and legal doctrine is in a state of utter confusion'). *See* also the reference work on the abuse of contractual prerogatives by Philippe Stoffel-Munck, *L'abus dans le contrat. Essai d'une théorie* (LGDJ 2000).
251. Angelo Dondi, *Abuse of Procedural Rights: Regional Reports for Italy and France*, in *Abuse of Procedural Rights: Comparative Standards of Procedural Fairness* (Michele Taruffo ed., Kluwer Law 1999) 109, 117–121. *See* also in French Cadiet & le Tourneau, *supra* n. 250, at paras 130–175.
252. *See* in English Peter E. Herzog & Martha Weser, *Civil Procedure in France* (Springer 1967) 277–278.

As is the case for the substantive rights, the French case law is torn between two positions: in some cases, mere negligence is sufficient to give rise to a compensation claim in tort, whereas other situations call for a stricter approach requiring intentional misconduct. In order to determine the scale for liability, trial judges do not mind considering other factors, such as the merits of the procedural initiative[253] or the harm which would be caused by the (allegedly abusive) proceedings.[254] One cannot say that the current state of tort law has consolidated; it appears more like shifting sands.[255]

§4. Injury to Reputation and Privacy

118. As in many other jurisdictions, the legal protection of personality rights has evolved quite spectacularly under French law over the course of the twentieth century. Based on the constitutional and international dimension of individual fundamental rights and on Article 9 Civil Code,[256] French courts have recognized numerous facets of personality interests which are protected by tort law against infringement by others:[257] right to privacy (*droit à la vie privée*),[258] right to one's

253. *See* most recently Civ 2, 3 October 2019, no. 18-19940 (the legal counsel of an abused child had relentlessly sued a youth leader who was not in contact with his client at the time the offence was committed).

254. Cadiet & le Tourneau, *supra* n. 250, at paras 141–161.

255. *See* Marie-Reine Renard, *L'abus du droit d'agir en justice*, Gaz Pal 2007, no. 144, 6 and, from another perspective, Michel Attal, *Les fondements multiples de la notion d'abus du droit d'agir en justice*, Droit et patrimoine 2017, no. 269, 18–24. *See* also the earlier work by Yvon Desdevises, *L'abus du droit d'agir en justice avec succès*, D 1979, chr 21.

256. According to this provision, 'everyone has the right to respect for his private life' and 'without prejudice to the right to recover indemnification for injury suffered, judges may prescribe any measures, such as sequestration, seizure and others, suited to the prevention or the ending of an infringement of the intimate character of private life; in case of emergency those measures may be provided for by summary proceedings'. On those provisions, *see* Roger Errera, *On the Origins and Content of Article 9 of the Civil Code on the Right to Privacy*, Franco-British Lawyers Society, London, 22–23 September 2011, http://www.rogererrera.fr/liberte_expression/docs/Article_9.pdf.

257. For a general overview in English, *see* Bell, Boyron & Whittaker, *supra* n. 17, at 376–380; the contributions on French law by Agnès Lucas-Schloetter in *Personality Rights in European Tort Law* (Gert Brüggemeier, Aurelia Colombi Ciacchi & Patrick O'Callaghan eds, CUP 2010). *See* also the contributions of Barbara C. Steininger, Eva Ondreasova, Monika Hinteregger and Ernst Karner in *The Legal Protection of Personality Rights: Chinese and European Perspectives* (Ken Oliphant, Zhang Pinghua & Chen Lei eds, Brill Nijhoff 2018) 13–100.

258. Huw Beverly-Smith, Ansgar Ohly & Agnès Lucas-Schloetter, *Privacy, Property and Personality: Civil Law Perspectives on Commercial Appropriation* (CUP 2005) 185–190; Étienne Picard, *The Right to Privacy in French Law*, in *Protecting Privacy* (Basil S. Markesinis ed., OUP 1999) 49; Jeanne M. Hauch, *Protecting Private Facts in France: The Warren & Brandeis Tort Is Alive and Well and Flourishing in Paris*, 68 Tulane Law Review 1219 (1994); Wenceslas J. Wagner, *The Development of the Theory of the Right to Privacy in France*, 45 Washington University Law Review 45 (1971). *See* also from a comparative perspective Joanna Krzeminska-Vamvaka & Patrick O'Callaghan, *Mapping out a Right to Privacy in Tort Law*, in *Fundamental Rights and Private Law in the European Union* (Gert Brüggemeier, Aurelia Colombi Ciacchi & Giovanni Comandé eds, CUP 2010) 111.

own image (*droit à l'image*),[259] honour and reputation (*droit à l'honneur*), personal name (*droit au nom*)[260] and presumption of innocence (*présomption de l'innocence*).[261]

119. The protection of those personality rights is provided by injunctions or damages if not directly by criminal law. In general, a claimant willing to obtain damages for an infringement shall base his claim on the general clause of liability for fault laid out by Articles 1240 and 1241 Civil Code. Although most authors agree that the assessment of fault does not differ fundamentally from that observed in other cases, the 'reasonable person' test is probably not the most commonly used reference in case law. The demonstration of a misconduct appears more like a matter of balancing (*mise en balance*) of conflicting rights. This is particularly palpable for the right to privacy and the right to one's own image, which often come into conflict with the principle of freedom of the media to inform society of matters of public interest[262] or with another individual right (e.g., a right of usage acquired by the defendant). When taking a closer look at the case law, it appears that the method used by courts to determine whether or not a fault was committed by the defendant is very similar to the one adopted for the purposes of constitutionality review or *contrôle de conventionnalité*: it is primarily a question of estimating the respective weight of two competing principles and determining the proportionality of the defendant's infringement.[263] Obviously, an accurate presentation of the current state of French law would show a more casuistic pattern in this matter.

120. Two distinctive features must be mentioned for the civil liability arising from injuries to personality rights. The first one concerns the requirement of harm (*dommage*). In the field of privacy litigation, it is very common that an infringement did not cause any pecuniary consequences (*préjudices patrimoniaux*) so that the only reparable harm would be a pure non-pecuniary loss (*préjudice moral pur*).[264] Far from denying monetary compensation in these cases, the French courts

259. Elisabeth Logeais & Jean-Baptiste Schroeder, *The French Right of Image: an Ambiguous Concept Protecting the Human Persona*, 18 Loyola of Los Angeles Entertainment Law Journal 511 (1998). *See* also Wenceslas J. Wagner, *The Right to One's Own Likeness in French Law*, 46 Indiana Law Journal 1 (1970).

260. Roderick Munday, *The French Law of Surnames: A Study in Rights of Property, Personality and Privacy*, 6 Legal Studies 79 (1986); Audrey Guinchard, *Is the Name Property? Comparing the English and the French Evolution*, 1 Journal of Civil Law Studies 21, 48–49 (2008).

261. *See* in English François Quintard-Morénas, *The Presumption of Innocence in the French and Anglo-American Legal Traditions*, 58 American Journal of Comparative Law 107 (2010).

262. Logeais & Schroeder, *supra* n. 259, at 528–532. *See* also Kathryn F. Deringer, *Privacy and the Press: The Convergence of British and French Law in Accordance with the European Convention of Human Rights*, 22 Penn State International Law Review 191 (2003).

263. In 2013, the First Civil Chamber of the Court of Cassation introduced an explicit (and exclusive) reference to Art. 10 ECHR in its case law on civil liability arising from an 'abusive exercise of the freedom of expression'. *See* Civ 1, 10 April 2013, no. 12-10177. On the (potentially far-reaching) consequences of this decision, *see*, for example, Geneviève Viney, *La sanction des abus de la liberté d'expression*, D 2017, 787.

264. Brun, *Responsabilité*, *supra* n. 147, at paras 216–225 (the author distinguishes between non-pecuniary harm arising from personal injury and *préjudice moral pur* which encompasses bereavement damages and the harm related to the infringement of personality rights).

assess damages on the basis of several indices that are not necessarily linked to the claimant's situation. There is a clear tendency in French case law to take into account the gravity of fault and the economic situation of the defendant as well as the profit made through the infringement.[265] It may be argued that the assessment of non-pecuniary damages in those cases reveals the existence of 'punitive damages' (*dommages-intérêts punitifs*) that are not openly identified as such.[266] Moreover, it is not unusual for courts to infer the reparable loss from the mere demonstration of the injury to privacy or to other personality rights.[267]

121. The second unusual feature is the inapplicability of general liability for fault (Articles 1240 and 1241 Civil Code) to acts which fall under the scope of two criminal offences created in 1881.[268] According to the Freedom of the Press Act of 23 July 1881, *diffamation* is defined as the allegation of facts, true or not, offending the honour or the reputation of another person, whereas *injure* consists of the use of offensive statements which do not impute particular facts to another person. In a landmark decision of 2000, the Court of Cassation held that a compensation claim could not be raised on the basis of a simple fault; the claimant had to establish the existence of one of those two offences which require the demonstration of malice.[269] Furthermore, a claim for damages brought before a criminal court (by way of an *action civile*)[270] or a civil court shall be subject to all procedural requirements and limitation periods laid out in the 1881 Act. Given those restrictions, it is often difficult to be awarded damages for a *diffamation* or an *injure*, which was precisely the aim of this case law. Paradoxically, in press litigation, this interpretation causes journalists to demonstrate that there is indeed evidence for one or another of those offences simply to be eligible for the procedural regime of the 1881 Act and, thus, avoid civil liability.[271] However, there are signs in recent case law that under the pressure of Article 10 ECHR, the Court of Cassation might abandon its position and authorise a more widespread use of civil liability for fault under Articles 1240 and 1241 Civil Code in press litigation cases.[272]

122. The protection of personality rights is not specific to natural persons under French law. The Court of Cassation has repeatedly recognized the possibility for legal persons and, in particular, for commercial firms, to invoke civil liability in

265. *See* the references cited by Lepage, *supra* n. 57, at paras 253–274.
266. *See* already Galand-Carval, *supra* n. 56, at para. 22 ('There is no doubt, for the French legal doctrine, that civil liability arising from an infringement of personality rights does not only have a compensatory function, but also a strong punitive character.').
267. Civ 1, 5 November 1996, no. 94-14798 ('the mere infringement of privacy gives rise to compensation'). On the technique of 'presumption of harm' (*présomption de dommage*) in this area, *see* also Gratton, *supra* n. 125.
268. On this specific feature, *see* Julie Traullé, *L'éviction de l'article 1382 du Code civil en matière extracontractuelle* (LGDJ 2007) paras 106–119; Viney, *Introduction*, *supra* n. 55, at paras 208–222.
269. According to Art. 34(1) of the 1881 Freedom of the Press act, criminal sanctions of *diffamation* and *injure* are subject to the proof of the willingness to harm another person's honour or reputation.
270. *See* para. 50 above.
271. Viney, *Introduction*, *supra* n. 55, at para. 216.
272. For an illustration, *see* Civ 1, 10 April 2013, no. 12-10177.

cases of reputational damage, breach of business name rights or even infringement of the right to control the use of their image.[273] Even though there is no explicit right to privacy in a strict sense, French courts consider that corporations shall enjoy protection of their trade secrets and business premises.[274] The monetary compensation awarded under civil liability is explicitly qualified as non-pecuniary damages by the legal doctrine.[275]

§5. Interference by a Third Person with Contractual Relations

123. Civil liability for interference with contractual relations is closely related to two concepts which are deeply ingrained in the French law of contracts: the *effet relatif des contrats* (which is the equivalent to the common law doctrine of privity of contract) and the contract's *opposabilité* towards third parties.[276] According to the 'relative effect of the contract' laid out in Article 1199 Civil Code, contracts only create obligations between the contracting parties, but this does not hinder them to 'oppose' the contract against third parties as a so-called *fait social*. Although this facet of the *opposabilité* doctrine is endorsed by almost every legal scholar, it is impossible not to point out its inconsistencies and lack of clarity. In particular, legal literature does not really explain why the legal force of a contract is limited to contracting parties while third parties should owe a specific respect to it.[277]

124. Despite the relative hollowness of the *opposabilité* doctrine, the French legislator in 2016 recognized the analysis built by the legal doctrine and the courts relating to the relative effect of contracts and their opposability.[278] Article 1200(1) Civil Code now provides that 'third parties must respect the legal situation created

273. *See* the references cited by Viney, Jourdain & Carval, *Conditions*, *supra* n. 129, at para. 260.

274. This position follows the ECHR case law. *See* for example ECHR, 16 April 2002, no. 37971/97, *Société Colas Est v. France*. On this topic, *see* Piet Hein van Kempen, *The Recognition of Legal Persons in International Human Rights Instruments*, in *Corporate Criminal Liability: Emergence, Convergence, and Risk* (Mark Pieth & Radha Ivory eds, Springer 2011) 355.

275. Véronique Wester-Ouisse, *Le préjudice moral des personnes morales*, JCP G 2003 I no. 145; Philippe Stoffel-Munck, *Le préjudice moral des personnes morales*, in *Mélanges en l'honneur de Philippe le Tourneau* (Dalloz 2007) 959. For a critical assessment of what has been described as an 'anthropomorphic drift of the concept of legal personality', *see* in particular Véronique Wester-Ouisse, *La jurisprudence et les personnes morales*, JCP G 2009 I no. 121 and *Dérives anthropomorphiques de la personnalité morale*, JCP G 2009 I no. 137.

276. On those legal concepts, *see* in English Stefan Vogenauer, *The Effects of Contracts on Third Parties: The* Avant-projet de réforme *in a Comparative Perspective*, in *Reforming the French Law of Obligations* (John Cartwright, Stefan Vogenauer & Simon Whittaker eds, Hart 2009) 235; Denis Mazeaud, *Contracts and Third Parties in the* Avant-projet de réforme, in *Reforming the French Law of Obligations* (John Cartwright, Stefan Vogenauer & Simon Whittaker eds, Hart 2009) 207. *See* also Bell, Boyron & Whittaker, *supra* n. 17, at 335–340; Barry Nicholas, *French Law of Contract* (Clarendon Press 2d ed. 1992) 177.

277. *See*, in particular, Robert Wintgen, *Étude critique de la notion d'opposabilité* (LGDJ 2004) 89–95; Pascal Ancel, *Force obligatoire et contenu obligationnel du contrat*, RTD civ 1999, 771, paras 49–53.

278. *See* in English Jean-Sébastien Borghetti, *The Effects of Contracts and Third Parties*, in *The Code Napoléon Rewritten: French Contract Law after the 2016 Reforms* (John Cartwright & Simon Whittaker eds, Hart 2017) 227, 245–253.

by a contract'; this provision has become the explicit legal basis for the civil liability of third parties for tortious interference with contract.[279] The courts have recognized liability in many different cases, for example, the hiring of an employee away from a competing business (*débauchage*) despite a non-competition clause, purchasing goods from a distributor bound by an exclusivity clause or real estate transactions concluded in violation of contractual preferential or pre-emptive rights. However, in spite of its practical importance, the academic work on the liability for wrongful interference with contract has not given rise to a consistent position in case law.[280] Of course, the claimant has to demonstrate the third party's civil fault, but it is not yet clear whether this implies knowledge of the other contract, an intention to harm one of the contracting parties or even a collusion with the other contracting party.[281] Even though recent case law does not impose proof of collusion,[282] the Court of Cassation seems to follow a differentiated approach on a case-by-case basis, which is obviously detrimental to legal certainty.[283] From a comparative standpoint and despite its lack of precision, French case law offers relatively broad protection to the contracting parties, thereby giving increased stability to contractual relations, especially since a compensation of pure economic loss may be awarded under extra-contractual liability.[284]

§6. Liability for Fault in a Sporting Context

125. The assessment of civil liability cases arising from sports has always been linked to the question of a specific standard of care or, using French legal terminology, to the relationship between civil fault and unsporting misconduct (*faute sportive*).[285] Whereas in ordinary cases the concept of fault refers to a comparison of the tortfeasor's conduct with that of a reasonable person,[286] one has to take into

279. On this issue, *see*, in particular, Viney, *Introduction*, *supra* n. 55, at paras 332–345.
280. For a presentation of the historical background, *see* in English Vernon V. Palmer, *A Comparative Study (from a Common Law Perspective) of the French Action for Wrongful Interference with Contract*, 40 American Journal of Comparative Law 297, 302–320 (1992) and by the same author *Historical Origins of the Civilian Action Against Interference with Contract in France: Louisiana Perspective on a Road Not Taken*, 6/7 Tulane Civil Law Forum 131 (1991–1992). *See* also Olivier Moréteau, *France* in *ETL 2008 (2009)*, 264, paras 38–43.
281. Viney, *Introduction*, *supra* n. 55, at paras 343–344.
282. Civ 3, 20 December 2018, no. 17-31461. *See* Patrice Jourdain, *Non-cumul des responsabilités du contrat aux tiers*, RTD civ 2019, 338.
283. But *see* Palmer, *Comparative Study*, *supra* n. 280, at 334 (according to the author, 'whereas the French action can be stated simply and applied predictably, the common law tort has evolved into a far more complex and indeterminate type of liability').
284. *See* Palmer, *Comparative Study*, *supra* n. 280, at 338. *See* also the more recent comparative study in Dutch Laura M. van Bochove, *Betrokkenheid van derden bij contractbreuk* (Wolf Legal Publishers 2013) 125–150.
285. On this general issue, *see* Aurélie Cappello, *La faute civile et la violation des règles régissant une activité sportive ou professionnelle*, RTD civ 2013, 777 and in English, the brief reference made by Rosmarijn van Kleef, *Reviewing Disciplinary Sanctions in Sports*, 4 Cambridge Journal of International and Comparative Law, 3, 12 (2015). From a comparative standpoint, *see* von Bar, *supra* n. 142, at paras 253–273.
286. *See* paras 73–76 above.

account the risk of causing physical injury inherent to most sports. This leads the Court of Cassation to a more restrictive approach of fault-based civil liability in sports cases where only a 'deliberate failure to comply with sports rules' gives rise to a right of compensation.[287] The distinction between a simple *faute sportive* (not subject to civil sanctions) and deliberate failures regarded as civil faults was developed by the courts in personal injury cases, primarily when a player injured his opponent, on the basis of the idea that all participants have accepted a certain risk inherent to the sport.[288]

287. *See* Civ 2, 20 November 2003, no. 02-13.653 and more recently Civ 2, 20 November 2014, no. 13-23759.

288. For a more detailed presentation, *see* Brun, *Responsabilité*, *supra* n. 147, at para. 327; Jourdain, *supra* n. 136, at 559; Frédéric Buy, Jean-Michel Marmayou, Didier Poracchia & Fabrice Rizzo, *Droit du sport* (LGDJ 6th ed. 2020) 597–604. *See* also in English the brief exposé by Jean-Michel Marmayou, *Sports Law in France* (Wolters Kluwer 2d ed. 2019) paras 151–157. On the doctrine of *acceptation des risques*, *see* also para. 214 below.

Part II. Liability for Acts of Others

Chapter 1. Liability of Employers for Acts of Their Employees

126. According to Article 1242(5) of the Civil Code, 'masters and employers (are liable) for the damage caused by their servants and employees in the functions for which they have been employed'. This text is one of the many examples of French tort law provisions reminding us of the legislator's inertia in this field. It goes without saying that the reference to 'masters' and 'servants' has long since fallen into disuse given that the relationship between home-owners and their domestic staff is nowadays included in that of employer/employee. It is, therefore, sensible and logical that none of the reform drafts reiterates the antiquated terminology of the current text. Consequently, the following chapter will deal exclusively with liability of employers for acts of their employees, which corresponds to the regime of vicarious liability as known in the common law world.

127. Before getting into the substance of the matter, it is important to address a preliminary issue related to the terminology used in French law. The terms *commettant* and *préposé* are often improperly translated into English as 'employer' and 'employee,' but Article 1242(5) is not confined to the employer/employee relationship but extends to other situations in which a person is employed to conduct a mission on behalf of another.[289] As will be seen, the scope of application of the vicarious liability *à la française* is much wider and encompasses very diverse relationships, such as between neighbours or even within families.[290]

128. French tort law provides for strict liability of the employer, although the wording of Article 1242(5) Civil Code is silent on this point. Even though the case law from the early nineteenth century refers to an irrebuttable presumption of fault in the choice or surveillance of the employee (*culpa in eligendo* or *culpa in vigilando*), the current state of the law is very explicit on the ratio of vicarious liability. *Commettants* are liable for the damages caused by *préposés* in the functions for which they have been employed, regardless of any misconduct of the employer. There is no doubt among French academics that the liability of *commettants* is a

289. Giliker suggests a translation of *commettant* as 'principal', but she uses the term 'employer' for the sake of convenience throughout her work. *See* Giliker, *Vicarious Liability, supra* n. 197, at 25–26 and *Vicarious Liability or Liability for the Acts of Others in Tort: A Comparative Perspective*, 2 JETL 31, 47 (2011). This will also be the approach here.

290. *See* para. 133 below.

strict one and that the only defences available are force majeure and the employee's *abus de fonctions*, that is, in cases when the *préposé*'s conduct has exceeded the assigned tasks. The reason for this strict approach to the civil liability of employers, which leaves very little room for civil irresponsibility, lies in the idea of guarantee. According to French legal scholars and to the Court of Cassation, an innocent victim should not suffer from the impecuniosity of an employee who acted negligently when there is a solvent employer drawing benefits from the employee's actions. In other words, the liability without fault of *commettants* is closely linked to the idea that creating a risk by 'using' another person should lead to a stricter liability regime than in the cases of liability for one's own acts.[291]

129. Two caveats must, however, be expressed: first, the employer can also be liable on the basis of civil fault. The liability for *faute* under Article 1240 Civil Code coexists with the specific liability regime applicable to *commettants* and *préposés,* and it is perfectly possible to invoke employer misconduct (incorrect instructions, lack of surveillance) in order to establish civil liability. Second, it is important to realize that cases in which damage has been caused by an employee often arise in a contractual context and, thus, fall under the *non-cumul* rule, forcing the claimant to raise his action in contract and not in tort.[292] For example, if the employee of a construction company negligently damages property on the client's premises, the case will be dealt with on the grounds of the company's contractual liability.[293]

130. Lastly, it must be remembered that the French Court of Cassation introduced in the famous *Costedoat* case from 2000 a general 'civil immunity' for *préposés* so that they are preserved from the burden of liability in cases of harm caused by mere negligence.[294] As already mentioned, it is only when *préposés* deliberately commit a criminal act, albeit under the orders of the employer, that personal liability may be incurred.[295]

§1. Scope of Application

131. The central element of the liability regime is the relationship between the *commettant* and the *préposé.* The French doctrine and the relevant case law speak of a *lien de préposition,* which implies the right of a person to give orders or instructions to another person as to how to comply with entrusted tasks and to monitor the

---

291. *See* in French Patrice Jourdain, *La responsabilité du fait d'autrui à la recherche de ses fondements*, in *Études à la mémoire de Christian Lapoyade-Deschamps* (Presses universitaires de Bordeaux 2003) 67, 72. *See* also Birke Häcker, Fait d'autrui *in Comparative Perspective*, in *French Civil Liability in Comparative Perspective* (Jean-Sébastien Borghetti & Simon Whittaker eds, Hart 2019) 143, 146–147.
292. On this rule, *see* paras 55–64 above.
293. However, it is common for lower courts to not apply the *non-cumul* rule in those cases and to award damages in tort. *See* on this issue Aurélie Harmand-Luque & Alexis Collin, *La règle du non-cumul à l'épreuve de la responsabilité du fait d'autrui*, in *Mélanges en l'honneur du Professeur Didier R. Martin* (Lextenso 2015) 219, 228–231.
294. *See* para. 100 above.
295. Ass plén, 14 December 2001, no. 00-82066, *Cousin*.

implementation of the tasks.[296] Although regularly reiterated by French courts, this 'control test' receives a very flexible interpretation. In most cases, the *lien de préposition* is deduced from a contract of employment (*contrat de travail*) that implies a relationship of subordination. Even employees with a significant degree of autonomy, such as salaried doctors or lawyers (*avocats*), have been qualified as *préposés* in light of practical constraints (work schedules, technical staff) and the assigned objectives.[297]

132. A *lien de préposition* may also exist without a formal contract of employment since the power to give instructions can have another legal basis than a relationship of subordination (*lien de subordination*) in the sense of labour law. In case law, much attention has been given to temporary workers (*travailleurs intérimaires*), borrowed workers (*prêt de main d'œuvre*) and trainees who remain under the responsibility of their education centre while working in industry.[298] In all these cases, French courts have recognized a *lien de préposition* with the entity exercising authority over the wrongdoer, even in the absence of a contractual relationship. To put it in the words of legal academics, there cannot be a *cumul* of authority: what matters is the factual control over the wrongdoer which is thus subject to a transfer from the employer to another person.[299]

133. In case law, there are examples illustrating an even wider approach to the criterion of *préposition*. On several occasions, the courts have held that a family member, a friend, a neighbour, a member of a sports club or a supporter of a political party may be qualified as *préposés* during the performance of a specific task.[300]

134. Despite this exorbitant understanding of relationships leading to vicarious liability, the French courts have made it clear that there is a demarcation line that must not be crossed. In the presence of service contracts (*contrats d'entreprise*) or agency contracts (*contrats de mandat*), the autonomy granted to the contractor or agent is incompatible with a relationship of subordination or *préposition*. Therefore, 'a main contractor cannot be held liable, towards third parties, for the damage caused by its subcontractor'.[301] By the same token, parent and subsidiary companies cannot be qualified as *commettants* and *préposés*, even though there can be

296. *See* e.g. Com, 24 January 2006, no. 03-21153. On the various definitions suggested in legal literature, *see*, e.g., Viney, Jourdain & Carval, *Conditions*, *supra* n. 129, at para. 792 and Jérôme Julien, *La responsabilité civile du fait d'autrui: ruptures et continuités* (PUAM 2001) paras 154–166. The 2017 Reform Draft defines the *commettant* as 'a person who has the power to give orders and instructions to his employee in relation to the performance of [her] functions'.

297. *See*, e.g., Civ 2, 10 November 2005, no. 04-16501. For a more detailed analysis from a comparative perspective, *see* in English Giliker, *Vicarious Liability*, *supra* n. 199, at 61–65.

298. From a comparative perspective, *see* in English Giliker, *Vicarious Liability*, *supra* n. 197, at 81–100.

299. *See* le Tourneau (ed.), *Droit de la responsabilité*, *supra* n. 54, at paras 2235.51–2235.55. The 2017 Draft Reform explicitly refers to the transfer of the *lien de préposition* (Art. 1249(2) of the draft).

300. For case law references, *see* le Tourneau (ed.), *Droit de la responsabilité*, *supra* n. 54, at para. 2235.47.

301. Civ 3, 8 Septembre 2009, no. 08-12723.

strong economic bonds of dependency between them. In 2017, the French Parliament imposed a corporate 'duty of vigilance' (*obligation de vigilance*) on globally acting companies regarding human rights violations;[302] non-compliance with this duty may give rise to fault-based liability under Article 1240 Civil Code.[303]

§2. Requirement of Liability: A Harm Caused by the *Préposé*'s Fault

135. Once the relationship of *préposition* is characterized, the defendant has to prove a harm caused by the *préposé*'s fault. Even though the requirement of *faute* is not mentioned in Article 1242(5) Civil Code, it was clearly affirmed by the Court of Cassation in 1866 and has been reiterated on a regular basis since then.[304] Therefore, the *préposé*'s conduct has to be assessed according to the standard of fault under Article 1240 Civil Code.[305] Surprisingly, most legal writers do not consider that the fault has to be committed in the course of the functions for which the *préposé* was employed. The connection between fault and the functions of the *préposé* is often analysed only from the perspective of defences available to the *commettant*.[306] Except in extreme cases, French courts tend to presume a connection, which obliges the defendant to prove that the *préposé*'s conduct was entirely disconnected from the assigned tasks or that there was an *abus de fonctions*.[307]

136. It should not be forgotten that the liability of *commettants* for the acts of their *préposés* cannot be combined with the liability for the action of things (*responsabilité du fait des choses*). According to the case law, a *préposé* can never be the custodian of a thing over which control belongs to the *commettant* whether or not the thing was in the hands of the employee at the time of the damage.[308]

§3. Defences

137. Employers will be exonerated from liability if they can prove that the *préposé*'s fault was entirely disconnected from functions assigned to the *préposé*. The

302. Act no. 2017-399 of 27 March 2017 on a Duty of Vigilance of Parent and Subcontracting Companies. The provisions have been enshrined in the Commercial Code (Arts L 225-102-4 to 225-102-5).
303. *See* Sandra Cossart, Jérôme Chaplier & Tiphaine Beau de Lomenie, *The French Law on Duty of Care: A Historic Step Towards Making Globalization Work for All*, 2 Business and Human Rights Journal 317 (2017); Iris Barsan, *Corporate Accountability: Non-Financial Disclosure and Liability: A French Perspective*, 14 European Company and Financial Law Review 399, 422–426 (2017).
304. Req, 19 February 1866. *See* more recently Civ 2, 8 April 2004, no. 03-11653.
305. *See* paras 73–76 above.
306. *See* para. 138 below.
307. On the legal figure of *abus de fonctions*, *see* paras 133–139 below. Art. 1249(3) of the 2017 Reform Draft suggests to codify this interpretation. *See* on this provision, Häcker, *supra* n. 291, at 159 ('an "escape route" from liability').
308. *See* para. 171 below.

practical result is that harm caused by an employee outside his working hours, outside his workplace and without using a tool or other means provided by his employer will not give rise to vicarious liability.[309] This solution is of common sense and can be explained by the intermittency of the *lien de préposition*: before and after work, employees may not be considered as *préposés* since they are free to do what they want to do.

138. The more delicate cases are those in which the *préposé* has 'abused his functions' (*abus de fonctions*), that is, cases in which there is a certain but slight connection to the tasks the *préposé* was supposed to fulfil. The French case law is full of examples: fraud committed by an insurance agent, physical abuse from a nightclub bouncer, sexual harassment from a teacher or theft from a cleaning agent in a jewellery store. It took almost 40 years for the Court of Cassation to elaborate an adequate test for the assessment of the *abus de fonctions* criterion.[310] To put an end to a difference of opinion between the civil and criminal chambers, the Court of Cassation sitting in full bench (*Assemblée plénière*) issued in 1988 a landmark decision. In a case in which the employee of an insurance company had defrauded a client, the judges held that an employer can be exonerated from liability if the *préposé* acted 'without authorisation, for his own ends and outside the normal duties of his functions'.[311] All three requirements are cumulative and the subsequent judgments reveal that the central issue is often whether the act was 'outside the normal duties of the *préposé*'s functions'. For the lower courts, this condition is only fulfilled when the *préposé*'s tasks do not 'provide the opportunity and means for the wrongful act'.[312] In general, it is almost impossible for the employer to be exonerated if the *préposé*'s fault has been committed during working hours, at the workplace or with the means provided.[313]

139. In the (rare) cases in which an *abus de function* is acknowledged by the court, the issue of the civil liability of the *préposé* re-emerges. As stated above,[314] the Court of Cassation has enacted a civil 'immunity' for the *préposé*, making it almost impossible to hold an employee liable to a third-party victim. In the famous *Costedoat* case from 2000, the Court of Cassation, however, put a limit to this 'immunity', holding that only a *préposé* 'acting within the limits of his attributions' (*qui n'a pas dépassé les limites de sa mission*) could benefit from this exemption. Subsequent case law has failed to circumscribe the precise limits of the employee's 'immunity'. In a 2001 decision, the Court of Cassation found that if the employee

309. *See,* for example, Civ 2, 10 June 1999, no. 97-19614 (a harm caused by an employee during his free time in a staff apartment).

310. For a comprehensive assessment of this issue, *see* in English Giliker, *Vicarious Liability, supra* n. 197, at 181–188.

311. The 2017 Draft Reform formulates this test in the following terms: 'An employer … is not liable if he proves that the employee acted outside the functions for which [he] was employed, without authorisation and for purposes alien to [his] attributions' (Art. 1249(3) of the draft).

312. Civ 2, 3 July 1991, no. 90-13302.

313. For an illustration, *see* Civ 2, 6 February 2003, no. 00-20780, commented in Fabien Lafay, Olivier Moréteau & Catherine Pellerin-Rugliano, *France* in *ETL 2003 (2004)*, 157, paras 14–23.

314. *See* para. 100 above.

has deliberately committed a criminal act, even under the orders of his employer, he remains liable.[315] Nevertheless, more than 20 years after the *Costedoat* case, it is still unclear to what extent the seriousness of the wrongful act has to be taken into consideration. To remedy this situation, the 2017 Draft Reform suggests a codification of the employee's liability and a clear assertion of its limits. According to Article 1249(4) of the Draft, 'an employee is not subject to any personal liability except in the case of intentional fault, or where without authorisation he acted for purposes alien to his attributions'.[316]

140. As for other defences available to the defendant, such as force majeure or contributory fault, reference should be made to Part IV of this monograph.[317]

§4. A Specific Liability Regime for Craftsmen and Apprentices?

141. According to Article 1242(6) Civil Code, the liability of craftsmen for acts of their apprentices follows the same rules as set out for teachers. Initially, both were presumed liable for damages caused by their pupils or apprentices during the time when they were under their supervision unless they could prove that a correct supervision would not have prevented the accident. The assimilation of the teacher/pupil and craftsman/apprentice relationships may be surprising at first glance, especially since the French Labour Code states in Article L 6221-1 that 'the contract of apprenticeship is a specific employment contract'. The drafters of the 1804 Civil Code sought to draw a parallel between teaching pupils and training apprentices at a time when labour law did not yet exist as a separate branch of private law.

142. Over the years, the liability regime for craftsmen and apprentices has gradually drifted away from the rules applicable to teachers, who have benefitted from a preferential treatment since 1937, thereby exempting them from the presumption of fault enshrined in Article 1242(6) and, in case of public sector teachers, even from all personal liability.[318] Contrary to what one may think, this did not lead to an equal treatment of employees and apprentices but brought the liability regime for craftsmen much closer to the liability rules governing parents and their children. Historically, an apprentice was fed and lodged free of charge by the master and belonged in a certain way to the master's family. Therefore, from the 1940s on, French courts applied the same rules governing parents and their children to compensation claims directed against craftsmen for harm caused by their apprentices.[319]

143. Yet it is important to note that the specific treatment of craftsmen according to 1242(6) Civil Code has tended to fall into disuse. The latest decision of the

315. *See* in English Giliker, *Vicarious Liability*, *supra* n. 197, at 36–39.
316. For a commentary in English of this provision, *see* Häcker, *supra* n. 291, at 160–161.
317. *See* paras 205–232 below.
318. *See* para. 150 below.
319. Civ 2, 8 Decembre 1961, RTD civ 1962, 331, note André Tunc.

Court of Cassation dates back to 1983,[320] and it is more than likely that insurance companies and lower courts prefer to rely on more 'contemporary' regimes, such as the liability of employees, the liability of parents or fault-based liability. Unsurprisingly, the 2017 Draft Reform suggests nothing less than a repeal of any specific treatment of craftsmen and their apprentices.

320. Crim, 4 July 1983, no. 82-94063.

Chapter 2. Liability of Parents, Teachers and Guardians

§1. Parental Liability

144. For almost 200 years, French tort law has imposed on parents a liability based upon a presumption of fault (*présomption de faute*). According to Article 1242(7) Civil Code, the parents are held liable towards a third-party victim unless they can 'prove that they could not prevent the act which give rise to that liability'. In practical terms, the defendants had to establish that the damage caused by the child was not due to a lack of supervision or education (*faute de surveillance* or *faute d'éducation*). From the 1960s to the early 2000s, parental liability progressively shifted from a fault-based regime to strict liability, subject only to the defences of force majeure and contributory fault.[321] The reason for this spectacular drift, without any change in the wording of relevant provisions of the Civil Code, does not only lay in the difficulties to uphold a consistent approach to the *faute de surveillance ou d'éducation* test but also more generally to evolutions in French society. Harm caused by children is no longer considered as a fatality or an ordinary risk of life by a large part of the population but as a loss which cannot remain uncompensated, especially when their parents are covered by third-party liability insurance (which nowadays is generally the case).

145. In order to file a compensation claim on the grounds of parental liability, the claimant first has to demonstrate that the harm was caused by a minor who is indeed the son or the daughter of the defendants, which means that the proof of a direct 'bond of kindship' (*lien de filiation*) is necessary. Furthermore, parental liability is confined to those who exercised 'parental authority' over the child at the moment the harm was caused, which excludes those cases in which the courts have withdrawn parental authority from one of the parents due to violence or severe drug addiction. In practice, it is very rare that upon divorce or separation, only one of the parents is given parental authority (which is not to be confused with the child's residency),[322] as Article 373-2 Civil Code makes clear that 'separation of the parents has no influence on the rules of devolution of the exercise of parental authority'.

146. The shift towards a strict liability regime is palpable when it comes to the requirement of *cohabitation*. According to Article 1242(4) Civil Code, 'the father and mother … are jointly and severally liable for the damage caused by their minor children *who live with them*'. The proof of *cohabitation* was particularly important under a fault-based parental liability regime since the courts had to determine whether the defendant(s) had properly supervised their child, something that is only

---

321. For a presentation in English of the development of parental liability under French law, *see* Giliker, *Vicarious Liability*, *supra* n. 197, at 213–217 and by the same author *Parental Liability for Harm Caused by Children: A Comparative Analysis*, in *Responsible Parents and Parental Responsibility* (Rebecca Probert, Stephen Gilmore & Jonathan Herring eds, Hart 2009) 335. *See* also Ferreira, *supra* n. 156, at 142–145; Francoz-Terminal, Lafay, Moréteau & Pellerin-Rugliano, *supra* n. 156, at 169–215; Galand-Carval, *supra* n. 197, at 88–89. For a more detailed account in French, *see* le Tourneau (ed.), *Droit de la responsabilité*, *supra* n. 54, at Ch. 2233.

322. Gilikers developments are somewhat ambiguous on this point (*supra* n. 197, at 216).

possible when there is physical proximity between them. Over the years, the *cohabitation* test has progressively become less and less consistent. Nowadays, it is sufficient that the child 'usually lived' with his parents, a standard that is very widely interpreted by French courts. In an emblematic case, the Court of Cassation held that parents could be liable for the actions of their 13-year-old daughter, even though she had resided with her grandparents from the age of one.[323] In light of these case law developments, the *cohabitation* requirement is seen by many authors as a purely 'virtual' one,[324] leading to criticism that in some cases, the *cohabitation* test leads to the consequence that only the parent with whom the child resides is subject to parental liability while the other parent (in most cases, the father) can escape civil liability.[325] Due to these inconsistencies, the 2017 Draft Reform suggests a replacement of the *cohabitation* requirement with sole parental authority as the basis for parental liability.[326]

147. The judicial expansion of parental liability has also resulted from a notable change regarding the conduct of the child which gives rise to civil liability. In two leading cases from 1984 and 2002 (*Fullenwarth* and *Levert*), the Court of Cassation made clear that the liability of parents under Article 1242(4) Civil Code no longer depends on the existence of fault or an action of a thing under the custody of the minor child, but derives from any act that causes harm.[327] Thus, parental liability is based under French law on a purely causal theory (*théorie du fait causal*), as it suffices that the child's action is a direct cause of the damage to the claimant. From a legal policy standpoint, this evolution implies a paradigm shift. Children are regarded as a source of risk rather than individuals whose immaturity should induce a differentiated regime of civil liability both for themselves and their parents. For some academics, the treatment of children as tortfeasors in case law has led to a certain 'reification' of minors since the parental liability rules are now very close to those governing liability for things. The 2017 Draft Reform suggests a step backwards, with Article 1245(2) of the Draft stating that a person's liability for damage caused by others always 'rests on proof of an action of a nature to engage liability in the direct author of the harm'.[328]

148. By far, the most spectacular case law development regarding parental liability is related to the defences available to parents. As already mentioned, Article 1242(7) Civil Code allows the defendant(s) to escape from parental liability on

323. Crim, 8 February 2005, no. 03-87447. In the light of this case, it goes without saying that trips to relatives, holiday camps and even residency at boarding schools do not terminate *cohabitation* between children and their parents.

324. *See* Denis Mazeaud, *La condition de cohabitation dans la responsabilité des parents: chronique d'un escamotage annoncé*, D 2000, 469.

325. Civ 2, 21 December 2006, no. 05-17540. On this controversial issue, *see,* for example, Laurent Bloch, *Résidence alternée de l'enfant: responsabilités solidaires des parents?*, Resp civ assur 2013, alerte no. 35.

326. For a presentation in English, *see* Häcker, *supra* n. 291, at 156–158.

327. Ass plén, 9 May 1984, no. 79-16612, *Fullenwarth*; Civ 2, 10 May 2001, no. 99-11287, *Levert*. For a comprehensive presentation of those two cases in English, *see* Giliker, *Vicarious Liability*, *supra* n. 197, at 214–215. *See* also Brun, *ETL 2002 (2003)*, *supra* n. 183, at paras 86–92.

328. *See* Häcker, *supra* n. 291, at 157.

proof 'that they could not prevent the act which give rise to that liability'. In the *Bertrand* case of 1997, the Court of Cassation decided to abolish the *faute de surveillance/éducation* test by 'deactivating' Article 1242(7) Civil Code and the exculpation defence laid out in its text. This radical step by which the French Supreme Court definitely transformed the fault-based parental liability into a strict liability regime can be explained by the difficulties of the lower courts to establish clear standards for supervision and education of children.[329] It is very unlikely that the future civil liability reform will reverse this development since insurance companies were able to easily absorb the economic consequences of the shift from a fault-based to a strict liability regime without any major financial impact on parents (who benefit very largely from insurance coverage).[330]

§2. Liability of Teachers for the Acts of Their Pupils

149. Originally, the liability of teachers was governed by the same rules as the liability of parents and craftsmen. Teachers were held personally liable for damage caused by their pupils during school time, the presumption being that their supervision was at fault. Subsequently, an act of 1937 repealed the doctrine of presumed fault and shifted the burden of proof to the claimant who now has to establish the teacher's fault,[331] which generally is non-compliance with supervision duties. In case law, teachers have been held liable, for example, because they allowed children to play dangerous games while under their supervision.[332]

150. More importantly, since 1937, if the claimant can prove fault on the part of a public sector teacher (or a teacher of a publicly-funded private school),[333] the state will assume full liability for the harm caused by the pupil. This gives most French teachers civil immunity,[334] and the scarcity of case law reveals that it is unusual in France to sue the state for a loss related to a teacher's lack of supervision. It is much

329. *See* François Terré, Yves Lequette & François Chénedé, *Les grands arrêts de la jurisprudence civile* (13th ed., Dalloz 2015) vol 2, 424. *See* also Christophe Radé, *Le renouveau de la responsabilité du fait d'autrui (apologie de l'arrêt Bertrand)*, D 1997, chr 279 (who considers that the solution of the *Bertrand* case is still covered by the wording of Art. 1242(7) Civil Code).

330. On the insurance environment of parental liability, *see* the interesting developments of Häcker, *supra* n. 291, at 172–177.

331. According to Art. 1242(8) Civil Code, 'as to teachers, the faults, imprudence or negligent conducts invoked against them as having caused the damaging act must be proved by the claimant at the trial, in accordance with the general law'.

332. Civ, 9 January 1939, Dalloz hebdomadaire 1939, somm 20. For more references, *see* e.g. le Tourneau (ed.), *Droit de la responsabilité, supra* n. 54, at paras 2236.31–2236.39.

333. *See* also among the social sciences literature, Roger Magnuson, *Law and the Teacher in England and France*, 6 Comparative Education 85, 93–94 (1970).

334. The 1937 act also states that a teacher shall not be required to appear personally in court to give testimony in the case. Moreover, even though the state is allowed to claim reimbursement of the damages if there is gross negligence by the teacher, this right of recourse is hardly ever invoked by the state.

more convenient for parents of an injured child to obtain damages from the playmate's liability insurer since fault-based liability is independent of the mental capacity of the wrongdoer.[335] The availability of third-party liability insurance coverage facilitates compensation by the insurer of the child and parents rather than through a claim against the state.

§3. Liability of Guardians for the Acts of Vulnerable Individuals

151. French courts have extended Article 1242(1) Civil Code to create other cases of liability for acts of other persons, in particular in cases in which harm was caused by a vulnerable person under the control of a guardian or an association. In the famous *Blieck* case of 1991,[336] the Court of Cassation held that Article 1242(1) should not only be treated as the legal basis for the strict liability principle for things[337] but that it could also be invoked to hold a person strictly liable for the acts of others.[338] In the *Blieck* case, the *Assemblée plénière* found that an association caring for mentally handicapped adults was strictly liable for the acts of one of their charges who had set fire to a forest next to the training centre in which he worked. For the Court of Cassation, strict liability was based on the fact that 'the association had accepted the responsibility to organise and to control, permanently, the way of life of this handicapped person'.

152. The principle laid out in the *Blieck* case has been applied to similar cases characterised by the organization and control of the way of life of vulnerable individuals by an institution or even a private person. Educational services dealing with juvenile offenders or vulnerable minors[339] and guardians (*tuteurs*) of minor children[340] have been held liable under Article 1242(1) for harm caused to third persons. To circumscribe the liability regime based on Article 1242(1), the Court of Cassation has stated, however, that grandparents who look after their grandchildren on an occasional basis should not be subject to strict liability.[341]

153. Should these cases of liability be regarded as the crucible of a general principle of strict liability for the acts of others similar to the liability for the acts of

335. *See* paras 80–83 above.
336. Ass plén, 29 March 1991, no. 89-15231. For a presentation of the case and its consequences, *see* Giliker, *Vicarious Liability*, *supra* n. 197, at 133–135.
337. *See* paras 165–168 below.
338. In 1956, the *Conseil d'État* recognized the strict liability of public institutions for harm caused by delinquent minors (CE, 3 February 1956, *Thouzellier*). The *Blieck* decision is also seen as an attempt made by the Court of Cassation to treat equally victims of the misconduct of vulnerable persons, regardless of the public or private status of the institutions which take care of them.
339. Crim, 26 March 1997, no. 95-83606.
340. Crim, 28 March 2000, no. 99-84075. Yet in another case (Civ 2, 25 February 1998, no. 95-20419), the Court of Cassation held that the guardian of an adult should not be subject to strict liability based upon Art. 1242(1) Civil Code.
341. Civ 2, 18 September 1996, no. 94-20580. *See* also Gérard Blanc, *À propos de la responsabilité des grands-parents*, D 1997, chr 327.

things? While some authors vigorously defend such an interpretation,[342] most tort law scholars consider that the *Blieck* decision and the subsequent case law have only led to an extension of parental liability on a case-by-case basis.[343] Due to the fact that the Court of Cassation does not traditionally reveal the underlying rationale of its decisions,[344] the attempts of the French legal doctrine to present a coherent framework for the cases of liability for the acts of others based on Article 1242(1) Civil Code have more to do with divinatory arts than with sound legal analysis.

154. It is to be hoped that the future tort law reform will restore some coherency in this field of tort law. The 2017 Draft Reform suggests equating for civil liability purposes a child's guardian (*tuteur*) with any other 'physical or legal person charged by judicial or administrative decision with organising and controlling the minor's way of life on a permanent basis' (Article 1246 of the draft).[345] In Article 1247 of the draft, the *Blieck* principle is upheld for cases in which an adult whose life is being controlled and organised by the defendant on a permanent basis (i.e., by judicial or administrative decision) has caused harm to a third party. However, if a person has voluntarily accepted the supervision of a minor or an adult by contract and as part of a professional activity, liability is not of a strict nature but based on a (rebuttable) presumption of fault (Article 1248 of the draft).[346]

342. Le Tourneau (ed.), *Droit de la responsabilité, supra* n. 54, at Ch. 2232; Matthieu Poumarède, *L'avènement de la responsabilité civile du fait d'autrui*, in *Mélanges Philippe le Tourneau* (Dalloz 2007) 839.
343. *See* e.g. Brun, *Responsabilité, supra* n. 147, at para. 482.
344. On the judicial style *à la française* and recent reform plans, *see* Steiner, *supra* n. 16, at 140–148.
345. For a presentation in English of the following draft provisions, *see* Häcker, *supra* n. 291, at 156–159.
346. This provision shall apply, in particular, to babysitters and to nursing homes. In both situations, French courts have always refused to apply the *Blieck* principle of strict liability.

Chapter 3. Other Cases of Liability for Acts of Others

§1. Liability of Sports Clubs for the Acts of Their Members

155. From 1995 on, the *Blieck* principle has been extended to a different type of situation in which a defendant organised and controlled risk-producing activities. In line with the logic of the liability of employers, strict liability has been imposed on sports clubs for injuries caused by their members to other players or members of the public on the basis of Article 1242(1) Civil Code.[347] In other cases, the organisers of a majorette parade have been held strictly liable for the harm caused by a twirling baton.[348] On the other hand, the Court of Cassation made clear that hunting associations and unions were not subject to strict liability based on Article 1242(1) Civil Code.[349]

156. Given that there are only a handful of decisions that extend the *Blieck* principle to sports clubs and other leisure associations, it is even more difficult to identify a coherent legal framework than it is in the case law related to vulnerable individuals. Case law shows that, according to the principles governing the liability of *commettants*,[350] only fault on the part of the player or, more broadly, of the member who has caused the harm will lead to strict liability of the club or the association and that the risk of causing physical injury inherent to most sports must be taken into account.[351] This leads the Court of Cassation to a restrictive approach in which only a 'deliberate failure to comply with sports rules' gives rise to a right of compensation against the sports club.[352]

157. Due to the difficulties to circumscribe strict liability based on the idea that the defendant controlled and organised the activity of another person[353] and given that the relationship between sports players and their clubs might also be seen as a *commettant/préposé* relationship,[354] the 2017 Draft Reform does not uphold a specific tort law provision for sports clubs and other leisure associations.

347. Civ 2, 22 May 1995, nos 92-21197 and 92-21871 (injury caused during a rugby match).
348. Civ 2, 12 December 2002, no. 00-13553. *See* also CA Paris, 9 June 2000, no. 1998/10517, Resp civ assur 2000, comm 74 (liability of a scout association for the harm caused by one of the scouts).
349. Civ 2, 11 September 2008, no. 07-15842 (hunting association); Civ 2, 26 October 2006, no. 04-11665 (union).
350. *See* para. 135 above.
351. *See* para. 125 above.
352. Ass plén, 29 June 2007, no. 06-18141, commented in Olivier Moréteau, *France* in *ETL 2007 (2008)*, 274, paras 19–28. On this case law development, *see* Jérôme François, *Fait générateur de la responsabilité du fait d'autrui: confirmation ou évolution ?*, D 2007, chr 2408.
353. On these difficulties, *see* also in English Giliker, *Vicarious Liability*, *supra* n. 197, at 133–135.
354. *See* on this issue Jean Mouly, *Les paradoxes du droit de la responsabilité civile dans le domaine des activités sportives*, JCP G 2005 I no. 134.

§2. Liability of Legal Entities for Acts of Their Organs

158. French courts have developed a specific regime for corporate entities of all kinds which will be held liable for the acts of their 'organs', that is, for their executives.[355] For a long time, the legal basis of this liability has not been entirely clear. Until the 1960s, the Court of Cassation accepted that the misconduct of an executive could lead to both fault-based liability under former Article 1382 Civil Code and to vicarious liability under former Article 1384(5) Civil Code. However, in a leading case in 1967, the Second Civil Chamber stated that 'a legal person is liable for a fault committed through its organs and owes compensation to the victim without the need to involve the said organs as *préposés* under [former] Article 1384(5) Civil Code'.[356] This means that the civil liability of legal entities for acts of their organs is not seen as a subspecies of vicarious liability. Unless the executive has the legal status of an employee,[357] the organ's *faute* is purely and simply considered as the *faute* of the legal entity, giving rise to liability under Article 1240 Civil Code. This solution complies with the so-called reality of corporate personality doctrine (*théorie de la réalité des personnes morales*), which also presides over corporate criminal liability.[358] According to this conception, the organ whose actions are attributed directly to the legal person is not a third party but an inherent part of the entity. Despite some discordant voices in case law and legal doctrine,[359] the misconduct of managers or presidents of associations is regarded as the misconduct of the entity they were supposed to represent even if the actions were outside the perimeter fixed by the corporation or the association.[360] Accordingly, it is not necessary for the claimant to establish the misconduct of one of the guiding officers since French courts acknowledge the liability of legal persons in cases in which there is a mere failure in organization or functioning.[361]

159. The 2017 Draft Reform suggests the introduction of a specific provision on the liability of legal entities which codifies the judge-made solutions. According to Article 1242-1 of the Draft, 'fault in a legal person results from fault in one of its organs or a failure in its organisation or its functioning'. Although the wording is supposed to reformulate existing case law solutions, it has given rise to massive criticism both from legal academics (mostly with a business law background) and

355. *See* also in English Katrin Deckert, *Corporate Criminal Liability in France*, in *Corporate Criminal Liability: Emergence, Convergence, and Risk* (Mark Pieth & Radha Ivory eds, Springer 2011) 147, 149–150.
356. Civ 2, 17 July 1967, RTD civ 1968, 149, note Georges Durry. *See* also Civ 1, 16 November 1976; Civ 2, 27 April 1977.
357. On this specific case, *see* Véronique Magnier, *La responsabilité des dirigeants sociaux à l'égard des tiers: le dirigeant est-il un préposé?*, Resp civ assur 2013, dossier 18.
358. *See* Viney, Jourdain & Carval, *Conditions*, *supra* n. 129, at para. 853.
359. *See* Civ 2, 15 May 2008, no. 06-22171. Le Tourneau (ed.), *Droit de la responsabilité*, *supra* n. 54, at para. 2112.51; Wester-Ouisse, *La jurisprudence*, *supra* n. 277.
360. A limitation of the organ's authority, as stipulated in the corporation's or association's statutes, will not be effective against third parties. *See* Arts L 221-5(3), L 222-2, L 223-18(5), L 225-35(3), L 225-51(4) and L 225-64(3) Commercial Code and Art. 1849(1) and (3) Civil Code.
361. *See* e.g. Civ 1, 15 December 1999, no. 97-22652 (organisational fault of a clinic); Civ 2, 12 May 2005, no. 03-17994 (organisational fault of an association in charge of a rehabilitation centre).

from the business community.[362] It is argued that the formal recognition of civil liability in cases of a *défaut d'organisation ou de fonctionnement*, a legal figure borrowed from administrative law,[363] would lead to an excessive legal and economic burden for French corporations which are already weakened by the financial crisis of the late 2000s.[364] Furthermore, although the 2017 Draft does not mention any specific liability provisions for corporate groups (*groupes de sociétés*), it is said that Article 1242-1 could lead to a new form of corporate liability litigation if applied to the non-compliance with duties arising from corporate social responsibility (*responsabilité sociale des entreprises*).[365] However, in light of the current position of the French courts, it is likely that a codification of the *défaut d'organisation ou de fonctionnement* test would not bring about significant changes to the existing law.[366]

---

362. *See* e.g. Didier Poracchia, *La responsabilité civile des personnes morales*, Bulletin Joly Sociétés 2017, 357.
363. *See* para. 105 above.
364. See, in particular, the report of the Legal High Committee for Financial Markets of Paris which was issued in 2018 on this specific subject (Haut Comité Juridique de la Place financière de Paris, *Rapport sur l'introduction de règles spécifiques aux personnes morales dans le droit de la responsabilité extracontractuelle* (2018) paras 33–66).
365. Haut Comité Juridique de la Place financière de Paris, *supra* n. 364, at paras 54–56.
366. *See* Viney, Jourdain & Carval, *Conditions*, *supra* n. 129, at para. 854 (with references to cases in which a *défaut d'organisation ou de fonctionemment* was regarded as sufficient). *See* also Patrice Jourdain, *Responsabilité fondée sur la faute : Responsabilité du fait personnel* in *JurisClasseur Civil* (2014), paras 8–17.

Part III. Forms of Strict Liability

Chapter 1. Liability for Things and Animals

§1. Liability for Animals and Ruined Buildings

160. In 1804, the French Civil Code only provided for two cases of liability detached from the idea of fault. Following the Roman Law institutions known as *actio de pauperie* and *cautio damni infecti*, Articles 1385 and 1386 (now 1243 and 1244) Civil Code codified strict liability for the action of animals and ruined buildings. [367]

161. According to Article 1244 Civil Code, 'the owner of a building is liable for the damage caused by its collapse, where it happens as a result of lack of maintenance or of a defect in its construction'. At first sight, this provision could be seen as a duplicate of Article 1240 Civil Code and its general principle of liability for fault. However, what makes Article 1244 the legal basis of *strict* liability is the fact that a defect in construction or a lack of maintenance does not necessarily involve the actions of the present owner, the first having probably existed since the building was constructed and the second able to result from neglect by a tenant who bears a share in the maintenance of the property. It is therefore understandable that behind its innocuous appearance, this provision expresses the idea that a building owner can be liable without any fault.

162. Although it has somewhat fallen into scholarly oblivion since the recognition of a general principle of strict liability for things,[368] Article 1244 Civil Code is still used by courts, for example, in cases in which a passer-by, a neighbour or any other person on the premises is injured by the fall of the building structure (the 'ruin'). To obtain compensation in tort, the claimant has to establish an involuntary fall of the building or a part of it (e.g., a roof tile, a window glass or a balcony railing) due to a lack of maintenance or a construction defect. Once the claimant has proved these two conditions, the owner will be liable for the harm caused by the

367. On the origins of both, *see* Jonas Knetsch, *The Role of Liability without Fault*, in *French Civil Liability in Comparative Perspective* (Jean-Sébastien Borghetti & Simon Whittaker eds, Hart 2019) 123, 129–132.

368. See, however, the profound study by Valérie Depadt-Sebag, *La justification du maintien de l'article 1386 du Code civil* (LGDJ 2000).

ruin even if there is no personal fault.[369] If the claimant is related to the building owner by contract, for example, in a landlord–tenant relationship, the Court of Cassation has made clear that civil liability can only be established in contract according to the *non-cumul* principle.[370] The 2017 Draft Reform suggests omitting the provision of Article 1386 Civil Code and incorporating the liability for ruined buildings in the general principle of liability for things.[371]

163. Strict liability for harm caused by animals is enshrined in Article 1243 Civil Code. According to this text, 'the owner of an animal, or the person using it, during the period of usage, is liable for the damage the animal has caused, whether the animal was under his custody, or whether it had strayed or escaped'.[372] In recent times, the Court of Cassation has had the occasion to reaffirm the relevance of this liability regime[373] which has served as a model for the formation of a general principle of liability for things.

164. Under French law, the owner (*propriétaire*) or the user (e.g., a borrower, a leaseholder or even a thief) are held strictly liable for the harm caused by an animal, regardless of its nature.[374] While the claimant does not have to prove fault on the part of the owner or user, it is necessary to establish that an action of the animal (*fait de l'animal*) is at the origin of the harm. To do so, the proof of contact between animal and claimant will be generally sufficient; otherwise, the claimant is required to demonstrate that the animal's behaviour was abnormal.[375] Following the principles of strict liability, the owner or user can escape liability only in cases of force majeure or contributory fault of the claimant. The 2017 Draft Reform no longer

369. In 2000, the Court of Cassation stated that the owner's liability under Art. 1244 Civil Code does not exclude the parallel application of the general principle of liability for things to the building's guardian (who is not its owner). Civ 2, 23 March 2000, no. 97-19991.

370. *See* paras 58–60 above. *See* also in English Ferdinand F. Stone, *Liability for Damage Caused by Things*, in *International Encyclopedia of Comparative Law* vol XI (André Tunc ed., Brill & J C B Mohr 1983) para. 99.

371. In legal literature, there is strong support for this position. Most authors argue that there is no reason that victims of collapsed buildings should be subjected to a more difficult standard of liability (proof of a lack of maintenance or a construction defect) than victims of other things. *See,* e.g., Viney, Jourdain & Carval, *Conditions*, *supra* n. 129, at para. 739-1. *See* also in English Paula Giliker, *The Role of* la faute *in the Avant-projet de réforme*, in *Reforming the French Law of Obligations* (John Cartwright, Stefan Vogenauer & Simon Whittaker eds, Hart 2009) 289, 295 ('outdated').

372. On this liability regime from a comparative perspective, *see* Stone, *supra* n. 372, at paras 37–80. For a more detailed presentation in French *see* Jérôme Julien, *Responsabilité du fait des animaux* in *Répertoire de droit civil* (Dalloz 2018) paras 1–54.

373. Civ 2, 17 January 2019, no. 17-28861. *See* e.g. Patrice Jourdain, *Fait des animaux et absence de contact*, RTD civ 2019, 351.

374. Only wild animals living in nature are excepted from the scope of application of Art. 1243 Civil Code. Damage caused by game is subject to a specific compensation regime which attributes to local hunters' associations the duty to compensate the losses. *See* Art. L 426-1 Environmental Code.

375. In the forementioned 2019 case (*see supra* n. 375), the Court of Cassation held that a dog running towards a pony and causing it to rear and plunge behaved in such an 'abnormal' way.

mentions a specific liability provision for animals, considering that a general principle of strict liability for things is able to encompass cases which are today subject to Article 1243.

§2. General Principle of Liability for Things

I. Origins[376]

165. In 1804, when the Code Napoléon came into force, it was totally inconceivable that the guardian of a thing which caused harm to another person should be liable without fault. Yet in Article 1384(1) Civil Code, it could be read at that time that 'a person is liable not only for the damages he causes by his own act, but also for that which is caused by the acts of persons for whom he is responsible, or by things which are in his custody'. It was generally acknowledged that the last part of this provision ('or by things which are in his custody') referred to Articles 1385 and 1386 then dealing with the liability for harm caused by animals and ruined buildings.[377] In other words, Article 1384(1) Civil Code was seen as a formal announcement of the liability provisions that follow and are disconnected from the then dominant principle of fault-based liability.

166. With the rise of industrial accidents at the end of the nineteenth century, the supremacy of *faute* as the legal and moral basis of civil liability was increasingly questioned by legal academics and politicians. The idea of leaving victims of labour-related accidents uncompensated because they could not establish the employer's fault[378] became more and more disputed. Prominent legal academics such as Louis Josserand and Raymond Saleilles vehemently urged the courts to move away from the sole doctrine of *faute* by interpreting the last part of Article 1384(1) Civil Code as the legal basis of strict liability for damages caused by things. Developing a so-called doctrine of 'created risk' (*théorie du risque créé*), both authors considered that the ownership over a thing should go hand in hand with liability for the damage caused by it. After the *Conseil d'État* suggested its eagerness to embrace these new ideas in the field of administrative liability,[379] the Court of Cassation held in the famous *Teffaine* case of 1896 that liability could indeed be based on (former) Article 1384(1) Civil Code. In a case in which a mechanic was fatally injured by the explosion of a boiler attached to a tugboat, the Civil Division ruled that the owners of the vessel were strictly liable, implying that they could not

376. *See* also the extensive study by Edward A. Tomlinson, *Tort Liability in France for the Act of Things: A Study of Judicial Lawmaking*, 48 Louisiana Law Review 1299, 1322–1357 (1988).

377. Tomlinson, *supra* n. 376, at 1301 ('Everyone understood it to be a transitional provision preparing the reader for the special rules imposing liability on the owners of animals and collapsing buildings, the specific 'things' enumerated in the two articles that immediately followed it.'). *See* also Frederic Henry Lawson and Basil S. Markesinis, *Tortious Liability for Unintentional Harm in the Common Law and the Civil Law* (CUP 1982) vol 1, 146 ('a mere *élégance de style*').

378. *See,* e.g., Civ, 19 July 1870, *Painvin*, D 1870, 1, 361.

379. CE, 21 June 1895, *Cames*, Sirey 1897, 3, 333, note Maurice Hauriou.

escape liability by proving that they had not committed any *faute* and that the accident was due to an unknown defect in the boiler's tube.[380]

167. Two years after the *Teffaine* case, the French Parliament voted into law an important act on the liability for 'accidents to workers in the course of their employment'. This highly disputed legislation provided injured workers with a right to compensation by their employer or their insurer without proof of fault. With this improvement of workers' rights, the number of cases brought before the courts on the basis of Article 1384(1) Civil Code greatly diminished and some commentators thought that the trend initiated by the *Teffaine* case had come to a halt. However, with the increase of motor vehicle accidents in the first decades of the 20th centuries, the Court of Cassation reaffirmed its determination to see in Article 1384(1) Civil Code not only a *figure de style* but a genuine basis for strict liability.

168. This interpretation was definitely sanctioned in 1930 by the Court of Cassation sitting in Plenary Session (then called *Chambres réunies*) in the famous *Jand'heur* case.[381] In this case, a girl was seriously injured by a motor truck owned by a department store. Ending a five-year judicial saga, the *Chambres réunies* held that 'for the purpose of applying the presumption of liability (*présomption de responsabilité*) laid down in Article 1384, the law does not distinguish between things causing damage when handled by men or causing damage by themselves; nor is it necessary that the damage resulted from an inherent defect in the object'.[382] For the Court of Cassation, the mother of the injured girl could base her claim on the sole Article 1384(1) Civil Code without establishing any fault whatsoever of the driver or the car owner. Ever since, the courts have recognized strict liability attached to the guardianship (*garde*) of a thing, regardless of any defect or any misconduct. The 2017 Reform Draft suggests incorporation of the main rules of this liability regime in Article 1243, confirming one of the most spectacular developments of French tort law in the twentieth century.

II. Scope of Application and Requirements for Liability

169. Since the *Jand'heur* decision, the liability regime based upon Article 1242(1) Civil Code covers all kind of 'things' (*choses*), whether intrinsically defective or not, whether moving or inert, whether dangerous or not, whether liquid, gaseous or in solid form and whether movable or immovable.[383] There are many examples that illustrate the diversity of *choses* for which strict liability has been adopted by courts. In 2011, the guardian of a cliff was held liable for the harm caused by a rock to a third person;[384] in 1992, an instance court even recognized the liability of a TV company for the loss caused to a French corporation from showing

380. For a more detailed presentation of the *Teffaine* case in English, *see* Tomlinson, *supra* n. 376, at 1322–1332.
381. *See* Tomlinson, *supra* n. 376, at 1337–1351.
382. The translation is by Steiner, *supra* n. 16, at 270.
383. Steiner, *supra* n. 16, at 270.
384. Civ 3, 3 March 2011, no. 09-69658.

advertising signs during a world cup football match.[385] This inclusiveness of the term *chose* should not conceal the limitation of the scope of application. Things which are governed by specific tort law provisions, such as animals, ruined buildings, nuclear plants, aircraft and motor vehicles, do not fall within the ambit of Article 1242(1) Civil Code. Furthermore, a 1922 act excluded from the strict liability for things cases in which the spreading of a fire (*propagation d'incendie*) is the origin of harm.[386] Finally, it must be noted that there is uncertainty about incorporeal things (*choses incorporelles*) and things of microscopical nature (viruses, bacteria, etc.).[387] For the time being, French courts have never acknowledged that the strict liability principle under Article 1242(1) Civil Code could apply to those cases. For greater clarity, the 2017 Draft Reform intends to limit the scope of application to corporeal things (*choses corporelles*).[388]

170. According to the case law, the 'thing' must have played an 'active role' (*rôle actif*) in the occurrence of the damage, that is, the *chose* has to be 'the instrument of the harm caused',[389] which leads authors of tort law textbooks to state that the trigger of liability is not so much the *chose* itself or its guardianship as its 'active action' (*fait actif d'une chose*). In practice, this means that the defendant has to establish the causal link between the thing and the damage.[390] To do this, the claimant can rely on a subtle system of presumptions which distinguishes three groups of cases. If a thing is in motion (*en mouvement*) and has direct physical contact with the property damaged or the person injured, the 'active role' is presumed. In the case of an inert *chose* or if there was not any direct contact between the thing and the property or the injured person, the claimant has to establish its 'active role', for example, an internal defect (*vice inhérent*), a wrong position or 'behaviour' (*position ou comportement anormal*) or inadequate maintenance (*état d'entretien insuffisant*). The 2017 Draft Reform sanctions this nuanced approach by providing that 'an action of a thing is presumed wherever, while moving, it comes into contact with the person or property which is harmed' (Article 1243(2) of the Draft).[391]

385. TGI Paris, 27 February 1992, JCP G 1992, 2, no. 21809, note Philippe le Tourneau.
386. The vast majority of authors assert that this exception should be abandoned. *See* e.g. Guy Courtieu, *Communication d'incendie : une loi à éteindre*, Gaz Pal 1995, 1, doctr 610; Marie-France Steinlé-Feuerbach, *De l'opportunité de la suppression de l'alinéa 2 de l'article 1384 du code civil*, JCP N 1993, 1, no. 38.
387. On this issue, *see,* e.g., Emmanuel Tricoire, *La responsabilité du fait des 'choses immatérielles'*, in *Mélanges en l'honneur de Philippe le Tourneau* (Dalloz 2008) 983. *See* also in English Jean-Sébastien Borghetti, *Liability for False Information in French Law. The Limits of Civil Law*, in *Tatsachenmitteilungen und Werturteile: Freiheit und Verantwortung* (Helmut Koziol ed., Jan Sramek Verlag 2018) 133.
388. Art. 1243(1) of the draft: 'A person is liable strictly for harm caused by the action of corporeal things within his keeping.'
389. *See,* e.g., Civ 2, 25 October 2001, no. 99-21616.
390. *See* Bell, Boyron & Whittaker, *supra* n. 17, at 386 ('the courts have taken a broad but nuanced approach to the causal relation between the thing and the injured person's harm, using causation to reflect a normative sense of the proper attribution of responsibility for the claimant's harm').
391. In Art. 1243(3) of the draft, it is said that 'in other cases, it is for the victim to prove the action of the thing by establishing either its defect or the abnormality of its position, its state or its behaviour'. For a critical assessment in English, *see* Bell, Boyron & Whittaker, *supra* n. 17, at 387–388.

171. The liability for the action of a thing is attributed to its guardian (*gardien*). The Court of Cassation had the occasion to define the legal concept of *garde* at a very early stage. In the famous *Franck* case from 1941, the *chambres réunies* held that a guardian was the person who possesses the 'use, direction and control' (*usage, direction et contrôle*) of the thing.[392] In the *Franck* case, a car belonging to a doctor was stolen and the thief who was driving the car fatally injured a third person. By attributing guardianship to the thief rather than to the owner, the *Chambres réunies* departed from the *legal* status of the guardian and adopted a more *fact-based* approach.[393] Soon after this case, the courts began to apply this formula on condition that the owner would be presumed to be the guardian of a thing unless this presumption could be rebutted by showing that the guardianship had been transferred. It is now well established that the owner can invoke such a transfer of guardianship by contract[394] or factual circumstances.[395] In detail, French case law provides a nuanced approach to the transfer of guardianship, revealing a case-by-case approach which is difficult to summarize. However, the case law is consistent when it comes to things which are under the control of employees or other *préposés*. In those cases, the employer or *commettant* remains the guardian of the thing due to the relationship of subordination.[396] Paradoxically, it has been held that a lack of discernment or a state of unconsciousness does not exclude the possibility of being the guardian of a thing: a young child before the age of seven can be regarded as guardian as can a person suffering from an epileptic seizure at the time the harm was caused.[397]

III. The Future of the General Principle of Liability for Things

172. In 2010, a doctrinal controversy arose between two distinguished tort law scholars over the opportunity of a general principle of liability for things in French law. Under the heading 'liability for things, a doctrine which has seen its day', it was argued that the circumstances under which this liability regime was developed in the first half of the twentieth century do not reflect the current situation and that the French tort law system would be more consistent if the excessively wide general principle of liability of things was abandoned.[398] His opponent noted in

392. Ch réunies, 2 December 1941, S 1941, 1, 217, note Henri Mazeaud.
393. In French legal doctrine, it is said that the Court of Cassation made a shift from *garde juridique* to *garde matérielle*. On this issue, *see* the more detailed presentation by Bell, Boyron & Whittaker, *supra* n. 17, at 387–388; Steiner, *supra* n. 16, at 272–273.
394. A person who hires a thing becomes its *gardien*.
395. It is not necessary that a person has control over the thing for a long time to become its guardian. It has been held that a client of a supermarket becomes the guardian of a shopping-trolley while he is on the premises (Civ 2, 13 January 2012, no. 11-11047). The same applies to a person holding a door or a child kicking a bottle.
396. In reality, this solution is necessary to protect the employee from civil liability. On the *préposé*'s civil immunity, *see* paras 100, 139 above.
397. Ass plén, 9 May 1984, no. 80-14994, *Gabillet*; Civ 2, 18 December 1964, *Trichard*.
398. Jean-Sébastien Borghetti, *La responsabilité du fait des choses, un régime qui a fait son temps*, RTD civ 2010, 1.

response that the actual case law has become very scarce, especially since the enactment of the *loi Badinter* on motor vehicle accidents, and that the general principle of liability for things adequately covers some residual cases of liability in which fault-based liability would be too harsh (e.g., railway accidents).[399] He further contested the analysis according to which the *non-cumul* principle is closely related to the appearance of strict liability on the basis of Article 1242(1) Civil Code.[400]

173. In light of the multiple reform proposals and drafts presented since 2005, it is very unlikely that a future tort law reform will abandon the general principle of liability for things, which is deeply rooted in the imagination of French tort lawyers despite its little weight in practice. A limitation to corporeal things, as suggested by the 2017 Draft Reform, would help to dispel the doubts concerning the scope of application. There is actually no doctrinal support for the proposal, made by the *Terré* working group in 2010, to restrict the liability regime to personal injury cases, although it would not be unreasonable to limit the principle of liability for things since French tort law is already characterized by an extremely wide-ranging principle of liability for *faute*.[401]

399. Philippe Brun, *De l'intemporalité du principe de responsabilité du fait des choses*, RTD civ 2010, 487. *See* also Georges Durry, *L'irremplaçable responsabilité du fait des choses*, in *L'avenir du droit : Mélanges en l'honneur de François Terré* (Dalloz, PUF & JurisClasseur 1999) 707.

400. Brun, *supra* n. 399, at 488–492.

401. *See* also the arguments presented by Jean-Sébastien Borghetti, *Des principaux délits spéciaux*, in *Pour une réforme du droit de la responsabilité civile* (François Terré ed., Dalloz 2011) 163, 173–175.

Chapter 2. Road and Traffic Accidents

174. Since 1985, the general principle of liability for things laid out in the *Teffaine* and *Jand'heur* cases no longer applies to road traffic accidents. The reasons which led to the enactment of a specific liability regime lay in the general developments of French tort law. Even though the interpretation of Article 1242(1) Civil Code by the French courts made it much easier for victims to claim damages from car drivers and their insurers than under the doctrine of *faute*, there was growing dissatisfaction in legal doctrine and among practitioners as to the adequacy of this liability regime for the specific situation of traffic accident victims. In particular, the shift from a subjective to an objective vision of *faute*[402] had the effect that the defendant could very easily invoke contributory fault in order to escape partially or totally from liability. In the 1960s and 1970s, it was not uncommon for motor vehicle insurers to submit to the claimant an offer for a compensation agreement which almost automatically took into account the slightest negligence committed by the victim. If the offer was rejected, the claimant had to bring the case in court, resulting in a further delay in compensation for the loss.[403] The sometimes dramatic consequences of traffic accidents for families and private households thus led to several reform proposals,[404] but it was not until the 1981 presidential election and the nomination of *Robert Badinter*, a successful lawyer and former law professor, as minister of Justice that *André Tunc*, a distinguished tort law scholar, was able to bring the work of a reform commission to success.[405] Despite considerable opposition from the bar and the insurance companies, the Parliament in May 1985 passed a law 'designed to improve the situation of the victims of road accidents and to accelerate compensation procedures'.[406]

---

402. *See* paras 80–83 above.
403. For a full account of the situation before the enactment of the 1985 *loi Badinter*, *see* André Tunc, *The French Law of Traffic Victims Compensation: The Present and the Possible*, 31 American Journal of Comparative Law 489, 492–497 (1983); *Traffic Accident Compensation: A French Proposal*, 16 Revista Juridica de la Universidad Interamericana de Puerto Rico 125 (1981). *See* also from a comparative standpoint André Tunc, *Traffic Accident Compensation: Law and Proposals*, in *International Encyclopedia of Comparative Law* vol XI (André Tunc ed., Brill & J C B Mohr 1983).
404. The most important and audacious was probably the Tunc proposal of 1966 which included provisions which were widely inspired by the famous 1965 Keetan/O'Connell plan: André Tunc, *La sécurité routière. Esquisse d'une loi sur les accidents de la circulation* (Dalloz 1966). For a full account of this text in English, *see* André Tunc, *Traffic Accident Compensation in France: The Present Law and a Controversial Proposal*, 79 Harvard Law Review 1409 (1966).
405. For a presentation of the political context of the *loi Badinter*, *see*, e.g., André Tunc, *'Loi Badinter' – On Traffic Accidents and Beyond*, 6 Tulane Civil Law Forum 27, 29–30 (1991–1992).
406. For a full account of this act in English, *see*, e.g., Ruth Redmond-Cooper, *No Fault Liability on the French Roads*, Journal of Personal Injury Litigation 1995, 291; *The Relevance of Fault in Determining Liability for Road Accidents: The French Experience*, 38 ICLQ 502 (1989); André Tunc, *It is Wise not to Take the Civil Codes too Seriously: Traffic Accident Compensation in France*, in *Essays in memory of Professor F. H. Lawson* (Peter Wallington & Robert M. Merkin eds, Butterworths 1986) 71; *'Loi Badinter'*, *supra* n. 405, at29–30; *Traffic Accidents Compensation Under Tort Law and under a Specific Law: The French Experience*, in *The Law of Obligations: Essays in Celebration of John Fleming* (Peter Cane & Jane Stapleton eds, Clarendon Press 1998) 363–376 and, more recently, Jean-Sébastien Borghetti, *Extra-Strict Liability for Traffic Accidents in France*, 53 Wake Forrest Law Review 265 (2018).

175. Contrary to what was expected in 1985, the *loi Badinter* has caused significant litigation, which can be explained by the unusual structure of the first six articles dealing with the compensation of road traffic accidents. It took almost a decade to stabilize the judicial interpretation of the act as the basis of a strict liability regime[407] and to define the precise limits of new legal concepts such as 'involvement' (*implication*), 'motor vehicle' (*vehicle terrestre à moteur*) and 'inexcusable fault' (*faute inexcusable*). It is nowadays accepted that in order to get compensation, claimants have to establish that their damages are attributable to a traffic accident (*accident de la circulation*) in which a motor vehicle driven or owned by the defendant was involved.

176. The *loi Badinter* does not define the term 'motor vehicle' (*véhicule terrestre à moteur*), but there is no doubt that the definition should be the same as in Article L 211-1(1) Insurance Code which governs the scope of compulsory motor vehicle insurance. According to this text, 'any motor vehicle intended for travel on land and propelled by mechanical power, but not running on rails, and any trailer, whether or not coupled' is subject to compulsory insurance.[408] Trains and trams running on their own tracks are excluded from the ambit of the *loi Badinter*, but the 2017 Draft Reform suggests to abandon this exception as a measure of simplification.[409]

177. Neither does the *loi Badinter* set out any specific standards to circumscribe the notion of 'traffic accident'. It was up to the French courts to decide on a case-by-case basis which events fall into the ambit of the regime and which do not. Over the years, it has emerged that a traffic accident in the sense of the *loi Badinter* is any unforeseen and potentially harmful event arising in connection with the circulation of a motor vehicle.[410] According to this broad definition, it has been held that it made no difference that the event occurred on a public road or on private premises or if it implied a moving or a stationary vehicle. On the other hand, there is no traffic accident if the event is only connected to a 'tool function' of a commercial vehicle[411] or if the driver voluntarily intended to cause harm.[412]

---

407. There has been uncertainty as to the legal nature of the rules (liability or compensation regime). *See* in English Bell, Boyron & Whittaker, *supra* n. 17, at 401.
408. Some vehicles are exempt from compulsory insurance but are still subject to the *loi Badinter*: Government vehicles, snow mobiles, ride-on mowers, cement mixers, etc. *See* on this issue Redmond-Cooper, *supra* n. 406, at 510–511.
409. For a long time, accidents between trains and cars at a level crossing created many difficulties and the actual case law is not satisfying since the *loi Badinter* may apply as against the driver of the vehicle in case of a compensation claim by the railway company but not vice-versa. However, an extension of the scope cannot be accomplished without difficulty as the compensation procedure laid out by the act is not compatible with the specific situation of railway carriers. *See* Jonas Knetsch, *Réforme de la responsabilité civile: faut-il soumettre les accidents ferroviaires au régime de la loi Badinter?*, D 2019, 138.
410. Tunc, *'Loi Badinter'*, *supra* n. 405 and, more recently, Borghetti, *Extra-Strict Liability*, *supra* n. 406, 273. *See* also Redmond-Cooper, *supra* n. 406, at 509–510.
411. *See,* e.g., Civ 2, 19 October 2006, no. 05-14338.
412. *See,* e.g., Civ 2, 22 January 2004, no. 01-11665. In those cases, the claimant may claim compensation from a guarantee fund (*Fonds de garantie des assurances obligatoires de dommages*). *See* also Borghetti, *Extra-Strict Liability*, *supra* n. 406, at 285.

178. The most controversial element of the *loi Badinter* is without any doubt the requirement of an 'involvement' (*implication*) of the motor vehicle in the traffic accident. Once again, there is no statutory definition of this notion and case law has to be consulted to gain a better understanding. According to the Court of Cassation, a vehicle is involved in the accident when it has intervened 'in any way whatsoever' (*d'une manière ou d'une autre*).[413] Similar to what has been decided for the *fait actif d'une chose* in the area of liability for things,[414] the courts have developed a system of presumptions for the purpose of assessing the requirement of *implication*. In case of physical contact between the vehicle and the injured person or the property damaged, the involvement is presumed and the defendant may not rebut this presumption, even though the vehicle did not present any abnormality. In case there was no physical contact, the vehicle is nevertheless involved in the accident if it had a 'disturbing effect' (*rôle perturbateur*) on someone or something, even a slight one.[415] Unlike the general principle of liability for things, the concept of involvement does not require in those cases that the vehicle played an active role in the occurrence of the accident. For example, it has been decided that in cases in which a vehicle was parked in such a way as to obstruct another motorist's, a cyclist's or a pedestrian's view, the vehicle in question, although not physically involved in the accident, is nevertheless *impliqué* for the purpose of the *loi Badinter*.[416] This extensive vision of the concept of *implication* is of particular interest in cases of so-called complex accidents, when several collisions occur at the same place within a short period of time.[417] The Court of Cassation has decided that multiple collisions should be treated as a unique traffic accident and that all vehicles must be regarded as 'involved' in the accident. This means that any victim of this mass accident can claim compensation from the insurer of any of the vehicles involved, even if it was not technically the cause of the claimant's harm. In other words, the concept of involvement is much larger than the traditional requirement of causation.

179. The originality of the liability regime arising from the *loi Badinter* is also illustrated by the limitation of the defences available to the driver or guardian of the vehicle and to the insurer. Article 2 of the *loi Badinter* provides that the defendant cannot escape from liability, even in cases of force majeure or acts of a third party. Accordingly, the victim's right to compensation will not be reduced if the accident is due, for example, to weather conditions (black ice, fog, etc.) and could not have been avoided. As for contributory fault, Articles 3 to 6 of the *loi Badinter* make eligibility depend on the nature of the harm for which compensation is demanded and on the legal status of the claimant. Following the wish of André Tunc, the 'spiritus rector' of the act, non-drivers (such as pedestrians, cyclists or passengers) are more protected than drivers and particular attention is given to personal injuries. When a non-driver claims compensation for personal injury caused by a traffic accident, the

---

413. *See,* e.g., Civ 2, 24 March 2012, no. 11-19339.
414. *See* para. 170 above.
415. Borghetti, *Extra-Strict Liability, supra* n. 406, at 277.
416. *See* e.g. Civ 2, 20 January 1993, no. 91-15707.
417. Borghetti, *Extra-Strict Liability, supra* n. 406, at 277–278.

only defence that may be raised is 'inexcusable fault' (*faute inexcusable*) and only to the extent that such fault was the 'exclusive cause' (*cause exclusive*) of the accident.[418] However, in practice, it is very seldom that the defendant can escape from liability, either totally or partially, as the Court of Cassation has adopted a very restrictive approach to the notion of *faute inexcusable*.[419] The protection is even stronger for victims younger than sixteen, older than seventy or who suffer from a disability of 80% or more as their right to compensation is excluded only if they 'voluntarily sought the harm suffered'.[420] On the other hand, drivers who suffer personal injuries caused by a traffic accident are given significant less protection, as Article 4 of the *loi Badinter* provides that the fault of a driver limits or excludes the right to compensation,[421] which is the normal rule under French law.[422] As for the compensation of damaged property, Article 5 stipulates the very same rule.[423]

180. Thirty-five years after the *loi Badinter* came into force, it must be noted that the fears of the insurance industry and the bar have proved unfounded. As Jean-Sébastien Borghetti has observed, 'the *loi Badinter* has resulted neither in the sky-rocketing of costs nor in an explosion in litigation rates'.[424] One may add that the French bar, who feared losing a substantial part of its judicial activity, is not complaining about a decline of work over the last decades. By combining an extra-strict liability regime and a simplified compensation procedure with the insurance companies on the front line, the *loi Badinter* has succeeded in establishing an effective compensation system which has become an important part of French tort law.[425]

418. The 'exclusiveness' test consists of determining whether there is other fault (of the driver or a third party) that contributed to the traffic accident.
419. No French tort lawyer would think of invoking *faute inexcusable* in cases in which a pedestrian crossed the road when the light was red since the Court of Cassation has made clear that an inexcusable fault should be recognized only in extreme cases. For a full account of the notion of *faute inexcusable* in English, *see* Borghetti, *Extra-Strict Liability*, *supra* n. 406, at 279–280; Redmond-Cooper, *supra* n. 406, at 516–518 (with references to case law). For an example, *see* Lafay, Moréteau & Pellerin-Rugliano, *ETL 2003 (2004)*, *supra* n. 313, at paras 77–87.
420. Art. 3(2) of the *loi Badinter*. In legal literature, this category of claimants is often referred to as 'super-privileged victims'.
421. The 2017 Draft Reform suggests that a driver's right to compensation should be reduced only when he has committed an 'inexcusable fault' (Art. 1287 of the draft).
422. *See* paras 224–228 below.
423. According to this text, 'fault on the part of the victim has the effect of limiting or excluding compensation for physical damage to property which he suffered'.
424. Borghetti, *Extra-Strict Liability*, *supra* n. 406, at 277–278.
425. *See*, e.g., the testimonies of practitioners (*avocat*, judge and insurer) on the occasion of the 30th anniversary of the *loi Badinter*. Viviane Schmitzberger-Hoffer, Claude Creton & Jean-Marc Sarafian, *Les trente ans de la loi Badinter: bilan et perspectives*, Resp civ assur 2015, dossier 20–22.

Chapter 3. Product Liability[426]

181. Until 1998, there was no specific legislation on product liability under French law. Historically, the courts applied contract law to compensation claims filed against manufacturers or retailers of defective goods provided, of course, that there was a contractual relationship with the claimant. In cases of personal injury or damage to property, the contractual remedies were 'the cornerstone of the general product liability system in France'.[427] There was a good chance for the claimant to be awarded damages as there were various options to choose from to determine the basis of the claim. Sometimes courts found manufacturers or retailers liable on the grounds of non-compliance with their duty to correctly inform clients about the product's risk; sometimes the harm was regarded as the consequence of the breach of an *obligation de sécurité*. In most cases, however, the vendor's obligation to guarantee against defects (*garantie contre les vices cachés*), laid out in Article 1641 Civil Code, was an adequate legal basis of damages. In the absence of a contractual relationship, the claimant could invoke the general liability for things of (former) Article 1384(1) Civil Code and claim that the manufacturer kept the guardianship of the 'structure' of the thing for which defectiveness was at the origin of the harm.[428]

182. The consumer-friendliness of the courts and the variety of legal grounds for compensation claims explain why the European Community product liability directive of 1985 did not generate boundless enthusiasm on the part of French legal scholars. For most authors and legal practitioners, it was difficult to understand why they had to abandon a system which proved effective for the purposes of consumer protection. As provided for in the 1985 Directive, the numerous defences available to defendants, the subsidiary nature of the retailer's liability and the restriction to the recoverable harm were perceived, not without reason, as a step back in consumer law. It therefore came as no surprise that in 1988 when the deadline for transposition of the directive expired, the French legislature had not taken any measure whatsoever to implement the EC directive. The process was delayed even further

---

426. For a more detailed presentation in English, *see* Jean-Sébastien Borghetti, *Product Liability in France*, in *European Product Liability* (Piotr Machnikowski ed., Intersentia 2016) 205; *The Development of Product Liability in France*, in *The Development of Product Liability* (Simon Whittaker ed., CUP 2010) 93; Duncan Fairgrieve, L'exception française? *The French Law of Product Liability*, in *Product Liability in Comparative Perspective* (Duncan Fairgrieve ed., CUP 2005) 84; Simon Taylor, *Harmonisation or Divergence? A Comparison of French and English Product Liability Rules*, in *Product Liability in Comparative Perspective* (Duncan Fairgrieve ed., CUP 2005) 221; *The Harmonisation of European Product Liability Rules: French and English Law*, 48 ICLQ 419 (1999); Olivier Debouzy & David Por, *Recent Evolutions and Foreseeable Trends of French Product Liability Rules: Apocalypse Later?*, Revue internationale de droit comparé 2002, 311. *See* also Simon Whittaker, *Liability for Products: English Law, French Law and European Harmonization* (OUP 2005); Bell, Boyron & Whittaker, *supra* n. 17, at 403–408.

427. Fairgrieve, *supra* n. 426, at 86.

428. The doctrine based upon the distinction of *garde de la structure* and *garde du comportement* has been applied in only a few cases (Civ 1, 12 November 1975, JCP G 1976, 2, no. 18479; Civ 2, 4 June 1984, Gaz Pal 1984, 2, 634). In the light of recent case law, it is now considered to be abandoned by the Court of Cassation.

when the country was shaken by a massive product safety scandal related to the supply of HIV contaminated blood to haemophiliacs and other patients. This scandal, also known as the 'infected blood scandal' (*affaire du sang contaminé*), provoked an intensive debate on whether the development risk defence should be implemented in French tort law.

183. Finally, with a ten-year delay, the French parliament transposed the 1985 Directive directly into the Civil Code.[429] In Articles 1245 to 1245-17, a tort lawyer from Europe will find the provisions, with slightly different wording, from the EC product liability directive. As this regime derives from European law and has been extensively presented in another monograph of this Encyclopaedia,[430] it suffices to focus on the specific features of the French implementation and the major case law developments since 1998:

EC Product Liability Directive 85/374	French Civil Code
Article 1	Article 1245
Article 2	Article 1245-2
Article 3	Articles 1245-5 and 1245-6
Article 4	Article 1245-8
Article 5	(Article 1245-7)
Article 6	Article 1245-3
Article 7	Article 1245-10
Article 8	Articles 1245-12 and 1245-13
Article 9	Article 1245-1
Article 10	Article 1245-16
Article 11	Article 1245-15
Article 12	Article 1245-14
Article 13	Article 1245-17
Article 14	-
Article 15	Articles 1245-2, 1245-10, 4° and 1245-11
Articles 16–22	-

429. In the meantime, the Court of Cassation had developed a case law based liability regime according to which the *obligation de sécurité* was interpreted 'in the light of the directive' (*à la lumière de la directive*). Those rules still apply to products put into circulation between 30 July 1988 and 21 May 1998. *See* on this point Jacqueline de la Rochère & Olivier Milhac, *France*, in *International Product Liability* (Dennis Campbell ed., Lloyd's of London 1993) 231; Taylor, *Harmonisation*, *supra* n. 426, at 234–235. For an illustration, *see* Com, 26 May 2010, no. 07-11744, ZEuP 2011, 919, note Jean-Sébastien Borghetti (in English).

430. *See* Gert Brüggemeier, *Tort Law in the European Union* (Kluwer Law, 2d ed. 2018) paras 361–451.

184. Given the discrepancy between the case law applicable prior to 1998 and the EC product liability directive, it is not surprising that the French Government and Parliament chose to use the entire margin left to the Member States and even to deviate from the EC law prescriptions in order to keep the same level of consumer protection as before. Contrary to what was laid down in the 85/374 Directive, the original text of the 1998 transposition act included damages of less than 500 ECU and provided that the supplier of a defective product was liable in all cases and on the same basis as the producer and that the producer had to prove that appropriate steps had been taken to prevent the consequences of a defective product in order to be eligible for the development risk defence. It needed two ECJ decisions and two legislative measures to bring the provisions of the French Civil Code in line with the text of the 1985 Directive.[431] There still remains a slight discrepancy between the wording of the directive and the Civil Code provisions,[432] but the ECJ made clear that it shall not be regarded as a violation of the obligation to transpose the directive.[433]

185. Over the last twenty years, there has been a significant increase in product liability litigation before French civil courts, and it is expected that the introduction of different types of class actions in 2014 and 2016[434] will accentuate this trend.[435] Although the provisions on product liability are still seen by many as an 'alien element' within French tort law, the coordination with the traditional case law is much clearer today than in the early 2000s. In a leading case in 2007, the Court of Cassation held that the judge-made product liability regime based upon an *obligation de sécurité* could no longer be invoked against a professional supplier and that even in cases in which the product was put into circulation before 1998, there should be no other liability regime applicable than the one arising from the directive.[436] Furthermore, the Court of Cassation decided that the liability for fault under Article 1240 Civil Code could only be relied on if the claimant characterizes the fault as 'distinct from the defect'.[437]

186. One of the thorniest difficulties in French product liability litigation is related to the assessment of the causal link between defect and damage in cases

431. *See* Michel Cannarsa *et al.*, *France* in *ETL 2004 (2005)*, 274, paras 20–25; Moréteau, *ETL 2006 (2007)*, *supra* n. 100, at paras 9–11.
432. Whereas Art. 9 of the directive provides that damage to property other than the defective product itself can be compensated only when 'the item of property is of a type ordinarily intended for private use or consumption, and was used by the injured person mainly for his private use or consumption', Art. 1241-2(2) Civil Code states that any damage caused to an item of property other than the defective product itself can be compensated.
433. ECJ, 4 June 2009, C-285/08, *Moteurs Leroy v. Dalka France*. In this case, the ECJ ruled that types of harm not covered by the directive lie outside its scope of application and that it is up to the national legislature to decide whether they are eligible to compensation or not.
434. *See* para. 287 below.
435. *See* in English Maria José Azar-Baud & Alexandre Biard, *The Dawn of Collective Redress 3.0 in France?*, in *Class Actions in Europe: Holy Grail or a Wrong Trail?* (Alan Uzelac & Stefaan Voet eds, Springer 2021) forthcoming. *See* also para. 287 below.
436. Civ 1, 15 May 2007, no. 05-17947. This judgement was preceded by ECJ, 10 January 2006, C-402/03, *Skov v. Bilka Lavrisvarehus*.
437. Com, 26 May 2010, no. 08-18545.

against pharmaceutical manufacturers. The debate focused in particular on claims made by individuals suffering from multiple sclerosis allegedly caused or exacerbated by vaccinations against hepatitis B.[438] Whereas Article 4 of the 1985 Directive states that 'the injured person shall be required to prove the damage, the defect and the causal relationship between defect and damage', some lower French courts decided that, despite scientific uncertainty on the link between the vaccination and the occurrence of demyelinating diseases, a number of circumstances (time coincidence, absence of other causes) allowed the presumption that the vaccination had caused the disease. After a few detours, the Court of Cassation acknowledged that the proof of damage, defect and causation 'could arise from circumstantial evidence (*présomptions*) provided they are serious, precise and corroborative'.[439] In a leading case in 2017, the ECJ confirmed this vision, holding that a national court 'may consider that, notwithstanding the finding that medical research neither establishes nor rules out the existence of a link between the administering of the vaccine and the occurrence of the victim's disease, certain factual evidence relied on by the applicant constitutes serious, specific and consistent evidence enabling it to conclude that there is a defect in the vaccine and that there is a causal link between that defect and that disease'.[440] However, this judgement did not lift all the uncertainty[441] and, in particular, it does not address the question of whether the defect and the causal link are two faces of the same coin or whether they have to be treated separately.

438. On this litigation, *see* in English Jean-Sébastien Borghetti, *Causation in Hepatitis B Vaccination Litigation in France: Breaking through Scientific Uncertainty?* 91 Chicago-Kent Law Review 543 (2016) (also published in *Uncertain Causation in Tort Law* (Miquel Martín-Casals & Diego M. Papayannis eds, CUP 2016) 11).

439. Civ 1, 22 May 2008, no. 05-20317, 06-14952, 05-10593, 06-10967, 06-18848, 07-17200 (six judgments). On this series of judgments, *see* Borghetti, *Causation in Hepatitis B*, *supra* n. 438, at 555–556; Taylor, Fairgrieve & Wester-Ouisse, *supra* n. 176, at 320–321.

440. ECJ, 21 June 2017, C-621/15, *W v. Sanofi Pasteur*. On this case in English, *see* Estelle Brosset, *Distinguishing between Law and Science in Terms of Causation and the Hepatitis B Vaccine: W v. Sanofi Pasteur*, Common Market Law Review 1899 (2018); Marco Rizzi, *A Dangerous Method: Correlations and Proof of Causation in Vaccine Related Injuries*, 9 JETL 289 (2018); Elisabet Ruiz Cairó, *The Lack of Medical Research Does not Prevent and Injured Person from Proving the Defect of a Product and the Causal Link between the Defect and the Damage*, 8 European Journal of Risk Regulation 798 (2017).

441. *See* also Rizzi, *supra* n. 440, at 306.

Chapter 4. Liability for Service

187. French tort law does not provide for any strict liability regime for services. As a 'service' cannot be regarded as a 'product' under the product liability regime,[442] a service provider is subject to the general provisions of contractual liability as well as the specific liability rules governing each type of contract. According to the *non-cumul* principle,[443] a compensation claim can be made on an extra-contractual basis, for example, under fault (Article 1240 Civil Code), only in those cases in which there is no contractual relationship between the claimant and the defendant.

442. On the EU draft service liability directive and the ECJ case law, *see* Brüggemeier, *supra* n. 430, at paras 452–458.
443. *See* paras 58–60 above.

Chapter 5. Environmental Liability

188. Over the last fifty years, the improvement of redress options for ecological harm has been a major concern for public authorities, environmental lawyers and a significant part of tort law scholars.[444] As in other countries, there is a vast academic literature on issues related to environmental liability litigation, especially since the enactment of the first landmark laws on waste disposal (1975) and hazardous installations (1976). It is important to note that an 'Environmental Charter' (*Charte de l'environnement*) has been incorporated in the French Constitution which provides that 'everyone must contribute to repairing damage which he causes to the environment in accordance with the requirements defined by legislation' (Article 4).[445]

189. Traditionally, tort law could play an important role in environmental litigation, where the ecological harm was accompanied by individual loss to health or to property. In those cases, the claimants could – and still can – bring a civil action to the courts on the grounds of liability for fault (Article 1240 Civil Code), for the action of things (Article 1242(1) Civil Code) or product liability (Article 1245–1245-17 Civil Code). There are also illustrations of the liability of public authorities, subject to the proof of administrative misconduct (*faute de l'administration*).[446] In the particular field of environmental litigation, claimants often seek remedies on the basis of private nuisance (*troubles anormaux de voisinage*), which has long been seen as a restriction on property rights rather than as a liability regime.[447] More specific liability regimes have been implemented over the years, mostly under the impetus of international organizations or the European Union, for nuclear accidents,[448] tanker accidents[449] and contamination arising from waste disposal sites.[450]

444. For a recent overview on this issue, *see* Geneviève Viney, Patrice Jourdain & Suzanne Carval, *Les régimes spéciaux et l'assurance de responsabilité* (LGDJ, 4th ed. 2017) paras 196–250.
445. On the Environmental Charter, *see* in English David Marrani, *The Second Anniversary of the Constitutionalisation of the French Charter for the Environment: Constitutional and Environment Implications*, 10 Environmental Law Review 9 (2008) and by the same author *The Intersection between Constitution, Human Rights and the Environment: The French Charter for the Environment and the New Ex Post Constitutional Control in France*, 16 Environmental Law Review 107 (2014).
446. The most blatant example is probably the 2004 *Conseil d'État* judgement in which the French state was ordered to pay damages to asbestos victims for having banned asbestos usage too late (CE, 3 March 2004, no. 241150). For a more detailed presentation, *see* Viney, Jourdain & Carval, *Régimes spéciaux*, *supra* n. 444, at para. 196, n. 20.
447. *See* paras 194–198 below.
448. Art. L 597-1–597-46 Environmental Code. Those texts incorporate into French law the provisions of the Paris Convention on Third Party Liability in the Field of Nuclear Energy.
449. *See* the provisions of the 2001 International Convention on Civil Liability for Bunker Oil Pollution Damages and the 1969 International Convention on Civil Liability for Oil Pollution Damage ('CLC Convention'). Both are directly applicable in France.
450. The tort law-related provisions laid out in EC Directive 75/442 of 15 July 1975 were implemented in Art. L 541-4 Environmental Code.

190. The situation is more complicated in cases in which the harm invoked is to the environment itself, also known as *préjudice écologique pur* under French law. There are two main difficulties with these tort law claims: first, it is well established that for a claim to be granted in tort, the claimant has to establish a 'personal loss' (*dommage personnel*); second, according to Article 31 of the Civil Procedure Code, a right to action is available only 'to all those who have a legitimate interest in the success or dismissal of a claim'. Not surprisingly, until the 2000s, civil and administrative courts had been very reluctant to award legal redress for ecological harm.

191. It was only in the famous *Erika* case, named after a tanker which sank in December 1999 off the Brittany coast and spilled 15,000 tons of heavy fuel oil in the Atlantic Ocean, that *préjudice écologique pur* became a reparable harm for the purposes of tort law. Given that the *Erika* shipwreck polluted wide stretches of the coastline and oiled thousands of seabirds, the State, a number of local authorities, associations and individuals initiated criminal proceedings, together with claims in damages against Total (the French multinational oil company owning the cargo), the carrier and other protagonists of the catastrophe. The Paris court of first instance found the ship owner as well as Total, the owner of the cargo, guilty and civilly liable.[451] A total of EUR 165 million was awarded to a wide range of victims, including an amount to compensate for 'damages resulting from harm to the environment' as separate from harm to property. Both the Paris Court of Appeal and the Court of Cassation confirmed this innovative approach and, thus, sanctioned the existence of *préjudice écologique pur* under French tort law.[452]

192. Recognising the importance of this case law development and taking up the proposals of several reports, the French Parliament decided to enact new legislation laying the foundation of a general and genuine environmental civil liability. However, the wide scope of the proposal was not to the liking of the government, which feared an excessive burden on the industry. Instead, it was considered preferable to add a series of provisions governing redress for ecological harm to the 2016 Act on Biodiversity. According to Articles 1246–1252 Civil Code, an action to 'repair ecological harm' is now open to the State, the French agency for the environment, local authorities and environmental protection associations, but unlike in the *Erika* case, priority was given to the 'repair of the environment' as a remedy for ecological harm rather than to monetary compensation.[453] Only if it is impossible to remedy the environmental harm will the judge be able to make an order for damages. There

451. Court of Appeal Paris, 30 March 2010, no. 08/02278, commented in Olivier Moréteau, *France* in *ETL 2010 (2011)*, 175, paras 48–58.

452. Crim, 25 September 2012, no. 10-82938, commented in Moréteau & On, *ETL 2012 (2013)*, *supra* n. 45, at paras 48–55. *See* also Danai Papadopoulou, *The Role of French Environmental Associations in Civil Liability for Environmental Harm: Courtesy of* Erika, 21 Journal of Environmental Law 87 (2009).

453. For a commentary on this legislation, *see* Simon Taylor, *Extending the Boundaries of Tort Law: Ecological Harm in the French Civil Code*, 9 JETL 81 (2018); Julie Foulon, *Recent Developments in French Environmental Law: Recognition and Implementation of Ecological Damage in French Tort Law*, 21 Environmental Law Review 309 (2019). *See* also Knetsch & Jacquemin, *ETL 2016 (2017)*, *supra* n. 45, at paras 4–8.

is no doubt that these rules have provided a more secure legal framework for environmental litigation by giving public authorities and associations more leeway to enforce environmental standards. However, the 2016 Act on Biodiversity failed to implement a specific liability regime for environmental harm since the provisions in Articles 1246–1252 Civil Code only apply to the consequences of liability and not to the assessment of whether there is an action in tort or not.[454] To that extent, the general rules on civil liability, whether strict or fault-based, remain applicable.

193. In addition to the 2016 legislation on ecological harm, it must be kept in mind that the 2004 EC Environmental Liability Directive introduced a further layer of complexity in an already complicated matter. Transposed in 2008, the provisions in Articles L 160-1 to 165-2 Environmental Code primarily focus on the prevention of ecological damage and do not implement into French law a genuine liability regime, instead of modifying existing rules on environmental governance (*police administrative*).[455] Although the wording is similar to that used in tort (*'dommages causés à l'environnement'*, *'lien de causalité'*, *'demander réparation'*), the legislative labelling is misleading.[456] Indeed, according to Article L 162-2 of the Environmental Code, an individual is not entitled to trigger the legal mechanism leading to the repair of the environment since it is up to public authorities (in particular, the *préfet* of each *département*) to engage a dialogue with the operator of a hazardous site and, when necessary, to oblige him to take preventive measures or to prescribe recovery operations.[457] In practice, the 2004 Directive and the 2008 transposition measures did not have a significant impact on environmental litigation until now.[458]

454. Laurent Neyret, *La consécration du préjudice écologique dans le Code civil*, D 2017, 924. Rather ambiguous on this point Taylor, *Extending*, *supra* n. 453, at 85 ('Liability is strict and is based on the causal link between the person "responsible" for the ecological damage and the harm.').

455. Viney, Jourdain & Carval, *Régimes spéciaux*, *supra* n. 444, at para. 204 ('hybrid regime').

456. Brüggemeier, *supra* n. 430, at para. 463 ('"Liability" means that public authorities are entitled to reimbursement of the costs spent for damage prevention or restoration from the commercial undertakings responsible for the ecological damage.').

457. Arts 162-6–162-12 Environmental Code.

458. A European Commission report on the application of the 2004 Directive found that no cases under the environmental liability regime had been brought in France from 2007 to 2013. European Commission, *Report from the Commission to the Council and the European Parliament on Environmental Liability with Regard to Prevention and Remedying of Environmental Damage*, COM (2016) 204 final, 3. The current situation is not very different from the one reported in 2016. For one of the very few judgements, *see* Administrative Appellate Court Nancy, 13 February 2014, no. 13NC00141.

Chapter 6. Others

§1. Private Nuisance (*Troubles anormaux de voisinage*)[459]

194. As in other jurisdictions, the remedy for disturbances between neighbours is based on the idea that in the enjoyment of their premises, individuals must take care not to interfere excessively with their neighbours. The Court of Cassation erected this maxim to an autonomous ground of civil liability,[460] progressively abandoning the reference to the doctrine of *faute* under Article 1382 Civil Code. In accordance with a landmark decision in 1844,[461] a claimant does not have to establish fault but only a *trouble anormal de voisinage*, that is, a serious disturbance exceeding the normal inconvenience or discomfort between neighbours. This departure from the *faute* doctrine means an owner or a tenant can be held liable even though every measure of precaution was taken which a prudent individual, anxious not to disturb his neighbours, would have taken.

195. For the purposes of the doctrine of *troubles anormaux de voisinage*, the term *voisinage* is not to be taken too literally. The regime is not limited to immediate neighbours but applies to all those living in the same 'neighbourhood' (*communauté de voisinage*), regardless of their legal status. An owner will thus be treated on an equal footing with a tenant or a beneficiary of any other right to use land or a building. According to case law, it is irrelevant whether the claimant is actually the occupier of the land or the building as long as it can be demonstrated that the disturbance resulted in a loss.[462]

196. Given the great variety of disturbances,[463] it is impossible to summarize the case law of the lower courts and to draw a line between *troubles* which must be endured by neighbours and those which exceed the *anormalité* threshold. For this purpose, judges take into account the properties of the neighbourhood, the frequency of the disturbances, their intensity, the existence of an easement (*servitude*) or other disturbances.[464] The Court of Cassation does not exercise a strict control on this test, holding that it is up to the lower courts to decide at their sole discretion whether the circumstances warrant liability on this basis.

197. Where a *trouble anormal* is characterized, the judge can award damages to compensate for the impossibility to cease the disturbance or, as is more frequent,

459. *See* also in English Pierre-Dominique Ollier & Jean-Pierre Le Gall, *Various Damages* in *International Encyclopedia of Comparative Law* (Mohr 1981) vol XI, Ch. 10, para. 66.
460. *See*, e.g., Civ 3, 19 March 2020, no. 18-26360 ('vu le principe selon lequel nul ne doit causer à autrui un trouble anormal de voisinage').
461. *See* Civ, 27 Novembre 1844, Sirey 1844, 1, 211. *See* also Req, 20 February 1849, D 1849, 1, 148.
462. Civ 2, 28 June 1995, 93-12681 (the owner of a building destined to be leased claimed damages on the ground that the disturbance caused a decrease in its rental value).
463. Noise, vibrations, smoke, smell, water pollution, unattractiveness of a building, shadowing, obstruction of views … .
464. For a complete survey, *see* e.g. le Tourneau (ed.), *Droit de la responsabilité*, *supra* n. 54, at paras 2242.21–2242.22.

make an order for a prohibitory injunction (*cessation de l'illicite*). The situation is more complicated when the inconvenience arises from an installation which was approved by public authorities, for example, relay antennas for mobile phones or classified facilities. In those cases, civil courts do not have jurisdiction to cancel or modify administrative authorizations (which falls under the competence of administrative courts). On the contrary, the mere existence of an administrative approval does not hinder the neighbour to seek redress before civil courts.[465]

198. Almost entirely case law based,[466] the doctrine of *troubles anormaux de voisinage* has long been seen as a part of property law, but it is now regarded by most legal scholars as an independent liability regime.[467] The 2017 Draft Reform confirms this interpretation, suggesting the introduction of a new Article 1244 according to which 'the owner, lessee, holder of a title whose principal object is a permission to occupy or exploit land or a building, or a person who commissions work on land or enjoys the latter's authority, who causes a nuisance exceeding the normal inconveniences of being neighbours, is liable strictly for the harm resulting from the nuisance'.

§2. Compensation Funds (*Fonds d'indemnisation*)

199. Beginning in the 1950s, public authorities have implemented numerous compensation funds which have become over the decades an autonomous legal instrument that is halfway between private insurance and social security and is designed to fill the gaps in civil liability regimes, in particular in the field of strict liability. One could say that the existing *fonds d'indemnisation* are the French answer to the common law debate on 'no-fault' compensation schemes. With more than 20 different schemes, it is difficult to give an extensive survey of the diversity of French compensation funds.[468]

200. A first group of compensation funds includes those that cover traffic accident and crime victims. The legislature established specific compensation schemes in order to assist victims who cannot claim damages either because the tortfeasor failed to stop at the scene of the road accident (*délit de fuite*) and thus could not be identified or in cases of criminal offences in which the tortfeasor cannot pay compensation. A Motor Guarantee Fund (*Fonds de garantie automobile*) was created in

465. On the interplay of administrative and civil law, *see* Valérie Gaillot-Mercier, *Troubles de voisinage* in *Répertoire de droit civil* (Dalloz, 2019) paras 16–17.

466. *See* in English, Ciara Kennefick, *Nuisance and Coming to the Nuisance. The Porous Boundary between Torts and Servitudes in England and France*, in *French Civil Liability in Comparative Perspective* (Jean-Sébastien Borghetti & Simon Whittaker eds, Hart 2019) 223.

467. However, the doctrine of *troubles anormaux de voisinage* does not exclusively apply. According to case law, claimants may choose to bring an action on the ground of *faute* if the occurrence of a *trouble anormal* can be regarded as a civil fault in the sense of Arts 1240 and 1241 Civil Code. *See* Gaillot-Mercier, *supra* n. 465, at paras 30–47.

468. For a more detailed presentation, *see* in English Jonas Knetsch, *Compensation Funds in France and Germany*, in *Compensation Funds in Comparative Perspective* (Thierry Vansweevelt & Britt Weyts eds, Intersentia) 2020, 45.

France in 1951, mainly funded by insurance companies through a premium supplement.[469] Today the fund is called *Fonds de garantie des assurances obligatoires de dommages* because hunting accidents and road accidents involving animals have been added to the initial field of application. As for the compensation of crime victims,[470] the French legislature has created a specific compensation fund. The Guarantee Fund for Victims of Terrorism and Other Offences (*Fonds de garantie des victimes d'actes de terrorisme et d'autres infractions*) has its origin in an act of 1977, and its range of action was significantly strengthened during the 1980s when France faced a wave of terror attacks.[471]

201. The second and most important group of compensation funds addresses victims of medical accidents and health-related serial damages.[472] In 1991, the 'infected blood scandal', previously mentioned in the context of product liability,[473] led to the implementation of a specific compensation scheme run by the *Fonds d'indemnisation des transfusés et hémophiles*.[474] In 2002, the French Parliament established a compensation fund with a much broader scope, the *Office national d'indemnisation des accidents médicaux* (ONIAM),[475] to organize the compensation of medical injuries that cannot be attributed to any misconduct (*aléa médical*).[476] In addition to those medical hazards, the 2002 Act also addressed victims of hospital-acquired infections, allowing them to seek compensation from the compensation office.[477] In 2004, the HIV-dedicated compensation fund originally created in 1991 was merged into the ONIAM. Since the establishment of the ONIAM in 2002, the legislature has added several other, more specific grounds for compensation: Hepatitis C infections through blood transfusions, infections resulting from mandatory vaccinations, injuries resulting from growth hormone therapy and bodily harm related to a drug called *Mediator* (widely prescribed as a weight-loss drug for

469. Suzanne Tunc, *France: Establishment of 'Fonds de garantie' to Compensate Victims of Motor Vehicle Accidents*, 2 American Journal of Comparative Law 232 (1953).
470. David Miers, *State Compensation for Victims of Violent Crime*, in *Justice for Victims: Perspectives on Rights, Transition and Reconciliation* (Inge Vanfraechem, Antony Pemberton & Felix Mukwiza Ndahinda eds, Routledge 2014) 105.
471. Art. L 422-1 Insurance Code. Olivier Moréteau & Fabien Lafay, *France*, in *Terrorism, Tort Law and Insurance: A Comparative Survey* (Bernhard A. Koch ed., Springer 2004) 29. See, for a comparative overview, Marshall S. Shapo, *Compensation for Victims of Terrorism* (OUP 2005); Rianne Letschert & Karin Ammerlaan, *Compensation and Reparation for Victims of Terrorism*, in *Assisting Victims of Terrorism: Towards a European Standard of Justice* (Rianne Letschert, Ines Staiger & Anthony Pemberton eds, Springer 2010) 215.
472. *See* also on this issue Olivier Moréteau, *Policing the Compensation of Victims of Catastrophes: Combining Solidarity and Self-Responsibility*, in *Shifts in Compensation Between Private and Public Systems* (Willem H. van Boom & Michael Faure eds, Springer 2007) 199, paras 28–64.
473. *See* para. 182 above.
474. Art. L 3122-1 Public Health Code.
475. On the legal background, *see* Helleringer, *supra* n. 183; Taylor, *Medical Accident Liability*, *supra* n. 174, at 53–58.
476. Art. L 1142-1 II Public Health Code.
477. Art. L 1142-1-1 Public Health Code.

overweight diabetics but leading to cardiovascular complications) and to an antiepileptic drug called *Dépakine* which caused serious abnormalities in female babies if taken during pregnancy.[478] Taking all types of injuries together, the ONIAM deals with more than 6,000 claims a year.

202. The third fund group contains the compensation schemes laid out for victims of environmental harm. France signed the 1971 International Convention on the Establishment of an International Fund for Compensation for Oil Pollution (IOPC) and the follow-up 1992 Convention.[479] There are also specific compensation schemes for asbestos victims,[480] sewage sludge-related harm[481] and agricultural damages caused by wild animals.[482]

203. The fourth and last group of compensation funds intervenes in the field of financial services. Different compensation schemes have been created to protect individuals from the consequences of the failure of a bank or an insurance company.[483]

---

478. As a result, ONIAM is now responsible for the compensation of six different kinds of medical accidents (medical hazard, vaccination damages, HIV blood transfusion cases, Hepatitis B and C blood transfusion cases, *Mediator* and *Dépakine* damages and health emergency-related damages). ONIAM is also in charge of the compensation in medical malpractice cases if the health professional was not insured, if the insurance guarantee is not sufficient or if the insurer refuses to offer compensation. *See* Thouvenin, *supra* n. 176, at 188.
479. For a recent overview, *see* e.g. Jingjing Xu, *The International Legal Framework Governing Liability and Compensation for Ship-Source Oil Pollution Damage*, in *Selected Issues in Maritime Law and Policy: Liber Amicorum Proshanto K. Mukherjee* (Nova Science Publishers 2015) 105.
480. Art. 53 of the Act no. 2000-1257 of 20 December 2000. *See* Annie Thébaud-Mony, *Justice for Asbestos Victims and the Politics of Compensation: The French Experience*, 9 International Journal of Occupational and Environmental Health 280 (2003); Cécile Manaouil, Marie Graser & Olivier Jardé, *Compensation of Asbestos Victims in France*, 25 Medicine and Law 435 (2006); Gakuto Takamura, *The French Indemnification Fund for Asbestos Victims: Features and Formative Historical Factors: Preliminary Observations for a Comparative Analysis of Asbestos Relief Frameworks*, in *Asbestos Disaster. Lessons from Japan's Experience* (Kenichi Miyamoto, Kenji Morinaga & Mori Hiroyuki eds, Springer 2011) 303.
481. On this topic, *see* European Commission, *Disposal and Recycling Routes for Sewage Sludge. Part 1: Sludge Use Acceptance Report* (Office of Official Publications of the European Communities 2001).
482. *Fonds d'indemnisation des dégâts de sangliers (Alsace-Moselle).*
483. For a recent comparative overview, *see* Luc Laeven, *Deposit Insurance in the European Union*, in *From Fragmentation to Financial Integration in Europe* (Charles Enoch, Luc Everaert, Thierry Tressel & Jianping Zhou eds, International Monetary Fund 2014) 279.

Part IV. Defences and Exception Clauses

Chapter 1. Limitation of Actions (*prescription extinctive*)

204. Along with other countries, France in the 2000s initiated a complete overhaul of the law of 'extinctive prescription' which had remained almost entirely unchanged since 1804 and dated back even further to the *Ancien Régime*. The law of 17 June 2008 substantially modified the rules of Title XX of Book III of the Civil Code. Since then, the rules governing the limitation of actions[484] are laid out in Articles 2219 to 2254. Unlike in common law jurisdictions, the legal institution of *prescription extinctive* does not only concern the procedural aspects of tort law but also refers to the substantive right to compensation. The predominant view in legal literature is that of a hybrid nature: after expiry of the period of prescription, the debtor is entitled to refuse performance on the level of substantive law, but the relevant obligation is not entirely extinguished since a debtor who has paid in spite of prescription having occurred is unable to recover.[485]

205. In the field of tort law, Article 2224 Civil Code provides for a general rule. According to this provision, 'personal actions or movable rights of action (*actions personnelles et mobilières*) prescribe in five years from the day the holder of a right knew or should have known the facts enabling him to exercise his right'. This means that actions in tort or on the basis of contractual liability are subject to a five-year prescription period which begins to run from the day on which the creditor (the 'victim') is aware or should have been aware of his right. As the commencement of prescription requires knowledge about the existence or the extent of the claim, it is generally considered as a 'subjective system' based upon a 'floating' starting point.[486]

484. The choice of terminology in this field is rather unsatisfactory for a civil lawyer as the term 'limitation of actions' only refers to a procedural institution. 'Extinctive prescription' in the sense of French law also has substantive effects. *See* on this issue Reinhard Zimmermann, *'Extinctive' Prescription under the* Avant-projet, ERPL 2007, 805 (note 1) and by the same author, *Comparative Foundations of a European Law of Set-Off and Prescription* (CUP 2002) 21.

485. Art. 2249 C Civ.

486. *See* in French Loïs Raschel, *Le droit processuel de la responsabilité civile* (IJLS éditions, 2010) paras 113–120; Cristina Corgas-Bernard, *La loi du 17 juin 2008 et le droit à réparation du dommage corporel*, in *La réforme de la prescription en matière civile* (Philippe Casson & Philippe Pierre eds, Dalloz 2010) 93. For a detailed assessment in English, *see* also Moréteau, *ETL 2008 (2009)*, *supra* n. 280, at paras 1–12; Reinhard Zimmermann & Jens Kleinschmidt, *Prescription: General Framework and Special Problems Concerning Damages Claims* in *ETL 2007 (2008)*, 26; Jean-Sébastien Borghetti, *Prescription in Tort Law: France*, in *Prescription in Tort Law* (Israel

206. One of the most notable exceptions to this general rule concerns claims 'based on civil liability arising from an event which has caused a bodily injury'.[487] According to Article 2226 Civil Code, those claims are governed by a ten-year period, running from the day of stabilising of the initial or aggravated injury (*consolidation du dommage initial ou aggravé*). In the specific case of personal injury caused by torture or acts of barbarism or by violence or sexual aggression committed against a minor, a twenty-year period applies. There are various other specific prescription periods applicable to different cases of contractual liability,[488] product liability[489] and civil liability of air, land or maritime carriers.[490]

207. The suspension of the prescription period[491] is governed by Articles 2233 to 2239 Civil Code. For the purposes of tort law, it is notable that prescription does not run or is suspended against minors and adults under *tutelle* (Article 2235) and, more generally, against individuals 'for whom it is impossible to act following an obstacle resulting from … force majeure' (Article 2234).[492] The 2008 reform also introduced two new causes for suspension: the mediation or conciliation attempt (Article 2238) and investigative measures ordered by a court prior to judicial proceedings (*mesures d'instruction* in futurum; Article 2239).

208. As for the interruption of the prescription period,[493] the provisions laid out in Articles 2240 to 2246 Civil Code should be familiar to lawyers of other jurisdictions. The legislation recognizes three major causes of interruption: the initiation of

---

Gilead & Bjarte Askeland eds, Intersentia 2020) 309. For a discussion of the provisions of the 2005 *avant-projet Catala*, *see* Robert Wintgen & John Cartwright, *Reforming the French Law of Prescription: A French Perspective and an English Perspective*, in *Reforming the French Law of Obligations* (John Cartwright, Stefan Vogenauer & Simon Whittaker eds, Hart 2009) 347; Zimmermann, *supra* n. 484, at 810; Moréteau, *ETL 2008 (2009)*, *supra* n. 280, at paras 1–12.

487. This rather long-winded term was used to apply the ten-year period even in complex compensation claims (personal injury and damage to property), as long as a part of the claimants' allegations concerned a personal injury.

488. For example, an action under a contract of sale (*contrat de vente*) for termination or reduction of price for certain defects in the goods has to be brought within a two-year period (Art. 1648 Civil Code). As for the contractual liability or warranty of building contractors, Arts 1792 to 1792-2 Civil Code provide for different prescription periods from two to ten years, depending on the seriousness of the defect.

489. The liability of the manufacturer of a defective product 'is extinguished after ten years following the putting into circulation of the actual product that caused the damage, unless the victim has in the meantime instituted proceedings' (Art. 1245-15 Civil Code) and is subject to a three-year prescription period running 'from the date the claimant knew or ought to have known of the damage, the defect, and the identity of the producer' (Art. 1245-16 Civil Code). On these provisions based on the 1985 EC product liability directive, *see* Brüggemeier, *supra* n. 430, at paras 443–446.

490. For details, *see* Viney, Jourdain & Carval, *Effets*, *supra* n. 129, at para. 604.

491. According to Art. 2230 Civil Code, 'suspension of the prescription temporarily stops its course without erasing the delay that has already run'. For a more detailed assessment, *see* Borghetti, *Prescription*, *supra* n. 485, at 325–331.

492. It has been held that a serious health condition can be regarded as an 'obstacle resulting … from force majeure' (Civ 1, 14 November 2012, no. 11-27853).

493. According to Art. 2231 Civil Code, 'interruption erases the delay that has elapsed' and 'causes a new period of the same duration as the former period to run'. For a more detailed assessment, *see* Borghetti, *Prescription*, *supra* n. 485, at 325–331.

judicial proceedings, even by way of summary proceedings (*référé*); the acknowledgement of an obligation by its debtor; and an act of forced execution (*exécution forcée*). Among those causes, the initiation of judicial proceedings is undoubtedly the most important cause of interruption in tort litigation. The Court of Cassation has decided that an action against the tortfeasor does not have any interruptive effect on the action against the tortfeasor's liability insurer.[494]

209. However, the 2008 reform of the law of prescription has introduced a general 20-year 'ceiling period' or 'long-stop period' (*délai butoir*), which makes it impossible to move the starting point of prescription or to suspend or interrupt extinctive prescription beyond twenty years from the moment the right starts to exist.[495] This 20-year period does not apply to personal injury cases which are subject to the specific 10-year period or to cases of personal injury caused by torture or acts of barbarism or by violence or sexual aggression committed against a minor for which the 20-year period applies regardless of the 'date of birth' of the right to compensation. In detail, the interpretation of Article 2232 is still controversial, especially regarding the interplay with specific prescription periods.[496]

494. Civ 2, 7 February 2013, no. 12-12875.
495. Art. 2232(1) C Civ. On this text, *see* in English, Borghetti, *Prescription*, *supra* n. 485, at 332.
496. *See* e.g. Jean-Denis Pellier, *Retour sur le délai butoir de l'article 2232*, D 2018, 2148.

Chapter 2. Grounds of Justification

210. Surprisingly, the Civil Code does not make any reference to defences such as consent (*consentement*), necessity (*état de nécessité*), self-defence (*légitime défense*) or legal duty/lawful authority (*ordre de la loi, permission de la loi, commandement de l'autorité légitime*). It was the responsibility of the courts and above all the Court of Cassation to develop a doctrine of *faits justificatifs* that limits the scope of fault-based liability.[497] Unlike in other tort law systems, grounds of justification under French law do not refer to 'defences' as they are understood in common law jurisdictions. For most French lawyers, *faits justificatifs* are not specific elements which are distinct from the cause of action but facts which preclude the element of *faute*. In this way, grounds of justification are folded into the concept of fault and thus merged into the elements of liability.[498] While some authors consider *force majeure*, the doctrine of abuse of rights (*abus de droit*) and contributory fault as grounds of justification in a broader sense, we would like to refer to other sections of this monograph as these concepts are more closely related to the definition of *fault* and to causation.[499]

211. Given the lack of explicit provisions in the Civil Code, the doctrine of *faits justificatifs* has been elaborated on the basis of the Napoleonic Criminal Code of 1810 which recognized in Articles 327 to 329 that under certain circumstances, legal duty, lawful authority and self-defence defeat criminal liability. Those defences as well as necessity (*état de nécessity*) are now enshrined in Articles 122-4 to 122-7 of the Criminal Code. There is agreement that in order to ensure the effectiveness of the primacy of criminal law over tort law (*le criminel tient le civil en l'état*), civil courts should follow as far as possible the solutions deriving from criminal law. From this perspective, it is not surprising that the 2017 Draft Reform adopts a series of texts which are largely patterned around the criminal law provisions.[500] Generally speaking, it can be said that, as in other jurisdictions, the grounds of justification have received much greater academic attention in the field of criminal law than in tort law, so that French tort lawyers tend, as a natural reflex, to refer to criminal law than to try to elaborate specific solutions.[501]

---

497. On the doctrine of *faits justificatifs* in the field of civil liability, *see* the reference work of Gill Dingomé, *Le fait justificatif en matière de responsabilité civile* (thesis Paris 1, 1986). *See* also more recently Hajer Rouidi, *Une notion pénale à l'épreuve de la responsabilité civile: les faits justificatifs*, Revue de science criminelle et de droit pénal comparé 2016, 17.

498. For a recent comparative analysis, *see* Sandy Steel, *Defences to Tortious and Contractual Liability in French Law*, in *French Civil Liability in Comparative Perspective* (Jean-Sébastien Borghetti & Simon Whittaker eds, Hart 2019) 285, 288. *See* also Jean Limpens, Robert M. Kruithof & Anne Meinertzhagen-Limpens, *Liability for One's Own Act*, in *International Encyclopedia of Comparative Law* vol XI (André Tunc ed., Brill & J C B Mohr 1983) Ch. 2, paras 165–192.

499. *See* paras 112–117 above (doctrine of abuse of rights) and paras 223–227 (contributory fault) and 258–260 (force majeure) below. *See* also on the *exceptio veritatis* defence in cases of media litigation, le Tourneau (ed.), *Droit de la responsabilité*, *supra* n. 54, at paras 2141.60–2141.93.

500. For an analysis in English, *see* Steel, *Defences*, *supra* n. 498, at 285. On the *Terré* draft, *see* also Clotilde Grare-Didier, *Des causes d'exclusion ou d'exonération de la responsabilité*, in *Pour une réforme du droit de la responsabilité* (François Terré ed., Dalloz 2011) 185, 187.

501. Steel, *Defences*, *supra* n. 498, at 295.

212. However, it would be wrong to presume that on the field of grounds of justification, the impact of criminal law on tort affects all kinds of *faits justificatifs*. As will be shown hereafter, civil courts as well as the drafters of the reform bill have not hesitated to cut the reliance on criminal law in order to give special attention to considerations of civil justice, especially when it comes to assessing the liability-defeating effect of claimant's consent (*consentement de la victime*) and necessity (*état de nécessité*).[502]

§1. CONSENT (*CONSENTEMENT DE LA VICTIME*)

213. In French law, the victim's consent is considered as a justification under certain conditions so that the defendant's unlawful act may not be regarded as fault (*volenti non fit iniuria*).[503] When it comes to interferences with property (*atteinte à des biens matériels*) and personality rights, such as privacy (*droit à la vie privée*)[504] or sexual self-determination,[505] the victim's consent precludes liability and bars the compensation claim based on fault. In other cases, however, consent is deemed irrelevant as individuals cannot dispose of inalienable rights. In particular, apart from medical action,[506] interference with bodily integrity or life may not be excluded from the scope of civil liability on the sole ground that the claimant consented. This nuanced approach to consent is reflected in Article 1257-1 of the 2017 Reform Draft according to which 'there is no room for liability where an action causing harm prejudices a right or an interest over which the victim has a power of disposal if the latter has consented to it'. Even though the criterion of disposable rights is pertinent, the difficulties which may arise when defining the concept of consent (*consentement*) should not be underestimated. The #MeToo movement has revealed to

502. *See*, e.g., Viney, Jourdain & Carval, *Conditions*, *supra* n. 129, at para. 557 ('the admission of the category of "grounds of justification" in civil law does not imply an automatic and comprehensive implementation of criminal law solutions'). *See* also the reference work of Jean Pélissier, *Faits justificatifs et action civile*, D 1963, chr 121.

503. In the field of tort law, it can be argued that consent is a general ground of justification and that this defence is excluded in specific cases. *See*, however, Limpens, Kruithof & Meinertzhagen-Limpens, *supra* n. 498, at para. 187 ('In French and Belgian law the consent of the victim does not remove the element of fault from the defendant's act.'). For a comparison of criminal and civil law, *see* Rouidi, *supra* n. 497.

504. In the law of press, the defendant may invoke the claimant's consent as a defence. However, according to the general provisions on proof in Art. 1353(2) of the Civil Code, it is up to the defendant to establish the claimant's consent to the interference (e.g., the publication of a photograph).

505. Likewise, there cannot be, in principle, any liability for sexual harassment or assault if the defendant can establish the claimant's (full) consent.

506. *See* Art. 16-3 C civ ('There may be no invasion of the integrity of the human body except in case of medical necessity for the person or exceptionally in the therapeutic interest of others. The consent of the person concerned must be obtained previously, except when his state necessitates a therapeutic intervention to which he is not able to assent.').

the greater public the existence of grey zones between consent and unlawful interferences with personality rights[507]; to tort and criminal lawyers, it has revealed one of the major challenges in the field of grounds of justifications.[508]

214. Closely related to the concept of consent, the doctrine of *acceptation des risques* ('acceptance of risk') has been used to raise the threshold of fault in cases in which personal injury was caused during sporting events.[509] According to the idea that the victim was aware of the risks when engaging in a dangerous activity, the Court of Cassation adopts a more restrictive approach of fault-based civil liability and recognizes a right to compensation only in cases of a 'deliberate failure to comply with sports rules'.[510] However, in 2010, it was ruled that the doctrine of *acceptation des risques* could not be upheld against a victim who based the claim on the general principle of liability for things[511] in order to improve the rights of victims. As a result of intense lobbying by motorsport organizations, the Parliament introduced a new provision in the Sports Code (*Code du sport*) according to which 'a competitor cannot be held liable for the damage to property caused to another competitor due to the action of a thing (*par le fait d'une chose*) under his custody during a sports event or a training session in preparation of this event, in a place permanently or temporarily dedicated to this sport'.[512]

§2. NECESSITY (*ÉTAT DE NÉCESSITÉ*)

215. There is no doubt that necessity (*état de nécessité*) excludes criminal liability because Article 122-7 of the Criminal Code provides that 'a person is not criminally liable if confronted with a present or imminent danger to himself, another person or property, he performs an act necessary to ensure the safety of the person or property, except where the means used are disproportionate to the seriousness of the threat'. Due to the scarcity of case law, it is much more difficult to determine the *civil* consequences of an act of necessity as defined by the Criminal Code.[513]

---

507. *See,* e.g., the contributions to Franklin G. Miller & Alan Wertheimer (eds), *The Ethics of Consent. Theory and Practice* (OUP 2010).
508. Alexia Boucherie, *Troubles dans le consentement : du désir partage au viol. Ouvrir la boîte noire des relations sexuelles* (Editions F Bourin 2019).
509. Surprisingly, French jurisdictions are reluctant to apply the doctrine to other dangerous activities. *See* on this point, Viney, Jourdain & Carval, *Conditions, supra* n. 129, at paras 573–573-1. In English, *see* Steel, *Defences, supra* n. 498, at 304.
510. *See* the references para. 125 above.
511. Civ 2, 4 November 2010, no. 09-65947.
512. Art. L 321-3-1 Code du sport. On this provision, *see* David Bakouche, *La loi de la course* JCP G 2012, no. 397; Éric Péchillon, *L'exception sportive en question : l'intervention ciblée du législateur en matière de responsabilité*, JCP A 2012, no. 228. *See* in English Moréteau & On, *ETL 2012 (2013), supra* n. 45, at paras 18–19.
513. In order to meet the conditions of Art. 122-7 Criminal Code, there has to be 'a present or imminent danger to a person or property' and 'proportionality between the unlawful act and the danger'. The courts also ensure that the act of necessity was 'socially useful' (*utile socialement*), i.e., the preserved interest is more important than the interest sacrificed, and that the author of the act did not

216. In almost every tort law textbook, it is stated that an act of necessity in the sense of Article 122-7 of the Criminal Code should exclude civil liability based on *faute* (Articles 1240–1241 Civil Code) but should not leave the victim of this act without any form of compensation.[514] However, there are profound differences when it comes to determining the legal basis of the victim's right of compensation. Whereas some authors call for the enactment of a specific strict liability regime, others refer to the 'law of quasi-contracts' (*droit des quasi-contrats*) and, in particular, to unjust enrichment or *negotiorum gestio*.[515] Strikingly, in the few cases in which necessity has been invoked before civil courts, the defence has been rejected on the grounds of the proportionality test or because an actual or imminent danger could not be characterized.[516] Accordingly, the doctrinal efforts to circumscribe the civil consequences of necessity are in sharp contrast to the little practical dimension of this issue.

217. The 2017 Reform Draft does not contain any specific reference to necessity but merely suggests that 'action causing harm does not give rise to liability where its author finds himself in one of the situations foreseen by Articles 122-4 to 122-7 of the Criminal Code'.[517] This means that the victim of an act of necessity shall not be awarded compensation, at least not on the basis of civil liability; the proposal of the *Terré* reform commission to grant an 'equitable compensation' in those cases[518] was not deemed sufficiently relevant.

§3. Self-Defence (*Légitime Défense*)

218. Related to the doctrine of *état de nécessité*, French courts also apply the concept of self-defence (*légitime défense*) in order to exclude civil liability in cases in which the defendant acted in response to a threat against person or property. Once again, the criminal law was the inspiration for this ground of justification as the Civil Code remains silent, for the time being, on *légitime défense*. According to Article 122-5 of the Criminal Code, 'a person is not criminally liable if, confronted with an unjustified attack upon himself or upon another, he performs at that moment an action compelled by the necessity of self-defence …, except where the means

cause the state of necessity by his own fault. On those conditions, *see* Patrice Jourdain, *Responsabilité fondée sur la faute : Faits justificatifs* in *JurisClasseur Civil Code*, Arts 1382 à 1386, fasc 121-20 (LexisNexis, 2012) paras 46–53.

514. *See,* e.g., Brun, *Responsabilité*, *supra* n. 147, at para. 346 (according to this author, a right of compensation should be granted 'in equity' [*équité*]). For an extensive survey, *see* Rouidi, *supra* n. 497, at paras 28–30.
515. Viney, Jourdain & Carval, *Conditions*, *supra* n. 129, at para. 571 (with further references). For a full survey, *see* Jourdain, *Responsabilité fondée sur la faute*, *supra* n. 513, at paras 54–62.
516. *See* the references in le Tourneau (ed.), *Droit de la responsabilité*, *supra* n. 54, at paras 2141.20–2141.24.
517. Steel, *Defences*, *supra* n. 498, at 296–297.
518. Art. 45 of the *Terré* Draft. On this issue, *see* Grare-Didier, *supra* n. 500, at 187.

of defence used are not proportionate to the seriousness of the attack'. If the requirements of self-defence are fulfilled (unjustified attack, actual or imminent;[519] concurrent response, necessary and proportionate), the courts will reject the victim's claim for compensation. The Court of Cassation has even held that *légitime défense* excludes not only fault-based liability but also strict liability under Article 1242 of the Civil Code.[520] Yet the legal ground of this extension is still unclear, and it is not certain that the exclusion of any civil liability whatsoever is consistent with the underlying rationale of the criminal concept of self-defence.[521]

219. As has been said, the 2017 Draft Reform does not refer to any specific grounds of justification, simply asserting in Article 1257 that 'action causing harm does not give rise to liability where its author finds himself in one of the situations foreseen by Articles 122-4 to 122-7 of the Criminal Code'. If adopted, the reform would dispel any remaining doubt as to whether *légitime défense* should be interpreted differently in civil and criminal cases. For consistency, the drafters of the reform favour a unitary over a more nuanced approach.

§4. Others

220. Even though there is little case law (and even less legal literature) on this topic, it is unanimously acknowledged that lawful authority (*permission de la loi*) is a defence which can be invoked in civil liability cases. Legal immunities awarded to civil servants[522], press agents,[523] pleading lawyers[524] and elected officials[525] are regularly cited to illustrate the exonerating effect of lawful authority in the field of civil liability.[526] On this point, civil law and criminal law apply the same solution,

519. Under criminal law, self-defence is not excluded if the person could reasonably believe that he responded to an actual or imminent threat. Even though the courts have not yet explicitly confirmed it, it is likely that self-defence would also be admitted with regard to civil liability.
520. Civ 2, 22 April 1992, no. 90-14586, RTD civ 1992, 768, note Patrice Jourdain.
521. For a critical assessment of the 1992 case, *see* Patrice Jourdain, *La légitime défense, fait justificatif de la responsabilité de l'article 1384, alinéa 1er*, RTD civ 1992, 768. *See* also in English Steel, *Defences*, *supra* n. 498, at 295–296.
522. Under French law, the personal liability of civil servants is excluded unless their attitude amounts to a 'personal fault' detached from 'public service'. *See* para. 109 above (with further references).
523. *See* para. 121 above (with further references).
524. According to Art. 41(4) of the 1881 Freedom of the Press Act, pleading lawyers and witnesses cannot be judged for defamation (*diffamation*) or for slander (*injure*) with regard to declarations made before court. However, this immunity only covers criminal liability and does not exclude compensation on the basis of civil liability.
525. Art. 41(1) of the 1881 Freedom of the Press Act provides that 'speeches held before the National Assembly and the Senate as well as any report or document printed by order of one of the two chambers cannot give rise to legal proceedings'.
526. One could also mention the immunity established in Art. 73 Criminal Procedure Code. According to this provision, 'in the event of a flagrant felony [*crime flagrant*] or of a flagrant misdemeanour [*délit flagrant*] punished by a penalty of imprisonment, any person is entitled to arrest the perpetrator and to bring him before the nearest judicial police officer'. For an illustration, *see* in English Walter van Gerven, Pierre Larouche & Jeremy Lever, *Cases, Materials and Text on National, Supranational and International Tort Law* (Hart 2000) 352/5.

even though an explicit legal provision which excludes liability in cases in which a person 'commits an act prescribed or authorized by legislative or regulatory provisions' is only available in criminal law.

221. A closely related question is to what extent administrative permission (*autorisation administrative*) may exclude civil liability.[527] More and more economic activities are subject to prior approval by public authorities: the manufacture of pharmaceuticals or other potentially toxic products, the operation of industrial facilities, the installation of mobile phone towers, etc. According to the traditional standpoint of French law, the mere fact that public authorities have granted a permit does not exclude civil liability in case of negligence.[528] The reason is that public authorities cannot carry out all the verifications that are necessary to ensure the protection of everyone's interests. Moreover, the authorization does not preclude the way the operator performs its activity, which explains why in the field of environmental protection, administrative permission is granted 'subject to the rights of third parties' (*sous réserve des droits des tiers*).[529] However, the legal relevance of authorizations has recently been requestioned in cases in which cell phone companies had been requested to demolish mobile towers (*antennes-relais*) that supposedly caused health issues to residents living nearby. In 2012, the *Tribunal des conflits* held that the jurisdiction of civil courts is limited to cases in which a mobile tower did not comply with the prescriptions made by the authorities or anormal private nuisances invoked by the claimant did *not* concern issues definitely addressed by a binding administrative decision.[530]

222. Finally, under certain circumstances, civil liability can also be excluded when a person has acted on an order emanating from a legitimate authority (*le commandement de l'autorité légitime*). According to Article 122-4(2) Criminal Code, 'a person is not criminally liable who performs an act prescribed … by legislative or regulatory provisions … or commanded by a lawful authority, unless the action is manifestly unlawful'. There is broad consensus that this rule should also apply in civil law, even though very little doctrinal attention has been given to this issue.[531]

527. On this point, *see* Viney, Jourdain & Carval, *Conditions*, *supra* n. 129, at para. 561 and, in English, Limpens, Kruithof & Meinertzhagen-Limpens, *supra* n. 498, at para. 183.
528. *See,* e.g., in the field of liability for toxical products, Civ 2, 14 June 1972, no. 71-11318 (the authorization 'does not relieve those who accomplish the act from the duty of care [*obligation de prudence et de diligence*] under Art. 1382 Civil Code').
529. Art. L 514-19 Environmental Code.
530. On this decision, *see,* e.g., Olivier Cachard, *Le droit face aux ondes électromagnétiques* (LexisNexis 2016) 155. *See* also in English Susan Perry & Claudia Roda, *Human Rights and Digital Technology: Digital Tightrope* (Palgrave Macmillan 2017) 40.
531. For a brief presentation, *see* Viney, Jourdain & Carval, *Conditions*, *supra* n. 129, at para. 562–562-1. *See* also in English Limpens, Kruithof & Meinertzhagen-Limpens, *supra* n. 498, at paras 181–182.

Chapter 3. Contributory Fault

223. French tort law recognizes that the claimant's own fault which has contributed to damage may reduce or exclude the right to compensation. While Articles 1240 to 1245 Civil Code do not contain any specific references to contributory fault (*faute contributive*), it is considered to be an obvious fact that the victim's negligence or intent shall have an effect on entitlement to damages. Contrary to what is sometimes said in comparative legal literature,[532] there is no significant theoretical debate in France about the underlying legal mechanism of the *faute contributive* doctrine.[533] There is broad consensus that the diminution of damages or the complete denial of liability due to the claimant's fault is the result of causation. Given that the claimant's attitude is a concurrent cause of the harm suffered, French courts tend to identify almost intuitively a 'joint liability' (*partage de responsabilité*)[534] between the tortfeasor and the victim or, if the claimant's fault outweighs the defendant's fault, the extinction of the right to compensation. Even though those solutions also express the idea of 'punishing' the blameworthy victim,[535] the issue of contributory fault is nowadays firmly grounded in the field of causation (*causalité*).[536]

224. The assessment of contributory fault is based on the rules governing the assessment of the defendant's fault as a basis of civil liability.[537] Accordingly, it comes as no surprise that some landmark cases on the *faute* doctrine have not addressed the defendant's, but the claimant's contributory fault. As already noted, the famous 1984 *Lemaire* and *Derguini* cases, in which the Court of Cassation decided to disconnect the concept of fault from capacity, ruled on how contributory fault could be opposed to children as claimants.[538] There is no sign that the French courts are willing to move away from a unitary approach of *faute* towards a more lenient assessment of the defendant's attitude. In particular, there are numerous cases in which the courts have taken a surprisingly strict approach towards the

532. Steel, *Defences*, *supra* n. 498, at 299.

533. *See* most recently Alexandre Dumery, *La faute de la victime en droit de la responsabilité civile* (L'Harmattan, 2011). *See* also the reference work of Christian Lapoyade-Deschamps, *La responsabilité de la victime* (thesis Bordeaux, 1977) and Marianne Éloi, Camille de Jacobet de Nombel, Marie Rayssac & Julia Sourd, *La faute de la victime dans la responsabilité civile extra-contractuelle*, in *Études à la mémoire de Christian Lapoyade-Deschamps* (PUB 2003) 47.

534. For a critical assessment of the idea of 'joint liability' between victim and tortfeasor, *see* Dumery, *supra* n. 533, at para. 301.

535. In a famous article, Louis Josserand considered that the doctrine of contributory fault expresses the idea of a 'liability towards oneself' (*La responsabilité envers soi-même*, Dalloz Hebdomadaire 1934, chr 73). Others speak of a 'duty to provide for one's own safety' (*obligation de veiller à sa propre sécurité*) as the dominant rationale. *See* le Tourneau (ed.), *Droit de la responsabilité*, *supra* n. 54, at para. 2144.42.

536. Every textbook on French tort law addresses contributory fault in the chapter on or from the angle of causation. *See,* e.g., Viney, Jourdain & Carval, *Conditions*, *supra* n. 129, at paras 426–433; le Tourneau (ed.), *Droit de la responsabilité*, *supra* n. 54, at paras 2144.30–2144.113; Brun, *Responsabilité*, *supra* n. 147, at paras 259–260.

537. *See* paras 68–83 above.

538. *See* para. 82 above.

behaviour of young children.[539] Even more importantly, the French courts do not assess contributory fault differently if invoked as a defence against fault-based liability or against strict liability,[540] although the apportionment of damages is supposed to be based on a comparison of the defendant's and the claimant's wrongful behaviour.[541]

225. In order to determine the consequences of contributory fault, French judges have a wide margin of discretion. The assessment of shares is made on the same basis as in the case of multiple tortfeasors, so that 'the relative blameworthiness of the parties and the relative causal potency of their conduct' will be taken into account.[542] In general, the acknowledgement of contributory fault will only lead to a partial reduction of damages. Under certain circumstances, the defendant may also invoke a total denial of damages, for example, in cases of intent or provocation, provided that the conditions of force majeure (unforeseeability and irresistibility) are met.[543]

226. From the 1970s on,[544] there have been calls among French tort law scholars to mitigate the effects of contributory fault. In particular, it has been argued that while the tortfeasor's liability has been shifted to liability insurers, the victim alone must now personally bear the consequences of wrongful behaviour. Those changes led to a paradoxical situation in which the principle of liability does not apply to those who create a risk of harm but only to those who are exposed to that risk. Taking into account those criticisms, the French legislator decided to partially exclude the defence of contributory fault under the special liability regime for traffic accidents. As already noted,[545] Articles 3 to 6 of the *loi Badinter* make its eligibility depend on the nature of the harm for which compensation is demanded and on the legal status of the claimant. When a non-driver claims compensation for a personal injury caused by a traffic accident, the only defence that may be raised is 'inexcusable fault' (*faute inexcusable*) and only to the extent that this fault was also the 'exclusive cause' (*cause exclusive*) of the accident.

227. The 2017 Reform Draft suggests the implementation of this tendency in the general civil liability rules.[546] According to Article 1254(2), in cases of personal injury, only a 'gross negligence' (*faute lourde*) may lead to a partial reduction.

539. For references, *see* Viney, Jourdain & Carval, *Conditions*, *supra* n. 129, at para. 433.
540. Le Tourneau (ed.), *Droit de la responsabilité*, *supra* n. 54, at paras 2144.111–2144.113.
541. Lapoyade-Deschamps, *supra* n. 533, at 196. *See* also on this point Éloi, de Jacobet de Nombel, Rayssac & Sourd, *supra* n. 533, 59.
542. Steel, *Defences*, *supra* n. 498, at 301–302. Unlike in other jurisdictions (United Kingdom, Germany), there are no fixed reductions in particular situations.
543. On force majeure, *see* paras 258–260 below.
544. *See*, in particular, Lapoyade-Deschamps, *supra* n. 533.
545. *See* para. 179 above.
546. For a critical assessment of the reform provisions, *see* Steel, *Defences*, *supra* n. 498, at 302–303.

Furthermore, it is advocated that the defendant's capacity be reintroduced in the assessment of *faute* with regards to contributory fault, with Article 1255 providing that 'unless it bears the characteristics of force majeure, fault in a victim who lacks discernment has no exonerating effect'.

Chapter 4. Exemption Clauses

228. Over the last decades, exemption clauses have aroused considerable interest among French legal academics. Even though most of the legal literature addresses the issue of exemption clauses in a *contractual* context,[547] extensive research has also been conducted on the possibility that two parties agree on an adjustment of *extra-contractual* liability.[548] To comply with the terminology used by French scholars, it is necessary to distinguish three types of clauses: clauses excluding liability (*clauses exclusives de responsabilité*),[549] clauses limiting the amount of damages (*clauses limitatives de responsabilité*) and clauses providing for the payment of a lump sum in case of civil liability (so-called penalty clauses or *clauses pénales*).[550]

229. In the field of extra-contractual liability, French courts have never recognized the possibility for contracting parties to exclude or adjust the consequences of liability. In a landmark case in 1955, the Court of Cassation held that delictual and quasi-delictual liability were matters of public policy (*ordre public*) and that those rules could therefore not be deactivated or altered in advance by agreement.[551] The idea that the rules governing extra-contractual liability are outside of the parties' freedom of contract is deeply rooted in the French twentieth-century legal doctrine. In the words of a leading textbook on tort law, those rules are 'based on the desire to reconcile freedom of action with the safety of individuals and groups' so that 'this balance is deemed so essential to all aspects of social life that it is neither legitimate nor appropriate to allow it to be modified'.[552] The prohibition of exemption clauses

547. For an extensive survey, *see* Viney, Jourdain & Carval, *Effets*, *supra* n. 129, at paras 323–443; le Tourneau (ed.), *Droit de la responsabilité*, *supra* n. 54, at paras 3222.00–3226.63 (with further references).

548. *See* the recent monographs of Johann Abras, *L'aménagement conventionnel anticipé de la responsabilité extra-contractuelle* (PUAM, 2008); Marie Leveneur-Azémar, *Étude sur les clauses limitatives ou exonératoires de responsabilité* (LGDJ, 2017); Henri Conte, *Volonté et responsabilité civile* (thesis Toulouse, 2017). *See* also in English Zoé Jacquemin, *Contracts Concerning Civil Liability*, in *French Civil Liability in Comparative Perspective* (Jean-Sébastien Borghetti & Simon Whittaker eds, Hart 2019) 309.

549. The terminology is not consolidated on this point. Some authors use alternative terms such as *clauses exonératoires de responsabilité*, *clauses d'irresponsabilité* or *de non-responsabilité*, *clauses élusives de responsabilité* or *clauses élisives de responsabilité*. On the variety of exemption clauses, *see* also in English Limpens, Kruithof & Meinertzhagen-Limpens, *supra* n. 498, at para. 274.

550. On the artificiality of penalty clauses in extra-contractual liability, *see* Denis Mazeaud, *La notion de clause pénale* (LGDJ, 1992) paras 482–493.

551. Civ, 17 February 1955, no. 55-02810. For an extensive assessment of this case, *see* Terré, Lequette & Chénedé, *supra* n. 329, at para. 185.

552. Viney, Jourdain & Carval, *Effets*, *supra* n. 129, at para. 355. *See* also Henri Mazeaud, Léon Mazeaud, Jean Mazeaud & François Chabas, *Traité théorique et pratique de la responsabilité civile délictuelle et contractuelle*, vol. 3/2 (Montchrestien, 6th ed. 1983) para. 2570.

applies to every kind of extra-contractual liability, whether fault-based or strict,[553] and has been confirmed for specific regimes of liability.[554]

230. The position of the French courts has been subject to considerable criticism over the last decades, and it is likely that in the coming years there will be a shift towards a more liberal approach. In particular, it is argued that exemption clauses are perfectly valid in contract, and it is not clear why 'public policy' considerations should prevent parties from adapting the rules governing extra-contractual liability since the same harm can be apprehended under both contract and tort.[555] It is also stressed that exemption clauses in tort are of increasingly practical importance, especially where neighbours intend to adjust the rules governing liability for private nuisance (*troubles anormaux de voisinage*) or environmental harm.[556]

231. The 2017 Draft Reform takes due account of this criticism and proposes that the traditional position of the Court of Cassation be overturned. According to Article 1281(1), 'contract terms whose object or effect is to exclude or to limit liability are in principle valid, in contractual as well as extra-contractual matters'. However, Article 1281(2) of the Draft states that 'in the case of personal injury, liability cannot be limited or excluded by contract'. This exception to the validity of exemption clauses is justified by the idea that the compensation of personal harm under tort law, which is considered a matter of public policy, should remain out of the reach of private parties.[557] The drafters intend to protect victims against the hasty acceptance of limitation clauses which compromise the full compensation of their injuries.[558] Another exception is made in the draft for fault-based liability, as Article 1283 provides that 'in extra-contractual matters, a person cannot exclude or limit his liability for fault'. The underlying rationale is not quite clear, even though many authors consider that while the entirety of the law of extra-contractual liability is not a matter of public policy, liability for fault certainly is.[559] All in all, the issue of exemption clauses shows that, unlike their counterparts in other countries, French tort law scholars still struggle with the idea that the rules of extra-contractual liability could be subject to the will of the parties.

553. Civ, 23 January 1959, no. 57-10063 (liability for the act of things under former Art. 1384(1) Civil Code).

554. According to Art. 1245-14 Civil Code (governing product liability) 'clauses that seek to eliminate or to limit the liability for defective products are forbidden and are deemed unwritten'. However, 'as to damages caused to things not used by the victim mainly for his own private use or consumption, such clauses stipulated between professionals are valid'. *See* also Art. L 415-6 Rural Code (prohibition of exemption clauses regarding the civil liability of hunters for the damage caused by wild game).

555. For a presentation in English, *see* Jacquemin, *supra* n. 548, at 315–316.

556. Jacquemin, *supra* n. 548, at 312–313 (with other examples).

557. On the idea of a hierarchy between the interests protected by tort law and the gradual emergence of specific tort rules governing personal injury, *see* para. 67 above.

558. However, the rationale of this exception is inconsistent with the rules governing out-of-court settlements in personal injury cases which can only be challenged by the victim under exceptional circumstances. *See* on this aspect, Liza Veyre, *Quel avenir pour les clauses et contrats excluant ou limitant la réparation?*, Contrats Concurrence Consommation 2016, étude 16, at para. 21.

559. Jacquemin, *supra* n. 548, at 320. *See* also Viney, Jourdain & Carval, *Effets*, *supra* n. 129, at para. 355.

Part V. Causation

232. The issue of causation is generally presented by French tort law scholars from two perspectives: in a positive way in the sense that a causal connection (*lien de causalité*) between the tortious conduct (*fait générateur de responsabilité*) and the harm is a necessary condition to civil liability; in negative terms, it is agreed that the tortfeasor's liability may be reduced or even dismissed if the injury is due to a foreign cause (*cause étrangère*). Although both statements have total unanimity in the legal literature and may seem obvious to French lawyers, the consensus disappears when it comes to the assessment of causation in a particular case, for example, when there is uncertainty in the causal chain or in the presence of multiple tortfeasors. Over the last three decades, the problem of causation has been much debated, especially in the field of medical and pharmaceutical liability.[560]

233. The particular difficulty in presenting the solutions under French law is a lesser degree of conceptualization, compared to other jurisdictions. A foreign lawyer will look in vain for the distinction between general and specific causation,[561] well established in common law jurisdictions, or for specific techniques designed to introduce legal policy considerations, such as the German theory of unlawful connection (*Lehre vom Rechtswidrigkeitszusammenhang*). Some might even be inclined to find French tort law solutions in the field of causation a bit simplistic given the scarcity of legal provisions in the Civil Code and the superficiality of most court decisions.[562] Indeed, while the Court of Cassation has intervened on several occasions as to certain aspects of causation, it is generally up to the lower courts (*juges du fond*) to assess the existence of a causal link, often on the basis of the statements made by technical experts.[563] Behind the screen of judicial discretion (*pouvoir souverain d'appréciation*), judges often use the condition of causation as an adjustment

560. *See*, e.g., the reference works of Florence G'sell-Macrez, *Recherche sur la notion de causalité* (thesis Paris 1, 2005); Christophe Quézel-Ambrunaz, *Essai sur la causalité dans le droit de la responsabilité civile* (Dalloz 2010).

561. There is, however, a tendency towards a distinction between causation and *imputabilité* in the field of product liability. *See* para. 247 below.

562. *See* Duncan Fairgrieve & Florence G'sell-Macrez, *Causation in French Law: Pragmatism and Policy*, in *Perspectives on Causation* (Richard Goldberg ed., Hart 2011) 111 ('French scholars have often been sceptical about the theoretical framework of causality, with commentators asserting that courts decide causation issues intuitively'). *See* also Olivier Moréteau, *Basic Questions*, *supra* n. 51, at para. 1/112.

563. Bell, Boyron & Whittaker, *supra* n. 17, at 410.

variable in litigation management.[564] It is not unusual that considerations of fairness and policy reasons are decisive factors, even though the judgments do not say so.

564. *See* also Marta Infantino & Eleni Zervogianni, *Unravelling Causation in European Tort Laws*, 83 Rabels Zeitschrift für ausländisches und internationales Privatrecht 647, 660–662 (2019).

Chapter 1. Concept of Causation

§1. Theories of Causation

234. In any textbook on tort law and in any tort law course, causation is always presented through two main theories that are seen as practicably incompatible alternatives. From a historical perspective, it is notable that it was only in the first half of the 20th century that French tort law scholars developed an interest in the theoretical foundations,[565] and it was solely through the reception of theories developed in Austria and Germany that a legal debate was initiated on the concept of causation. Nowadays, the issue of causation is still dominated by two main theories with roots that go back to the end of the nineteenth century.

235. The first theory is an extension of the so-called equivalence of conditions (*théorie de l'équivalence des conditions*) which was given a systematic shape by the German judge Maximilian von Buri.[566] According to Buri's analysis, every event is the product of numerous circumstances, and since it is impossible to determine the exact share of each of them, every one of them is to be deemed a cause if it was necessary to its realization. In other words, each necessary condition of an event has to be regarded as 'equivalent' to any other necessary condition. Initially designed for criminal liability,[567] this theory has become very popular in tort law and is now systemically taught to French law students in any course on law of obligations. Similar to the well-known 'but for' test in the common law world, the theory of 'equivalence of conditions' implies a reconstruction of the sequence of events had the circumstance in question not occurred: every condition 'sine qua non' of the damage is an element in the causation of the harmful act.[568]

236. It is well-established that the theory of 'equivalence of conditions', although logically sound, is not reliable in practice and may lead to inequitable results. The theory extends causation in an excessive way since there is no reason for interrupting the chain of causes and consequences. According to this theory, every *fait générateur de responsabilité* whatsoever should be deemed a cause of the harm, regardless of when it occurred. That is to say that a fault committed forty years ago which led to far-reaching consequences in the life of the claimant may well be seen as a cause of the harm. Thus, the 'sine qua non' doctrine was widely

565. An author has described the situation in the French legal scholarship at that time as an 'agnosticism regarding causation' (*agnosticisme causal*). *See* G'sell-Macrez, *supra* n. 560, at para. 4.

566. Maximilian von Buri, *Ueber Causalität und deren Verantwortung* (J. M. Gebhardt 1873). Buri's analysis was promoted in France by Pierre Marteau, *La notion de causalité dans la responsabilité civile* (thesis Aix-en-Provence, 1913).

567. On the historical background and the evolution of this theory, *see* e.g. Anthony M. Honoré, *Causation and Remoteness of Damage*, in *International Encyclopedia of Comparative Law* vol XI (A. Tunc ed., Brill & J C B Mohr 1983) ch. 2, paras 58–65 and more extensively H. L. A. Hart & Tony Honoré, *Causation in the Law* (Clarendon Press, 2d ed. 1985) 109–128. *See* also G'sell-Macrez, *supra* n. 560, at paras 139–150.

568. Pierre Catala & Tony Weir, *Delict and Torts: A Study in Parallel Part IV*, 39 Tulane Law Review 701, 709 (1965).

criticized for not offering a tool to keep the circle of potential tortfeasors sufficiently reasonable, as a damage is often the consequence of numerous tortiously relevant acts. This is why, despite its prestige and its simplicity, the theory of 'equivalence of conditions' is considered at best as a starting point for the assessment of causation.

237. The second theory refers to the legal figure of 'adequate causation' (*théorie de la causalité adéquate*), according to which a selection of causes is necessary in order to limit the scope of liability. Based upon the work of German criminal law scholars of the late 19th century,[569] this theory has been transposed to tort law and promoted throughout the second half of the 20th century in France. The rationale of the theory of 'adequate causation' may be summarized as follows: 'A man is in the legal sense the cause of an occurrence to the extent that he may be regarded as the condition by virtue of which what would be otherwise regarded as the regular course of events in human experience is altered.'[570] The influence of German literature was so strong that the formulation of authors such as von Bar, von Kries and Traeger was replicated almost identically in the French tort law doctrine. There is consensus that according to this theory, a *fait générateur de responsabilité* is only an 'adequate cause' when it is likely to produce the effect according to the ordinary course of things and in light of everyday occurrences.[571] This implies that other antecedents which would lead to harm only as a result of exceptional circumstances must be excluded.[572]

238. Even though this second theory does not lead to an excessive scope of liability and despite its major influence on tort law doctrine,[573] it did not give rise to unanimous enthusiasm. The establishment of a hierarchy of causes through an adequacy test is criticized for limiting the chance of obtaining compensation for a harm and for taking on the false appearances of a scientific theory. For many authors, the theory of adequate causation leaves too much room for subjective assumptions (how to understand the formula of the 'ordinary course of things'?) and tends to confuse the assessment of causation with the establishment of fault. Indeed, 'assessing causation in terms of probability, even in an objective way, will inevitably lead to the legal concept of fault',[574] at least under French tort law.

239. In response to the shortcomings of both approaches, the French tort law professor Noël Dejean de la Bâtie suggested that the test of causation should be

569. *See,* e.g., Honoré, *Causation and Remoteness*, *supra* n. 567, at paras 80–90; G'sell-Macrez, *supra* n. 560, at paras 80–86.

570. Carl von Bar, *Die Lehre vom Causalzusammenhange im Rechte, besonders im Strafrechte* (B. Tauchnitz 1871, reprint 1971). The translation is provided by Hart & Honoré, *supra* n. 567, at 466.

571. *See,* e.g., Viney, Jourdain & Carval, *Conditions*, *supra* n. 129, at para. 340-1; Brun, *Responsabilité*, *supra* n. 147, at para. 237.

572. François Terré, Philippe Simler, Yves Lequette & François Chénedé, *Droit civil : Les obligations* (Dalloz 12th ed. 2018) para. 1091.

573. Viney, Jourdain & Carval, *Conditions*, *supra* n. 129, at para. 340-1 ('had a major influence both in France and abroad').

574. Patrice Jourdain, *Détermination des causes du dommage* in *JurisClasseur Code civil*, Arts 1382 à 1386, fasc 160 (LexisNexis 2020) paras 137–142 with further references.

combined with principles of civil liability such as unlawfulness and abnormality.[575] Despite its lack of influence on case law, this alternative approach has to be regarded as one of the few genuinely French contributions to the legal analysis of causation. Dejean de la Bâtie considered that when many events occur between the initial act and the damage, each of the antecedents must contain an element of unlawfulness that explains the unlawfulness of the subsequent fact to be considered as a legal cause.[576] Dejean de la Bâtie called this idea the 'continued spread of the evil' (*l'empreinte continue du mal*) and illustrated the advantages of the theory with the example of a workplace accident. According to his analysis, if an illegal worker is injured at work, it is not possible to assert that the fact of hiring a person without papers is the cause of the accident since 'the unlawful presence of the worker does not explain at all the accident'.[577] In other words, the unlawfulness of the defendant's act must 'account for' the claimant's harm.[578]

§2. Causation in Legislation and Case Law

I. General Approach

240. As in other jurisdictions, the mere presentation of the various theories of causation does not reflect the current state of the law as they are not applied literally by the courts and are used at most as convenient guidelines in the day-to-day practice of civil judges. In France, the impact of the aforementioned theories presented is even less measurable. Not only are there no provisions in the Civil Code about the way causation in tort law should be assessed, but it is also the style of French judgments which makes it difficult to draw an accurate picture of the case law. It is indeed not very common that judges of either the lower courts or the Court of Cassation mention the analysis of causation or its underlying policy considerations. Probably more than in other legal systems, the assessment of the relevant case law reveals causation as 'a highly discretionary and unpredictable branch of the law'.[579]

241. French tort law scholars have spent considerable time and energy in trying to identify significant tendencies among the court solutions, with little success, one must say. The courts have always refused to take a position in the scholarly debate as to the different methods of assessment and even refuse, with few exceptions,[580] to mention the terms *équivalence des conditions* and *causalité adéquate*. It is quite

575. Fairgrieve & G'sell-Macrez, *supra* n. 562, at 119.
576. Charles Aubry, Charles Rau, André Ponsard & Noël Dejean de la Bâtie, *Droit civil français*, vol 6 (Librairies techniques 8th ed. 1989) para. 65 ('Causation is not an ordinary sequence of facts without any value judgment; it involves in fact a spread of evil from the defendant's conduct to the victim's harm.'). On this theory, *see* also Brun, *Responsabilité*, *supra* n. 147, at paras 241–245; Viney, Jourdain & Carval, *Conditions*, *supra* n. 129, at para. 346-1.
577. Aubry, Rau, Ponsard & Dejean de la Bâtie, *supra* n. 576, at para. 72.
578. Jourdain, *Détermination des causes*, *supra* n. 574, at para. 42.
579. Honoré, *Causation and Remoteness*, *supra* n. 567, at para. 105.
580. Civ 2, 27 March 2003, no. 01-00850 ('by virtue of the principle of equivalence of conditions').

telling that there is a doctrinal debate about the exact influence of each of the major theories of causation on case law. For some authors, the idea of equivalence of conditions appears as the principle, with adequate causation only applied in exceptional cases.[581] For others, a thorough analysis of the case law should lead to the exact opposite.[582]

242. In the past, there were attempts by legal scholars to systematize case law solutions on causation according to the nature of the liability, relating the equivalence of conditions to fault-based liability and the concept of adequate causation to strict liability, such as the liability for things.[583] However, those attempts did not give rise to unanimous adherence.[584] In particular, it was noted that such an approach did not provide an explanation for the practices of the courts which contained a number of contrary examples and, above all, 'this doctrinal position rests on the debatable proposition that the same notion [can] receive different definitions according to the [particular] *fait générateur de responsabilité*'.[585]

243. As has been said, it is extremely difficult to predict the outcome of causation issues brought before civil courts as there are cases in which the judges seem to follow the 'sine qua non' test (without saying so),[586] yet in others, a compensation claim is dismissed on the basis that a 'direct link' is missing between the defendant's conduct and the claimant's harm.[587] In cases in which a car accident victim was severely injured or died during hospitalization as a result of medical malpractice or a hospital-acquired infection, the Court of Cassation switched from one analysis to another, deciding either that the traffic accident was or was not the cause of the ultimate harm without stating any reason.[588] These shifts are symbolic of the casuistic approach of causation under French law in which policy reasons, availability of insurance coverage and equity considerations weigh more than the aim of finding and implementing a coherent causation system.[589]

---

581. Jourdain, *Détermination des causes*, *supra* n. 574, at para. 22 ('case law seems to promote, in the field of substantive law, the theory of equivalence of conditions'). *See* also Viney, Jourdain & Carval, *Conditions*, *supra* n. 129, at paras 354–358-2.
582. Terré, Simler, Lequette & Chénedé, *supra* n. 572, at para. 1091 ('case law is generally directed towards another approach, by enshrining preferably the theory of adequate causation').
583. Jacques Flour, Jean-Louis Aubert & Éric Savaux, *Droit civil. Les obligations*, vol 2 *Le fait juridique* (Sirey 14th ed. 2011) para. 162; Philippe Malaurie, Laurent Aynes & Philippe Stoffel-Munck, *Droit des obligations* (LGDJ 11th ed. 2020) para. 64; le Tourneau (ed.), *Droit de la responsabilité*, *supra* n. 54, at paras 2131.54–2131.56; for a more in-depth analysis, *see* Clotilde Grare, *Recherches sur la cohérence de la responsabilité délictuelle* (Dalloz 2005) para. 261.
584. *See,* in particular, Quézel-Ambrunaz, *supra* n. 560, at para. 130.
585. Mireille Bacache-Gibeili, *Les obligations. La responsabilité civile extracontractuelle* (Economica, 3d ed. 2016) para. 500.
586. For examples, *see* in English Fairgrieve & G'sell-Macrez, *supra* n. 562, at 120.
587. *Ibid.*
588. *See* in English Fairgrieve & G'sell-Macrez, *supra* n. 562, at 120–121 (with further references). *See* also Lara Khoury, *Uncertain Causation in Medical Liability* (Hart 2006) 26–29.
589. Despite this critical assessment of causation under French law, it must not be forgotten that whatever the degree of sophistication of the tort law system, a flexible approach to causation is common to all jurisdictions. *See,* in particular, the enlightening comments of Honoré, *Causation and Remoteness*, *supra* n. 567, at para. 105.

II. Alternative Concepts Related to Causation

244. While the general approach to causation is still very much based on a case-by-case approach and may seem vague and even erratic to an outside observer, the legal doctrine has tried to improve the concept of causation by separating related, alternative concepts used in statutory law or court decisions.

245. Since the enactment of the *loi Badinter* in 1985 on the compensation of traffic accident victims, French authors have emphasized the difference between proof of causation and the requirement of an 'involvement' (*implication*) of the motor vehicle in the accident.[590] As has been said, a vehicle is 'involved' in an accident when it has intervened in any way whatsoever,[591] which means that the concept of *implication* is much wider than causation. The difference between both concepts is particularly palpable in the cases of car pileups and other mass accidents as the Court of Cassation has decided that multiple collisions should be treated as a unique traffic accident and that all vehicles must be regarded as 'involved' in the accident regardless of their respective role in the occurrence of the claimant's harm.[592]

246. For some tort law scholars, another distinction has to be made between causation and the 'attributability' (*imputation*) of a tortious act to a specific defendant. This distinction is particularly helpful when it comes to explaining the underlying rationale of some liability regimes, such as civil liability for things or for the acts of others.[593] According to this analysis, it is necessary to distinguish the causal link between the alleged harm and the action of a thing (*fait d'une chose*) or the act of an employee or a child, and the connecting link between those *faits générateurs de responsabilité* and the defendant. Depending on the liability regime, the criterion of *imputation* will be the custodianship of the thing, the relationship of *préposition* or the parent-child relationship. The issue of 'attributability' has also been subject to debate in the field of medical liability in a case in which a patient could establish that her harm was caused by a medical error (a gauze compress was forgotten in the abdomen) but could not determine during which surgical operation this error had been committed.[594]

247. More recently, the concept of 'attributability' has been debated in the context of product liability under the term *imputabilité* (and not *imputation*). As has been said,[595] French lawyers are not accustomed to distinguishing between general

590. *See* para. 178 above.
591. *See* e.g. Civ 2, 24 March 2012, no. 11-19339.
592. On this point, Borghetti, *Extra-Strict Liability*, *supra* n. 406, at 277–278.
593. Fabrice Leduc, *Causalité civile et imputation*, Revue Lamy Droit civil 2007 (special issue to no. 40) 21; Jérôme Fischer, *Causalité, imputation, imputabilité, les liens de la responsabilité civile*, in *Libre droit : Mélanges en l'honneur de Philippe le Tourneau* (Dalloz 2008) 383.
594. Civ 1, 3 November 2016, no. 15-25348 (according to the Court of Cassation, 'the proof of a fault … implies that a health professional or health facility must be identified in order to attribute the fault').
595. *See* para. 233 above.

causation and specific causation. However, recent court decisions have led some authors to argue that a claimant should prove not only the causal link between the exposure to the defective product and the alleged harm but also the general capacity of a product to cause an injury of the sort alleged by the claimant.[596] Although this distinction did not receive unanimous support among tort law scholars,[597] there is a tendency in both case law and in the legal doctrine to separate causation and *imputabilité*.[598]

III. Proof of Causation

248. It is a general principle of any jurisdiction that the burden of proof rests with claimants as to the elements that establish their legal rights against a defendant.[599] In the field of tort law, this means that the claimant has to bear the 'risk of proof' (*risque de la preuve*) whenever one of the requirements of the right to compensation is encumbered by uncertainties. This is frequently the case with causation, in particular in medical or environmental liability, as science is not always capable of identifying the origin of a biological phenomenon.[600]

249. According to the general principles of the law of evidence, Article 1353(1) Civil Code provides that 'a person who claims performance of an obligation must prove it', which means that it is up to the claimant to establish the proof of the causal link between the tortious act (*fait générateur de responsabilité*) and the alleged harm. It is, therefore, not surprising that French courts regularly reject compensation claims based on tort when there is doubt about a causal connection between the claimant's action (or the action of a thing or a person under the claimant's control) and the alleged harm.[601] Although there is no specific rule on the standard of proof in civil liability cases, it is generally held that the judge must decide according to *intime conviction* ('free estimation'), which means that the claimant has to convince the court that a causal link is 'highly probable'.[602]

596. Jean-Sébastien Borghetti, *La responsabilité du fait des produits. Étude de droit comparé* (LGDJ 2004) para. 268; *Vers un régime spécial de responsabilité du fait des produits de santé?*, Rev contrats 2007, 1157 (according to the author, the distinction between causality and *imputabilité* is equivalent to the distinction between general and specific causation).
597. For a critical analysis, *see* Philippe Brun, *Raffinements ou faux-fuyants? Pour sortir de l'ambiguïté dans le contentieux du vaccin contre le virus de l'hépatite B*, D 2011, 316.
598. *See,* e.g., the case notes on Civ 1, 21 October 2020, no. 19-18689, JCP G 2020, no. 1276, note Béatrice Parance and no. 1432, note David Bakouche; Gaz Pal 15 December 2020, 18, note Marie Leveneur-Azémar; Rev contrats 2021, no. 1, 35, note Jonas Knetsch.
599. In English, *see* Sandy Steel, *Proof of Causation in Tort Law* (CUP 2015) 48.
600. *See* also Khoury, *Uncertain Causation*, *supra* n. 588, at 5.
601. *See* the many references given by Jourdain, *Détermination des causes*, *supra* n. 574, at para. 26.
602. On this point, *see* in English Steel, *Proof*, *supra* n. 599, at 59–60. In detail, the standard of proof is generally not seen as an adjustment variable and it is even struggling to find an equivalent term in French. For a comparative analysis, *see* Frédérique Ferrand, *Preuve* in *Répertoire de procédure civile* (Dalloz 2019) para. 66.

250. However, there are many situations in which the claimant can rely on so-called legal presumptions which are established by the legislator or by case law.[603] This is particularly true of mass or serial accidents in which the reversal of the burden of proof is deemed necessary because of the social impact of *catastrophes sanitaires*. Illustrations can be found in the provisions on nuclear liability[604] and in the field of liability for traffic accidents.[605] Statutory presumptions are even more present in compensation regimes which are distinct from tort law, such as the work accident compensation scheme (operated by the public health insurance providers)[606] and the compensation funds established for the victims of injuries related to contaminated blood transfusion[607] and for the victims of asbestos.[608]

251. French judges also frequently use presumptive evidence on the basis of (current) Article 1382 Civil Code according to which 'presumptions that are not established by legislation are left to the assessment of the court, which must allow only presumptions which are weighty, definite and corroborative, and only in the situations where legislation permits proof by any means'. Since causation is considered to be a legal fact (*fait juridique*) that can be proved by all means (*par tous moyens*), the existence of a causal link may thus be based on a 'bundle of indicia' (*faisceau de preuves*), that is, a factual presumption. This is particularly important in the field of product liability. In a series of highly remarked cases concerning the vaccine against Hepatitis B, the Court of Cassation held that, despite scientific uncertainty and lack of conclusive statistical data, a causal link between the vaccination and multiple sclerosis could be established by 'weighty, definite and corroborative' presumptions.[609] However, while departing from the concept of

603. Some authors use the term 'quasi-legal presumption' in this case. *See* e.g. Brun, *Responsabilité*, *supra* n. 147, at para. 253. *See* also the latest survey by Julie Traullé, *Le renouveau des présomptions en droit de la responsabilité civile*, D 2021, 360.

604. Arts L 597-12 and L 597-36 Environmental Code (the provisions refer to a list of diseases 'which are presumed, unless the contrary is proved, to be caused by the nuclear accident, taking into account the radiation dose and contamination received by the claimant and the period within which the disease has been recognized').

605. The Court of Cassation held that the causal link between the alleged harm and the traffic accident (which is sometimes called *imputabilité*) is to be presumed whenever the *implication* of a motor vehicle is established. *See* Civ 2, 28 June 1989, no. 88-16.149. *See* also Viney, Jourdain & Carval, *Conditions*, *supra* n. 129, at para. 365. For a similar presumption in the field of liability for things, *see* para. 170 above.

606. *See*, in particular, Art. L 411-1 Social Security Code ('A work-related accident is an accident, whatever the cause, arising out of or from a job performance by an employee or anyone who is hired, whatever the reason or the location, by one or several employers or business owners').

607. Arts L 1221-14 and L 3122-1 Public Health Code. Since 2012, this presumption applies to compensation claims related to HIV, Hepatis B or C and HTLV contaminations. *See* in English Steel, *Proof*, *supra* n. 599, at 263–264.

608. Art. 53 III of the Act of 23 December 2000. *See* in English Manaouil, Graser & Jardé, *supra* n. 480.

609. Civ 1, 22 May 2008, nos 05–20317, 06–14952, 05–10.593, 06–10.967, 06–18.848 and 07–17.200. For an analysis of these judgments in English, *see* Fairgrieve & G'sell-Macrez, *supra* n. 562, at 126 and Moréteau, *ETL 2008 (2009)*, *supra* n. 280, at paras 24–26. In practice, the claimant must establish the absence of alternative causes of multiple sclerosis (previous medical history, neurological problems in the family, short lapse of time between the vaccination and the first symptoms).

scientific causation,[610] the French tort law does not always allow claimants to overcome scientific uncertainty, and it is relatively rare that lower courts award damages in cases concerning the vaccine against Hepatitis B.[611] The balance between the preservation of principles of the law of evidence and their adaptation for the sake of fairness[612] is still fragile and does not provide sufficient legal certainty so far.

252. Another means to adapt the rules on the burden of proof in the field of causation is to use the concept of loss of a chance (*perte de chance*). As will be seen in part VI, French tort law recognizes the compensability of a lost chance (either of obtaining a gain or of avoiding a loss) and considers it as a valid type of damage.[613] In the context of medical liability, the *perte de chance* doctrine is extensively used by claimants and courts to such an extent that issues of causation tend to be absorbed by the assessment of a loss.[614] It is very common that in cases in which there is an uncertain causal link between a medical error (or the non-disclosure of risks to the patient) and the alleged harm, courts award partial compensation to the claimant on the grounds that the doctor's negligence did lead to a loss of a chance to avoid the complication of the medical act. To use the words of Christophe Quézel-Ambrunaz, 'the supposed autonomy of the loss of a chance is sometimes but a helpful expedient used to mask the integration of probabilistic reasoning in the field of causation. … The loss of a chance to avoid the realisation of a risk approximates to … a proportional liability'.[615]

IV. Alternative Causation or Defendant Indeterminacy

253. The most complex situation related to causation is the so-called indeterminate defendant problem which deals with cases in which there are at least two persons who may be at the origin of the alleged harm.[616] The central difficulty is the identification of the exact cause of the claimant's injury and thus the determination

610. Khoury, *Uncertain Causation, supra* n. 588, at 64–68. French authors emphasize almost systematically that scientific and legal causation are two distinct concepts. *See,* e.g., Christophe Radé, *Causalité juridique et causalité scientifique : de la distinction à la dialectique*, D 2012, 112 ; Philippe Brun, *Causalité juridique et causalité scientifique*, Revue Lamy Droit civil 2007, no. 40, 65.
611. *See,* e.g., Civ 1, 4 July 2019, no. 18-16.809 and the disenchanted commentary of Laurent Bloch, Resp civ assur 2019, comm no. 279 ('Considering the feeling of a lottery instilled by the court decisions on the issue of multiple scleroses and vaccination against Hepatitis B, … it is now obvious that the claimant is always the loser.').
612. *See* Steel, *Proof, supra* n. 599, at 268 ('The motivation is the simple one of compensating the victims of terrible illnesses.').
613. *See* paras 301–304 below.
614. Khoury, *Uncertain Causation, supra* n. 588, at 124–128.
615. Christophe Quézel-Ambrunaz, *Défaut d'information du patient: concurrence de l'indemnisation par l'Oniam et de la responsabilité civile*, Gaz Pal 25 March 2010, 10 (translation provided by Steel, *Proof, supra* n. 599, at 338). From a comparative point of view, *see* Thomas Kadner Graziano, *Loss of a Chance in European Private Law 'All or Nothing' or Partial Liability in Cases of Uncertain Causation*, 16 ERPL 1009, 1021–1027 (2008).
616. *See* in English Steel, *Proof, supra* n. 599, at 153–161; Khoury, *Uncertain Causation, supra* n. 588, at 84–88; Pinto Oliveira, *supra* n. 120, at 251–252.

of civil liabilities among the potential tortfeasors. Like in other jurisdiction, the classic example chosen by French tort law textbooks is the 'hunters case', a scenario in which it is impossible to prove which one of the multiple hunters fired the single shot that injured or killed the claimant.[617] This standard problem is also known to French lawyers as 'alternative causation' (*causalité alternative*).[618]

254. Given that the French Civil Code does not contain any indication on how to assess causation in cases of defendant indeterminacy, the Court of Cassation had to find its own way of balancing the interests of all parties. Until the mid-20th century, French courts tended to reject compensation claims on the grounds that the exact cause of the alleged harm could not be established by the claimant and that it would be a flagrant injustice to hold liable all defendants when it was clear that not all of them caused the damage.[619] A shift occurred from the 1950s on, when courts began to acknowledge the collective liability of all group members on the basis of 'group fault' (*faute collective*) or 'group guardianship' (*garde en commun*).[620]

255. As the doctrines of *faute collective* and *garde en commun* became more and more considered as artificial and obsolete, the Court of Cassation opted for a more direct approach beginning in the 2000s and recognized a presumption of causation in cases of pharmaceutical liability. In the so-called *Distilbène* cases,[621] claimants faced difficulty in determining which one of two pharmaceutical firms that manufactured the drug in France was at the origin of the defective drug causative to their injury. In two landmark decisions in 2009, the Second Civil Chamber held that the claimants did not have to establish the identity of the defendant that participated in the occurrence of the harm. Both firms were held solidarily liable (*in solidum*) because they could not prove that their product was not the cause of the damage.[622] The burden of proof was subsequently reversed in cases in which hospital-derived

617. *See* Ernest J. Weinrib, *Causal Uncertainty*, 36 Oxford Journal of Legal Studies 135, 140–144 (2016).

618. *See*, in particular, the reference work of Christophe Quézel-Ambrunaz, *La fiction de la causalité alternative, fondement et perspectives de la jurisprudence Distilbène*, D 2010, 1162 and Quézel-Ambrunaz, *Essai*, *supra* n. 560, at paras 578–581.

619. *See*, e.g., Henri Mazeaud & Léon Mazeaud, *Case Note on CA Montpellier, 8 November 1949*, RTD civ 1950, 191 (according to the authors, this solution would amount to 'a collective punishment in line with totalitarianism, that does not comply with French traditions').

620. Steel, *Proof*, *supra* n. 599, at 155–156. For a more detailed analysis, *see* Viney, Jourdain & Carval, *Conditions*, *supra* n. 129, at paras 377–378 (with further references).

621. Better known as DES in the English-speaking world, Distilbène was a drug put on the market by multiple manufacturers, which was used from the 1940s to the 1970s by pregnant women with a history of recurrent miscarriage or hormone therapy. The most important side-effects of the drug, namely, cervical cancer or female infertility, became apparent only 20 to 30 years after the birth. It was practically impossible for the claimants to determine which manufacturer exposed them to the defective drug.

622. Civ 1, 24 September 2009, nos 08-10081 and 08-16305 ('il appartenait … à chacun des laboratoires de prouver que son produit n'était pas à l'origine du dommage'). For an English commentary on those decisions, *see* Florence G'sell, *DES Daughters Cases: Cour de Cassation 24 September 2009 and 24 January 2010 and CA Paris 26 October 2012*, 21 ERPL 587 (2013) and by the same author, *Alternative Causation under French Law*, 25 ERPL 1109 (2018). *See* also Steel, *Proof*, *supra* n. 599, at 155–156.

infections (*infections nosocomiales*) could not be attributed to a specific health facility in which the claimant was hospitalized.[623]

256. As in other countries, the idea of 'market-share liability' in cases of alternative causation did not receive unanimously positive feedback in the legal doctrine and in case law. Apart from an isolated (but remarked) decision from the Nanterre District court,[624] this option has not been followed by French courts, either for the establishment of a right to compensation or in the aftermath for recourse actions.[625] Yet it is to be noted that the 2017 Draft Reform provides for an apportionment rule based on proportionality in cases of defendant indeterminacy but only for the purposes of recourse actions.[626]

257. The 2017 Draft Reform of Civil Liability suggests the introduction of a specific provision on alternate causation. According to Article 1240(1), 'where personal injury is caused by an undetermined person among two or more identified persons acting in concert or exercising a similar activity, each person is liable for the whole, unless he shows that he could not have caused it'. Despite the efforts of the drafters to codify existing case law, this provision faces criticism for its potentially unlimited scope of application.[627] When comparing the 2017 Draft Reform with the 2016 Preliminary Draft and the *Terré* and *Catala* reform project, the difficulty in finding adequate wording for a rule on alternate causation which preserves the case law *acquis* without opening a Pandora's box can be understood.[628]

---

623. Civ 1, 17 June 2010, no. 09-67011. On this judgment, *see* Olivier Moréteau, *Causal Uncertainty and Proportional Liability in France*, in *Proportional Liability: Analytical and Comparative Perspectives* (Israel Gilead, Michael D. Green & Bernhard A. Koch eds, de Gruyter 2013) 141, para. 14. Surprisingly, the Court of Cassation refused to extend this solution to cases in which a medical error could not be attributed to a specific health professional (Civ 1, 3 November 2016, no. 15-25348). On this decision, *see* already para. 246 above and Clotilde Aubry de Maromont, *Les tourments de la causalité alternative dans l'indemnisation des victimes de risques sanitaires*, Revue Lamy Droit civil 2017, no. 148, 14.

624. Nanterre District Court, 10 April 2014, nos 12/12349 and 12/13064. For a brief presentation in English, *see* Séjean & Knetsch, *ETL 2014 (2015)*, *supra* n. 180, at para. 54.

625. For a more detailed analysis, *see* Moréteau, *Causal Uncertainty*, *supra* n. 623, at 141.

626. Art. 1240(2) Draft Reform ('The persons so liable make contribution to each other in proportion to the probability that each had caused the harm').

627. For comparative remarks on Art. 1240 Draft Reform, *see* in English Pinto Oliveira, *supra* n. 117, at 254–255.

628. On this issue, *see* Jonas Knetsch, *Le projet de réforme de la responsabilité civile du 13 mars 2017 et les victimes de catastrophes et d'accidents collectifs*, in *Université et prétoire. Mélanges en l'honneur de Monsieur le Professeur Claude Lienhard* (Isabelle Corpart, Caroline Lacroix & Marie-France Steinlé-Feuerbach eds, L'Harmattan 2020), 127, paras 13–17.

Chapter 2. The Doctrine of *cause étrangère*

258. To avoid civil liability, the defendant in an action for compensation can plead the defence of *cause étrangère*. This term refers to any event which may impact the causal link between the defendant's action and the alleged harm and thus exempt the defendant in whole or in part from liability.[629] The French legal doctrine does not excel in terminological consistency as some authors define the term of *cause étrangère* in narrower terms and tend to assimilate force majeure and *cause étrangère*. However, it is widely acknowledged today that the terms need to be distinguished and that *cause étrangère* is to be understood as a general term (*notion-cadre*) which embraces different types of events: fortuitous events (*cas fortuit*), acts of a third party (*fait du tiers*) and acts of the injured person (*faute de la victime*).[630]

259. This is not to say that there is no room for a doctrine of force majeure, but it is used more as an additional criterion, as a qualifier (*qualificatif*), determining the strength of the exoneration effect.[631] The current understanding of the interplay of *cause étrangère* and force majeure is transcribed in Article 1253(1) of the 2017 Draft Reform, according to which 'a fortuitous event, or an act of a third party or of the victim, provide a total exoneration where they bear the characteristics of force majeure'. If they do not, the defendant will bear full liability or, in some cases, is eligible only for partial exoneration.

260. For a *cause étrangère* to qualify as force majeure, there are traditionally three requirements that must be met. First, the event has to be exterior (*extérieur*), which means that it is beyond the defendant's control or beyond the control of a person for which the defendant could be held liable (such as a minor or an employee). Second, the event must be unforeseeable (*imprévisible*), that is, the event could not reasonably have been anticipated by the defendant. Third, it has to be irresistible (*irrésistible*), which means that the event could not be reasonably avoided by the defendant. The criteria of *imprévisibilité* and *irrésistibilité* are assessed from the point of view of an average person in the same circumstances without taking into consideration the defendant's particular circumstances, such as skills, intelligence, emotional state or age.[632] Codifying the case law,[633] the 2017 Draft Reform provides in Article 1253 that 'in extra-contractual matters, force majeure is an event

629. Patrice Jourdain, *Droit à réparation. Lien de causalité* in *JurisClasseur Code civil*, Arts 1382 à 1386, fasc 161 (LexisNexis 2020) paras 1–4. For an extensive analysis of the *cause étrangère* doctrine, *see* Olivia Sabard, *La cause étrangère dans les droits privé et public de la responsabilité extracontractuelle* (LGDJ 2008).

630. Brun, *Responsabilité*, *supra* n. 147, at para. 275.

631. On the different terms, *see* Bacache-Gibeili, *Les obligations*, *supra* n. 585, at para. 532. *See* also from a comparative standpoint Honoré, *Causation and Remoteness*, *supra* n. 567, at para. 142.

632. On this abstract approach (*appréciation in abstracto*), *see* e.g. Viney, Jourdain & Carval, *Conditions*, *supra* n. 129, at para. 365.

633. In contractual matters, the concept of force majeure is defined in Art. 1218 Civil Code as 'an event beyond the control of the debtor, which could not reasonably have been foreseen at the time of the conclusion of the contract and whose effects could not be avoided by appropriate measures, prevents performance of his obligation by the debtor'. For a commentary on this text, *see* in English Bénédicte Fauvarque-Cosson, *Does Review on the Ground of* Imprévision *Breach the Principle of*

escaping the control of the defendant or of a person for whom he is responsible, whose occurrence and whose consequences the latter could not avoid by appropriate measures' and that 'in contractual matters, force majeure is defined by Article 1218'.

§1. Fortuitous Event (*Cas Fortuit*)

261. A fortuitous event (*cas fortuit*) refers to events which happen by forces of nature, independently of human volition, such as earthquakes, tornados, floods or volcano eruptions, but also to acts of people which cannot be attributed to any individual in particular (e.g., riots, strikes and wars). Apart from two single cases,[634] French courts have decided that a fortuitous event can only lead to the defendant's exoneration if it meets the characteristics of force majeure.[635] In other words, there cannot be an apportionment of liability in the sense that the alleged harm is deemed to be partly caused by the defendant's fault (or other tortious act) and partly by an act of nature which is neither foreseeable nor avoidable by taking appropriate measures.[636] This 'all or nothing' principle is generally justified by the victim's legitimate interest in a full compensation.[637]

§2. Act of a Third Party (*Fait du Tiers*)

262. An act of a third party (*fait du tiers*) may also break the chain of causation and exempt the defendant from civil liability if it bears the characteristics of force majeure. In such cases, the defence tends to establish that the defendant's act was not, in fact, the origin of the claimant's harm and that the third party's conduct is the sole cause of the injury. However, a full exoneration is very rarely recognized in case law.[638]

263. More often, the defendant invokes the liability of another person (*appel en garantie*) in order to prove that the third party's conduct is a concurrent cause of the harm. If it is, French courts hold that the defendant cannot rely on the coexistent tortious act of a third person as a ground for partial exoneration. Both defendants will be held liable *in solidum* so that the claimant can obtain full damages from

---

the Binding Force of Contracts?, in *The Code Napoléon Rewritten: French Contract Law after the 2016 Reforms* (John Cartwright & Simon Whittaker eds, Hart 2017) 187, 197.

634. Com, 19 June 1951, *Lamoricière*, commented in Olivier Moréteau, *Basic Questions*, *supra* n. 51, at para. 1/119. *See* also Civ, 13 March 1957, *Houillères du Bassin du Nord et du Pas-de-Calais*.

635. *See* Civ 2, 11 February 1970; Civ 2, 30 June 1971; Com, 14 February 1973. However, the Court of Cassation is still expected to reassert this solution as the former decisions are beginning to become obsolete.

636. Brun, *Responsabilité*, *supra* n. 147, at para. 256.

637. Viney, Jourdain & Carval, *Conditions*, *supra* n. 129, at para. 414. It is to be noted that under the *loi Badinter*, a fortuitous act is not even an eligible defence (*see* Art. 2 of the Act of 5 July 1985 and para. 179 above).

638. *See* e.g. Civ 2, 29 March 2001, no. 99-10735. For further references *see* Viney, Jourdain & Carval, *Conditions*, *supra* n. 129, at para. 416.

either of them.[639] It is only after the compensation payment is made to the victim that the shares of liability will be decisive to determine to what extent the author of the harm who made the payment is entitled to a recourse against a liable co-author. The justification for this case law-based rule is once again the protection of the legitimate interests of the victim, who should not bear the risk of insolvency or the lack of insurance of the concurrent tortfeasors.[640]

§3. Act of the Victim (*Fait de la victime*)

264. As was seen in part IV, French tort law recognizes that the claimant's own fault which contributed to the damage may reduce or exclude a right to compensation.[641] It was also stated that the assessment of contributory fault is based on the rules governing the assessment of the defendant's fault as grounds for civil liability[642] and that there is a tendency to limit the exonerating effect (*effet exonératoire*) of contributory fault to gross negligence and intent.[643] Unlike the solutions for fortuitous events and acts of third parties, there is no 'all or nothing' principle when it comes to assessing the impact of contributory fault on the victim's right to compensation. Depending on whether the claimant's fault bears or does not bear the characteristics of force majeure, the victim's conduct will give rise to a full or partial exoneration.[644] The limiting (or exclusionary) effect of contributory fault also extends to the right to compensation of indirect victims.[645]

265. In contrast, French courts do not take into account an act of the victim which does not amount to fault. This solution arises from several court decisions, although an explicit statement is still expected from the Court of Cassation.[646] In the same spirit, according to a widespread principle in comparative tort law, courts refuse to take into account the victim's predisposition in order to reduce compensation.[647]

639. *See* paras 266–268 below.
640. Brun, *Responsabilité*, *supra* n. 147, at para. 257. For an extensive overview of the case law related to this solution, *see* Viney, Jourdain & Carval, *Conditions*, *supra* n. 129, at paras 415–420.
641. *See* paras 223–227 above.
642. On the doctrine of *acceptation des risques*, *see* para. 214 above.
643. *See* para. 226 above.
644. Brun, *Responsabilité*, *supra* n. 147, at paras 259–260 (with further references).
645. It was only in 1981 after years of inconsistency that the Court of Cassation finally adopted this rule. *See* Ass plén, 19 June 1981, no. 78-91827 and for an extensive analysis, Viney, Jourdain & Carval, *Conditions*, *supra* n. 129, at paras 435–437-1.
646. Textbooks often refer to the *Mettetal* case (Civ 2, 6 avril 1987, no. 84-17748) in which the Court of Cassation held, albeit implicitly, that the claimant who is not at fault does not bear any restriction of his right to compensation. On this point, *see* the extensive work by Bernard Bonjean, *Le fait personnel non fautif dans le droit de la responsabilité civile* (thesis Grenoble, 1973).
647. According to established case law, 'the victim's right to compensation shall not be reduced on the ground of medical preconditions if the resulting injury has only been revealed or provoked by the tortious act' (Civ 2, 3 May 2018, no. 17-14985). For further references, *see* Viney, Jourdain & Carval, *Conditions*, *supra* n. 129, at paras 434–434-2. However, a pre-existing medical record can be taken into account for the purpose of the assessment of damages.

Chapter 3. Multiple Tortfeasors

§1. Obligation *in solidum*

266. Apart from rare exceptions,[648] the French Civil Code does not contain any provisions on the allocation of liability between multiple tortfeasors. Given that a solidary liability (*responsabilité solidaire*) cannot be recognized in the absence of legislative provisions,[649] the Court of Cassation has had to find an alternative solution to hold a tortfeasor liable for full compensation even though there was a concurrent cause of the harm.[650] As was stated in the chapter on the doctrine of *cause étrangère*,[651] the liability of a tortfeasor is not affected by another person's liability for the same injury in order to protect the victim from the possible insolvency of one of the tortfeasors.[652] Despite criticism and some isolated court decisions which have recognized a partial liability,[653] the Court of Cassation has repeatedly endorsed the doctrine that each tortfeasor is liable in full vis-à-vis the claimant.[654]

267. An alternative legal instrument to solidary liability can be found in the *obligation in solidum,* which can be described as an 'imperfect solidarity' or a 'reduced' joint and several liability.[655] The difference between solidary liability and liability *in solidum* is not immediately obvious as both types of liability lead to the same principal consequence: each tortfeasor is equally liable, and the victim can claim the full amount of damages from any of them. Unlike solidary liability, liability *in solidum* is not based on the idea that the obligation creates a community of interests between the debtors. The obligations giving rise to a liability *in solidum* are considered to be more separate than solidary ones so that the so-called secondary consequences of solidary obligations (*obligations solidaires*) related to the interruption of the limitation period and the application of the late payment regime will not apply

648. Regarding parental liability and the liability for defective products, Arts 1242(4) and 1245-7 Civil Code provide for a solidary liability (*responsabilité solidaire*) of the parents and the manufacturers of different parts of the same defective products.
649. Former Art. 1202 Civil Code provided that 'solidary liability may not be presumed: it must be expressly stipulated'. This provision was understood as a restriction to the normative authority of courts. *See* Jacques Flour, Jean-Louis Aubert & Éric Savaux, *Droit civil. Les obligations*, vol 3 *Le rapport d'obligation* (Sirey 7th ed. 2011) para. 312.
650. Weir, *supra* n. 88, at para. 79.
651. *See* para. 263 above.
652. *See* para. 263 above.
653. *See* Viney, Jourdain & Carval, *Conditions*, *supra* n. 129, at paras 418–419 and the reference work by Marc Mignot, *Les obligations solidaires et les obligations* in solidum *en droit privé français* (Dalloz 2002) paras 705–848. In English and from a comparative standpoint, *see* Weir, *supra* n. 88, at paras 80–86.
654. The solution is constantly reminded by the Court of Cassation. *See,* e.g., Civ 1, 11 September 2014, no. 13-16897, commented in Michel Séjean & Jonas Knetsch, *France* in *ETL 2015* (2016) 205, paras 40–47.
655. On this legal concept, *see* in English Carlos Gómez Ligüerre, *'Solidary' Liability and the Channelling of Liability*, in *French Civil Liability in Comparative Perspective* (Jean-Sébastien Borghetti & Simon Whittaker eds, Hart 2019) 263, 266–267 and Herman Cousy & Dimitri Droshout, *Multiple Tortfeasors under Belgian Law*, in *Unification of Tort Law: Multiple Tortfeasors* (W. V. Horton Rogers ed., Kluwer Law 2004) 29, 37 (Belgian law is identical to French law on this point).

to them. However, the primary effect of solidarity will apply, that is, the unity of the obligation shared by the liable persons.[656]

268. The 2017 Draft Reform suggests that in the field of tort law, the *in solidum* doctrine should be replaced with the principle of solidary liability. According to Article 1265(1), 'where one or more persons are liable for the same harm, they are jointly and severally bound to make reparation for it to the victim'. The consequence of this provision would be that multiple tortfeasors would be solidarily liable for the harm caused to their victim according to a general legislative provision, as is already the case for parents and manufacturers of different parts of a defective product. While such a reform has the merit of simplifying the French answer to the thorny issue of multiple wrongdoers and bringing it closer to other European legal systems, it probably will introduce some inconsistency in the understanding of the concept of solidary obligations, which in French law is traditionally based on the idea of an agency relationship (*rapport de représentation*) between solidary debtors.[657]

§2. Right to Recourse

269. To quote Carlos Gómez Ligüerre, 'the contribution between solidary debtors is the second step in the life cycle of the solidary obligation'.[658] Indeed, every French textbook on tort law distinguishes the external and internal dimension of solidary liability and liability *in solidum.*[659] Whereas every tortfeasor is held liable in full vis-à-vis the victim, the internal distribution of liability implies that in most cases the debtor who satisfied the compensation claim may recoup it from another debtor. Under French law, this right to recourse is based on the subrogation of the paying debtor (*solvens*) to the victim's rights against other liable persons.[660] Apart from a short period in the 1970s,[661] there has been no debate about the legal basis of the recourse as French courts continuously affirm that the recourse is a subrogative one and not an individual right of the tortfeasor.[662]

656. The primary effects of solidarity also include the possibility for any of the debtors to invoke vis-à-vis the creditor the defences of another debtor (Art. 1315 Civil Code).

657. For an analysis of Art. 1265(1) of the Draft Reform in English, *see* Ligüerre, *supra* n. 655, at 272–274. *See* also le Tourneau (ed.), *Droit de la responsabilité*, *supra* n. 54, at para. 2132.82 and, more recently, Antoine Touzain, *Obligation et contribution à la dette entre coresponsables : l'article 1265 du projet de réforme de la responsabilité civile*, D 2020, 1636.

658. Ligüerre, *supra* n. 655, at 275.

659. In French legal terminology, the terms *obligation à la dette* and *contribution à la dette* are also widely used. *See,* e.g., Brun, *Responsabilité*, *supra* n. 147, at para. 590.

660. For a comparative analysis, *see* Weir, *supra* n. 88, at para. 109; W. V. Horton Rogers, *Comparative Report*, in *Unification of Tort Law: Multiple Tortfeasors* (W. V. Horton Rogers ed., Kluwer Law 2004) 271–302.

661. *See* the reference work of Jacques Mestre, *La subrogation personnelle* (LGDJ 1979) paras 270–287. *See* also Patrick Canin, *Les actions récursoires entre coresponsables* (Litec 1996) and Marine Ranouil, *Les recours entre coobligés* (IRJS 2014).

662. *See,* e.g., Civ 1, 7 February 1989, no. 87-15409. For further references, *see* Viney, Jourdain & Carval, *Conditions*, *supra* n. 129, at paras 423–423-2.

270. The basic rule for the apportionment between multiple tortfeasors is that each party should bear an equal share of the compensation awarded to the claimant based on the idea that the award is a common burden.[663] This principle of equal division is, however, subject to certain exceptions. In the case of concurrent fault, the Court regularly decides that the criterion to apportion liability is to be found in the respective gravity of the tortfeasors' actions, leading to proportional liability among tortfeasors.[664] If one of the tortfeasors has been declared liable on the ground of fault and the other on the basis of strict liability, the courts enable the second to recover the whole amount from the first based on the theory that the fault of the first outweighs the act or omission giving rise to no-fault liability.[665] However, these are only guidelines and French courts enjoy a wide discretion in apportioning liabilities according to the 'respective shares of liability'.[666]

271. The 2017 Draft Reform suggests a more solid framework for the apportionment of liability in the internal relationship between multiple tortfeasors. Article 1265(2) provides that 'if all or certain of (the multiple tortfeasors) have committed a fault, they make contribution to each other in proportion to the seriousness and the causal role of the action giving rise to liability which is attributable to them. If none of them has committed a fault, they make contribution in proportion to the causal role of the action giving rise to liability which is attributable to them, or, if this is not possible, in equal parts'. Two of the many difficulties of this article are the uncertain nature of some liability regimes which borrow elements from fault-based and strict liability and the importance of causation for the sake of apportionment.[667] It is expected that the final draft of the civil liability reform will amend this article to provide more clarity.

663. For a recent application of this rule in the field of product liability, *see* Civ 1, 26 November 2014, no. 13-18819, commented in Michel Séjean & Jonas Knetsch, *France*, European Tort Law 2015 (2016), 205, paras 48–53.

664. *See,* e.g., Civ 1, 14 February 2008, no. 07-11710.

665. *See,* e.g., Civ 2, 25 November 1987, no. 86-16074.

666. For a critical assessment, *see* Viney, Jourdain & Carval, *Conditions*, *supra* n. 129, at paras 424-1–424-2.

667. *See* in English Ligüerre, *supra* n. 655, at 275. *See* also in French Touzain, *supra* n. 657, at paras 10–14.

Part VI. Remedies

272. The assessment of remedies under French tort law refers to the rules governing the consequences of civil liability. As in other jurisdictions, the prevailing remedy for harm caused by a tortious act is the award of damages (*dommages-intérêts*) to the claimant.[668] This monetary redress tends to fulfil the major aim of tort law, that is, compensation of the injury inflicted by the tortfeasor on another person. However, as will be seen, the same remedy may also be inspired by the idea of prevention and/or punishment, especially in the field of interference with personality rights such as reputation and privacy or – more subtly – by the mere purpose of declaring that the claimant suffered an unlawful harm.[669]

273. Instead of damages, a victim can also claim reparation in kind (*réparation en nature*), which under French tort law is equivalent to monetary compensation and, according to some authors, even a more adequate form of redress.[670] In cases of removal, destruction or unlawful detention of property, courts often favour its restoration or restitution.[671] It is also common for judges to order the tortfeasor to replace damaged property with a similar item or to carry out (or to allow the performance of) repair work in order to restore the *status quo ante*.[672] However, unlike in other tort law systems and except for the redress of ecological harm,[673] there is no principle of primacy of *réparation en nature,* and it is up to the court to decide whether the adequate form of reparation shall be monetary or in kind. When making this decision, the court has to take into account the interests of both the claimant

668. Viney, Jourdain & Carval, *Effets*, *supra* n. 129, at para. 110 ('the most common consequence of civil liability'). For a comparative survey, *see* Helmut Koziol, *Comparative Conclusions*, in *Basic Questions of Tort Law from a Comparative Perspective* (Helmut Koziol ed., Jan Sramek Verlag 2015) paras 8/311–8/317.
669. *See* already Hans Stoll *Consequences of Liability: Remedies* in *International Encyclopedia of Comparative Law*, vol XI (André Tunc ed., Brill & J C B Mohr 1983), Ch. 8, para. 6.
670. Le Tourneau (ed.), *Droit de la responsabilité*, *supra* n. 54, at para. 2311.51 (with further references).
671. Viney, Jourdain & Carval, *Effets*, *supra* n. 129, at para. 66.
672. For other examples, *see* Fabrice Leduc, *Régime de la réparation. Principes fondamentaux* in *JurisClasseur Responsabilité civile et assurances* (LexisNexis 2014) paras 34–38. *See* also in English Moréteau, *Basic Questions*, *supra* n. 51, at para. 1/210; Yves-Louis Sage, *French Law of Delict: The Role of Fault and the Prinicples Governing Losses and Remedies* 26 Victoria University of Wellington Law Review 1, 6–7 (1996). It is also possible for the court to authorise the claimant to have the reparation performed at the liable person's expense. On the contractual dimension of this *faculté de remplacement*, *see* Rowan, *supra* n. 82, at 114–117.
673. According to Art. 1249(1) Civil Code, 'as a matter of priority, reparation for ecological loss is to be effected in kind'.

and the defendant, and it is perfectly possible for the judges, under current case law,[674] to impose a reparation in kind against the will of the claimant. To attenuate the effects of this wide margin of appreciation, the Court of Cassation controls the lower courts' decisions and can quash judgments in which a reparation in kind was arbitrarily ordered or would have a disproportionate cost for the defendant.[675]

274. Specific mention has to be made of injunctive relief. As has been seen,[676] and subject to further developments,[677] some scholars argue that civil liability should not be restricted to the compensation of harm that has already occurred but should also address situations in which an individual is facing a risk of imminent harm.[678] In those cases, current civil procedure rules allow a claimant to request injunctive relief (*mesures conservatoires*) in accordance with Article 809 of the Civil Procedure Code.[679] The 2017 Draft contains a suggestion to transform the prohibitory injunction (*cessation de l'illicite*) into a tort law-related procedure which is generally available to all individuals confronted with the risk of imminent harm or exposed to unlawful nuisance (*trouble illicite*) that does not give rise to tortious loss.[680]

275. Finally, there is an ongoing discussion of the necessity to strengthen the punitive dimension of the law of damages.[681] An overcompensation of the claimant would be a derogation of the indemnity principle (*principe indemnitaire*) which is at the core of the French law of damages. However, the Court of Cassation occasionally assesses damages for non-pecuniary harm by taking into account the deliberate character of fault and the position of the tortfeasor.[682] A growing majority of tort law scholars consider that the current Civil Code provisions do not constitute a

674. The 2017 Draft Reform suggests a limitation of the court's discretion. According to Art. 1261, 'reparation in kind cannot be imposed on the victim'. Furthermore, it is suggested that a reparation in kind cannot 'be ordered in the case of impossibility or of manifest disproportionality between its cost for the person liable and its interest for the victim'.
675. For a comprehensive assessment of the current case law, *see* Viney, Jourdain & Carval, *Effets*, *supra* n. 129, at paras 91–109.
676. *See* para. 48 above.
677. *See* paras 354–355 below.
678. *See,* in particular, Bloch, *supra* n. 59.
679. According to Art. 809(1) of the Civil Procedure Code, 'the president (of a *tribunal judiciaire*) may always, even where confronted with a serious challenge, order in a summary procedure such protective measures or measures to restore the parties to their previous state as required, either to avoid an imminent damage or to stop a manifestly unlawful nuisance'. On this provision, *see* in English Cumming, Spitz & Janal, *supra* n. 60, at 212–215.
680. Art. 1266 of the 2017 Draft provides that 'in extra-contractual matters, independently of any reparation of loss which may have been suffered, a court may prescribe reasonable measures appropriate to prevent harm or to see that an unlawful nuisance to which a claimant is exposed is stopped'. On this proposal, *see* Giliker, *Injunctions*, *supra* n. 61, at 377.
681. For an overview, *see* Viney, *Introduction*, *supra* n. 55, at para. 114–117. *See* also the reference work Galand-Carval, *supra* n. 56 and para. 356 below.
682. *See* the examples cited by Lepage, *supra* n. 57, at paras 255–257.

sufficient legal basis for such 'disguised punitive damages'. Nevertheless, the proposal of a 'civil penalty' (*amende civile*) is still one of the most controversial issues when discussing the 2017 Draft of the civil liability reform.[683]

683. Art. 1266-1 of the 2017 Draft. *See* para. 47 above and para. 359 below.

Chapter 1. General Principles

276. One of the most distinctive features of French tort law is the breadth of its scope of application. All types of loss or damage, whether pecuniary or non-pecuniary in nature, are deemed compensable, and in principle, there is no restriction of interests protected by the rules of civil liability.[684] The general principle of liability for fault provided for in Articles 1240 and 1241 Civil Code does not make a distinction between interests relevant under tort law and those which are not protected. As a consequence, French lawyers find it very natural to seek compensation for pure economic loss, non-pecuniary damage or the loss of a chance (*perte d'une chance*) without even the slightest suspicion that in other jurisdictions, those concepts are subject to intense legal debate. Although this wide and, therefore, pro-victim approach in tort law[685] is based upon the wording of Article 1240 Civil Code, it would probably not exist without the generalization of liability insurance. Except for intentional acts, almost every facet of human life or economic activity is eligible for first- or third-party insurance coverage which is often compulsory,[686] thereby disguising the economic consequences of the victim-oriented stance of French tort law.

277. It is therefore not surprising that this broad approach is rarely criticized by legal scholars, and despite a trend towards more diversity, many scholars tend to regard the constant improvement of victim compensation as the only legitimate trend in tort law.[687] It is noteworthy, however, that the legal debate on the future of French tort law and, more specifically, of the law of damages is primarily based on cases in which the claimant invokes compensation for personal injury. It is often overlooked that while 'humanism may command that bodily injuries be compensated whenever possible … it does not require that people or companies undertaking profit-making economic activities in the market economy be compensated for pure-economic loss'.[688] Indeed, the academic fixation on examples from personal injury litigation might explain the existence of a comprehensive set of rules and guidelines for the assessment of pecuniary and non-pecuniary losses related to bodily harm,[689] while the ascertainment and assessment of economic losses are subject to a relatively poor legal framework.

684. On this issue, *see* also Christophe Quézel-Ambrunaz, *Fault, Damage and the Equivalence Principle in French Law*, 3 JETL 21 (2012).
685. For an assessment of this *idéologie de la réparation* ('compensation ideology'), *see* Loïc Cadiet, *Les faits et méfaits de l'idéologie de la réparation*, in *Le juge entre deux millénaires : Mélanges offerts à Pierre Drai* (Dalloz 2000) 495.
686. The risk of civil liability related to the personal life of private individuals living in France is covered by the so-called 'multirisk home insurance scheme' (*assurance multirisques habitation*) which is compulsory for tenants and flat owners.
687. For the 'cultural' background of this pro-victim stance, *see* Borghetti, *Culture*, *supra* n. 108, at 172–182.
688. Borghetti, *Culture*, *supra* n. 108, at 175. *See* also Moréteau, *Basic Questions*, *supra* n. 51, at para. 1/3.
689. *See* paras 324–339 below.

278. In both case law and legal doctrine, the foregoing elements are aggregated into a 'principle of full compensation' (*principe de réparation intégrale*), which is a key concept in French tort law.[690] This principle requires that every kind of harm caused by an unlawful act be compensated in its integrity without applying any gravity threshold, reduction clause or liability cap. Unlike in other jurisdictions, the development of strict liability has not prompted the idea that for the sake of insurability, there should be a cap on damages. As a consequence, the limitations arising from international or European legislation, especially in the field of transportation law and defective products, are regarded as alien to the French tort law tradition. To foreign lawyers, it might be confusing that the principle of full compensation is invoked even for the assessment of non-pecuniary harm despite its incommensurability. To resolve this contradiction, a statement of the late Jean-Pierre Dintilhac, then President of the Second Civil Chamber of the Court of Cassation, is referred to often and indicates that the idea of *réparation intégrale* has to be understood as a 'constructive utopia' (*utopie constructive*).[691]

279. The principle of full compensation is also a distinctive feature only of extra-contractual civil liability. The assessment of *contractual* damages is subject to exemption or limitation clauses and, more generally, to the expectations of the contracting parties.[692] Indeed, according to Article 1231-3 Civil Code, 'a debtor is liable only for damages which were foreseen or which could have been foreseen at the time of the contract'. This provision institutes a foreseeability test, the application of which by the lower courts is subject to control by the Court of Cassation. Yet except for cases in which contractual provisions explicitly limit recoverable damages for non-performance, the 'unforeseeability' defence has not always been consistently invoked before the courts, and until very recently, it was quite common for French lawyers to consider this limitation as obsolete. It was not until the 2010s that some decisions of the Court of Cassation returned to the forefront the limitation of contractual damages to foreseeable losses.[693]

690. For a recent survey of this principle, *see* Marie-Sophie Bondon, *Le principe de réparation intégrale du préjudice* (PUAM 2020).

691. Jean-Pierre Dintilhac, *La nomenclature et les recours des tiers payeurs*, Gaz Pal 2007, 218, 219.

692. *See* Rowan, *supra* n. 82, at 117–121; Nicholas, *supra* n. 276, at 228–231.

693. Civ 1, 28 April 2011, no. 10-15056; Civ 3, 11 March 2020, no. 18-22472. For a survey, *see* in English Jean-Sébastien Borghetti & Jonas Knetsch, *France*, in *Digest of European Tort Law*, vol 4 *Limits of Liability* (Ernst Karner et al. eds, de Gruyter) forthcoming.

Chapter 2. Kinds of Damages

§1. Remarks on Terminology: *Dommage* or *Préjudice*?

280. Before going into a presentation of the different kinds of damages, the reason the French legal literature on torts seems to hesitate between the terms *dommage* and *préjudice* should be explained. Until the late 20th century, French tort lawyers tended to confuse *dommage* and *préjudice* given that both words recover the same reality, that is, damages regarded as a prerequisite for any right to compensation.[694] However, over the last twenty-five years, a significant number of tort law scholars have expressed doubts on the synonym use of these two terms. Despite the opposition of some influential voices,[695] the majority view is now that *dommage* should describe the harm (to personal integrity, property, rights, etc.), whereas *préjudice* refers to the consequences of harm. While the former should be treated as a matter of fact, the latter is supposed to refer to a *legal* concept.[696] The idea that *dommage* and *préjudice* relate to different levels of reasoning[697] is of particular importance in the field of personal injury as the rules governing the assessment of bodily harm (*dommage corporel*) distinguish between pecuniary and non-pecuniary losses (*préjudices patrimoniaux et extrapatrimoniaux*).[698] On a more educational level, the distinction between the terms is helpful in explaining the concept of indirect victims (*victims par ricochet*) whose losses arise from the harm suffered by the direct victim. Yet it is acknowledged by some authors that the separation of *dommage* and *préjudice* is not suitable in any tort law case. Especially in cases of breach of personality rights, pure economic loss or precontractual liability, it is difficult to identify a purely factual 'harm' and to distinguish it from its consequences.[699] The definition of 'reparable loss' given in Article 1235 of the 2017 Reform Draft seems

694. Moréteau, *Basic Questions*, *supra* n. 51, at paras 1/91–1/93; Sirena, *supra* n. 107, at 205. *See* also Viney, Jourdain & Carval, *Conditions*, *supra* n. 129, at para. 246-1 (with further references).
695. Viney, Jourdain & Carval, *Conditions*, *supra* n. 129, at para. 246-1 ('we admit that the benefit of this distinction, that was given up by modern legal terminology long ago, is not quite clear to us'). *See* also Brun, *Responsabilité*, *supra* n. 147, at para. 176.
696. Le Tourneau (ed.), *Droit de la responsabilité*, *supra* n. 54, at para. 2122.12; Yvonne Lambert-Faivre & Stéphanie Porchy-Simon, *Droit du dommage corporel* (Dalloz 8th ed. 2016) para. 29. *See* also in English Moréteau, *Basic Questions*, *supra* n. 51, at para. 1/93 ('the former is fact and the latter is legal in essence').
697. From a historical point of view, the distinction between *dommage* regarded as a fact and *préjudice* as a legal concept goes back to the rediscovery of the Latin origins of both words by the Mazeaud brothers in the late 1940s. *See* Henri Mazeaud & Léon Mazeaud, *Traité théorique et pratique de la responsabilité* vol 1 (LGDJ 4th ed. 1947) 208.
698. *See,* in particular, Lambert-Faivre & Porchy-Simon, *supra* n. 696, at para. 29.
699. *See,* in particular, Fabrice Leduc, *Faut-il distinguer le dommage et le préjudice ? Point de vue privatiste*, Resp civ assur 2010, dossier 3.

to refer to the terms as two different concepts,[700] but the ambiguous wording of this provision reveals that the issue is still under debate.[701]

§2. INDIVIDUAL AND COLLECTIVE DAMAGE

I. General Approach

281. It has traditionally been held that, to be recoverable, damage needs to be 'personal, direct and certain'.[702] Whereas the direct character of the damage refers to the causal link between the tortious act and the harm,[703] the requirement of its personal and certain character needs to be further developed in this chapter since recent case law developments have largely attenuated these conditions.

282. The assertion that only a *dommage personnel* is actionable under French tort law has traditionally meant that only individuals who have personally suffered from the tortious act could claim compensation for their losses. The Civil Code of 1804 did not leave any place for a collective damage whatsoever or did it mention the rights of indirect victims, such as the spouse or the children of the victim. In the spirit of the Civil Code's drafters, the establishment of civil liability could only be based upon the one-to-one relationship between the tortfeasor and the injured person, whether natural or legal.[704]

283. However, from the 19th century on, the traditional requirement of 'personal' damage has been put aside to award damages to indirect victims, so-called *victimes par ricochet*,[705] in particular in cases of serious personal injury or death caused to the direct victim.[706] Under French law, members of the (direct) victim's family can claim compensation for distress, bereavement, loss of dependency and funeral expenses.[707] In a landmark decision from 1970, the Court of Cassation decided that unmarried partners could also claim damages, even though they could

---

700. According to this provision, 'any certain loss is reparable where it results from harm and consists of an injury to a lawful interest, whether patrimonial or extra-patrimonial'. The translation is provided by S. Whittaker, *Appendix*, in *French Civil Liability in Comparative Perspective* (Jean-Sébastien Borghetti & Simon Whittaker eds, Hart 2019) 477, 480 (*see* also 479, n. 2).
701. *See* also in English Dorota Leczykiewicz, *Loss and its Compensation in the Proposed New French Regime of Extra-contractual Liability*, in *French Civil Liability in Comparative Perspective* (Jean-Sébastien Borghetti & Simon Whittaker eds, Hart 2019) 181. For a parallel with the Italian distinction between *danno-evento* and *danno-conseguenza*, *see* Sirena, *supra* n. 107, at 207–209.
702. *See,* for example, Civ 2, 16 April 1996, no. 94-13613. In the legal doctrine, *see* le Tourneau (ed.), *Droit de la responsabilité*, *supra* n. 54, at para. 2123.00.
703. *See* paras 240–252 above.
704. It has never been disputed that a legal person could defend its pecuniary interests by the means of civil liability. On the issue of non-pecuniary loss, invoked by *personnes morales*, *see* para. 122 above.
705. A literal translation would be 'rebound victims'.
706. There is a tendency to lower the threshold of seriousness of the direct victim's injury. It is not uncommon that a significant monetary compensation is awarded to the relatives of direct victims with minor injuries.
707. For a more detailed presentation, *see* paras 336–339 below.

not invoke a legal relationship with the deceased.[708] Since then, the courts have expanded the class of secondary victims, requiring only the proof of a 'direct relationship' (*lien de proximité*) between the claimant and the deceased.[709] In light of recent case law, it is unlikely that those who only had a professional or economic relationship, such as employers or contracting parties, may claim damages for their loss.[710]

II. Compensation of Collective Damage (Substantive Law and Procedural Aspects)

284. While traditional French tort law adhered to a strictly individualistic approach, legal developments in the late 20th and the early 21st century have led to the idea that the assessment of recoverable loss should also take into account collective interests. Both in substantive and procedural law, the requirement of a personal loss, that is, individual loss, has been minimized to such an extent that scholars today do not hesitate to include collective loss in the category of actionable damage.[711] It therefore comes as no surprise that the 2016 Preliminary Draft of civil liability reform suggested a wide definition of reparable loss as an 'injury to a lawful interest, whether … *individual or collective*'.[712]

285. On a substantive level, the recognition of 'ecological harm' (*préjudice écologique*) as a reparable damage under the 2016 Law on Biodiversity has already been mentioned.[713] In addition, over the past 20 years, influential tort law scholars and practitioners have argued for a greater acknowledgement of the specific situation of mass accident victims (*victimes d'accidents collectifs*). It is argued that victims of terror attacks, stadium disasters and flight or rail accidents along with their relatives should be awarded damages in order to compensate for the specific impact of mass accidents on the victims' mental states.[714] Even though one might argue that there is no proof that the claimant's psychological distress depends on the individual or collective character of the damaging event, public authorities have been sensitive to the arguments raised by the proponents of such a specific 'tort law of

708. Ch mixte, 27 February 1970, no. 68-10276, *Dangereux*. On this case, *see* in English Steiner, *supra* n. 16, at 266.
709. Such a relationship is presumed for members of the deceased's family (parents, grandparents, grandchildren, siblings, spouse). *See* para. 337 below.
710. Le Tourneau (ed.), *Droit de la responsabilité*, *supra* n. 54, at para. 2123.173.
711. *See,* for example, Brun, *Responsabilité*, *supra* n. 147, at paras 199–201.
712. Emphasis added. This 'clarification' was dropped in the 2017 draft.
713. *See* paras 190–193 above.
714. *See,* for example, the contributions to the proceedings of conferences on 'Collective traumatic event and individual harm' (Gaz Pal 2019, 639–685) and on 'The compensation of mass accident victims' (Gaz Pal 2014, 1321–1341). *See* also Anne Guégan-Lécuyer, *Dommages de masse et responsabilité civile* (LGDJ 2006); Caroline Lacroix, *La réparation des dommages en cas de catastrophes* (LGDJ 2008).

catastrophes'.[715] In 2017, the board of the Guarantee Fund for Victims of Terrorism and Other Offences decided to award a specific amount which is in addition to ordinary damages dedicated to the compensation of a *préjudice exceptionnel spécifique*. This amount is paid to the direct victim of a terror attack or, in case of death, to relatives (spouse, children, parents, grandparents, grandchildren and siblings).[716] In tort law cases, it is still relatively uncommon to allocate specific amounts of damages to victims of mass accidents.[717]

286. On a procedural level, it is important to note that non-profit organizations, such as consumer protection associations, professional colleges or trade unions, are allowed to bring tort law actions in cases in which collective interests which they defend have been violated. In most cases, the compensation claim is made through an *action civile* before criminal courts.[718] Even though the Code of Criminal Procedure contains a list of organizations which are eligible for such an *action civile*,[719] French courts are eager to award compensation even to those organizations that do not have official authorization.[720]

287. Another important step towards a greater acknowledgement of collective damages was the enactment of three specific redress mechanisms.[721] 'Class actions *à la française*' were implemented in 2014 for consumer protection and, in 2016, for tort law claims in the health care sector, in the field of anti-discrimination and personal data protection law and for environmental harm. Over a three-year period, the French legislator tried to fill the gap in effective collective redress mechanisms that had been discussed for more than thirty years. However, it is regrettable that this legislative frenzy did not lead to a coherent legal framework of those *actions de*

715. Marie-France Steinlé-Feuerbach, *Le droit des catastrophes et la règle des trois unités de temps, de lieu et d'action*, Petites Affiches 28 July 1995, 9; Claude Lienhard, *Pour un droit des catastrophes*, D 1995, chr 91. For a more nuanced approach, *see* Knetsch, *supra* n. 628, at 127.
716. For direct victims, an extra compensation of EUR 10,000 minimum is awarded, whereas indirect victims can seek compensation up to an amount of EUR 17,500 for *préjudice exceptionnel spécifique*. For more details, *see* FGTI, *Guide pour l'indemnisation des victimes d'actes de terrorisme* (FGTI 2017) 27–28.
717. However, for a counterexample *see* Criminal Court Thonon-les-Bains, 26 June 2013, no. 683/2013 (after a crossing accident caused the death of seven school children and serious injuries to twenty-five other individuals, the court awarded compensation for a specific 'prejudice of anxiety' both to the direct victims and to their relatives).
718. *See* para. 51 above for more details.
719. Arts 2-1–2-21 Criminal Procedure Code. The list of authorized associations ranges from organisations dedicated to the defence of the French language and cultural heritage (Arts 2-14 and 2-21) and of the rights of animals (Art. 2-13) to those whose actions are dedicated to the protection of deprived children (Art. 2-3) and victims of racial discrimination (Art. 2-1).
720. Civ 3, 26 September 2007, no. 04-20636 ('an association is allowed to bring an action in order to defend collective interests that fall within the scope of its mandate [*objet social*]'). For a presentation of a follow-up case in English, *see* Jean-Sébastien Borghetti, *France*, in *Digest of European Tort Law*, vol 2 *Essential Cases on Damage* (Bénédict Winiger, Helmut Koziol, Bernhard A. Koch & Reinhard Zimmermann eds, de Gruyter 2011) 1009–1010. *See* also le Tourneau (ed.), *Droit de la responsabilité*, *supra* n. 54, at para. 2123.265 ('clear and unequivocal abandonment of the requirement of a legislative authorization').
721. For a recent study from a comparative standpoint, *see* Csongor István Nagy, *Collective Actions in Europe* (Springer 2019) 71–112.

groupe. There are currently two procedural regimes, a specific one for class actions related to consumer protection[722] and a general regime for all other class actions.[723] Both regimes provide for a two-stage procedure: first, a registered association initiates a class action before the *tribunal judiciaire* of the defendant's domicile on the basis of representative individual cases presented by the association. The court will decide both on the admissibility of the class action and the liability of the defendant; if these are found, the court will define the scope of liability, the recoverable loss, available remedies and the criteria and timeframe that have to be met in order to join the class. In a second phase, individuals who wish to join the class and who fulfil the criteria have to communicate their willingness to be part of the class, by notification either to the association or to the defendant directly.[724] An individual who chooses not to opt into the class within the timeframe set out by the court loses the right to seek compensation for a loss compensable under the collective redress scheme. In detail, there are many differences between the different types of class actions which are in regard to the recoverable loss and actionable harm (personal injury, damage to property, non-pecuniary loss), the opt-in period and eligible associations. It is generally agreed that the sector-based approach chosen by the French legislator made the system unduly complex and jeopardizes the success of the *action de groupe*. Since 2014, only 25 class actions have been brought to French courts, with very limited success.[725]

§3. DIRECT AND INDIRECT DAMAGE

288. In the field of non-contractual liability, French tort law does not give a specific meaning to indirect (or consequential) damage.[726] The principle is that every loss is to be compensated, with the scope of compensation controlled through the requirement of causation. It is therefore not rare that a loss which would be qualified as 'indirect damage' in other jurisdictions is deemed unrecoverable by French courts on the grounds that the claimant did not prove a direct causal link with the tortious act.[727]

---

722. Arts L 423-1–423-26 Consumer Code. *See* in English Bénédicte Fauvarque-Cosson, *The New Collective Redress Mechanism in French Law: An Oddity?*, 3 Journal of European Consumer and Market Law 141 (2014); Séjean & Knetsch, *ETL 2014 (2015)*, *supra* n. 180, at paras 1–13; Knetsch & Jacquemin, *ETL 2016 (2017)*, *supra* n. 45, at paras 9–12. *See* also the reference work by Maria José Azar-Baud, *Les actions collectives en droit de la consommation* (Dalloz 2013).
723. Arts 848–849-21 Civil Procedure Code. This general procedural framework must be combined with specific provisions set out for each sector (Arts L 1143-1–1143-22 Public Health Code; Art. L 142-3-1 Environmental Code; Art. L 1134-6 Labour Code). For more details, *see* also Alexandre Biard & Rafael Amaro, *Resolving Mass Claims in France: Toolbox and Experience*, BACT Working Papers Series 2016, para. 5.
724. Azar-Baud & Biard, *supra* n. 435 ('late opt-in system').
725. For more details, *see* Azar-Baud & Biard, *supra* n. 435 ('a "half-full" glass').
726. Jacques Herbots, *Why It Is Ill-Advised to Translate Consequential Damage by* Dommage Indirect, 19 ERPL 931, 945–949 (2011).
727. For examples, *see* Borghetti & Knetsch, *supra* n. 693.

289. However, the term *dommage indirect* is not completely unknown to French tort lawyers. As has already been seen,[728] according to Article 1231-3 Civil Code, 'a debtor is liable only for damages which were foreseen or which could have been foreseen at the time of the contract', which means that the right to seek compensation for the consequences of a breach of contract does not embrace any kind of loss. As a consequence, the assessment of contractual damages implies taking into account not only exemption and limitation clauses but also more generally the expectations of the contracting parties. While exemption or limitation clauses can be put aside in case of intent or gross negligence (*faute lourde*), Article 1231-4 Civil Code provides that contractual damages in any case 'should include only what is the immediate and direct consequence of the non-performance'. However, the distinction between foreseeability and directness of a loss is not entirely clear.[729] In general, it is argued that the limitation to the 'immediate and direct consequence' refers to the requirement of a causal link between the non-performance and the loss.[730]

290. The limitation to direct loss is also known in French insurance law.[731] Insurance policies often exclude compensation of indirect losses, especially for business companies. Due to the uncertainty surrounding the concept of *dommage indirect*, warranty exclusions of this sort are not exempt from the risk of being ruled out by courts because of their lack of clarity. Indeed, according to Article L 113-1 Insurance Code, exclusion clauses must be 'formal and limited', which is not always the case when referring to the exclusion of *dommages indirects*. In recent case law, the Court of Cassation has not hesitated to invalidate exclusion clauses that mentioned 'indirect losses of any kind, loss of profit and paralysis'.[732]

§4. PECUNIARY AND NON-PECUNIARY LOSSES

291. In French tort law, both pecuniary and non-pecuniary losses are deemed recoverable. While the compensability of *préjudice matériel* (or *préjudice patrimonial* according to modern legal terminology) has never raised criticism and embraces the suffered loss and denied profits, the right to seek compensation for *préjudice moral* (or *préjudice extrapatrimonial*) has constantly been challenged by legal scholars, mostly for moral and ethical reasons. As in other jurisdictions, it has

728. *See* para. 279 above.
729. *See* in English Nicholas, *supra* n. 276, at 229–230.
730. *See,* for example, le Tourneau (ed.), *Droit de la responsabilité, supra* n. 54, at para. 2131.11.
731. For an introduction to French insurance law in English, *see* Sabine Abravanel-Jolly, *French Insurance Law* (Éditions universitaires européennes 2016).
732. Civ 2, 6 February 2020, no. 18-25377; Civ 2, 5 March 2020, no. 18-15164. On the formal requirements applicable to exclusion clauses referring to 'operating losses' (*pertes d'exploitation*), *see* Anne Pélissier, *Les pertes d'exploitation dans tous leurs états*, RGDA 2020, no. 5, 29.

been argued that recovery for non-pecuniary losses would lead to a disputable quantification and monetarization of pain and suffering[733] and that a judicial assessment would lead to arbitrary amounts because of their incommensurability.[734] Putting aside these objections, and despite the lack of specific provisions in the Civil Code, the Court of Cassation decided in 1833 to award monetary compensation in a case in which a group of Parisian pharmacists claimed damages for the reputational harm caused by the unauthorized practice of pharmacy.[735] Yet, this early recognition of 'moral harm' as a source of monetary compensation should not lead to the conclusion that the legal debate on *préjudice moral* was over after this landmark decision. It is quite telling that in state liability cases, the *Conseil d'État* waited until 1962 to abandon its resistance to the recoverability of non-pecuniary loss.[736] Even though the scope of recoverable *préjudice moral* has steadily expanded since the 19th century (and in particular, over the past 25 years), there is still a debate on the assessment of non-pecuniary loss and the limits of its compensation.[737]

292. Monetary compensation for non-pecuniary loss is particularly important in cases of personal injury for which the French law of damages provides for a great variety of items of loss. Indeed, *préjudice moral* is not understood as a single head of damage but as an umbrella term for a large number of categories into which the victim's suffering is divided.[738] In 2005, a working group under the supervision of Jean-Pierre Dintilhac, former President of the Second Civil Chamber, published a list, today known as the *nomenclature Dintilhac*, which distinguishes the various items of non-pecuniary loss deemed recoverable.[739] This repository has become an important guideline for civil and administrative courts as well as insurance companies; in addition to this list, a detailed handbook on the monetary assessment (*référentiel d'indemnisation*) has been elaborated in order to harmonize the practices in civil courts.[740]

---

733. *See* for example Louis Josserand, *La personne humaine dans le commerce juridique*, Dalloz Hebdomadaire 1932, chr 1; Paul Esmein, *La commercialisation de la douleur morale*, Recueil Dalloz 1954, chr 113.
734. *See* also in English Steiner, *supra* n. 16, at 261.
735. Ch réunies, 15 June 1833, Sirey 1833, part I, 462–463, presented in English by Borghetti, *France*, *supra* n. 720, at 521–522. *See* also Vernon V. Palmer, *General Introduction*, in *The Recovery of Non-Pecuniary Loss in European Contract Law* (Vernon V. Palmer ed., CUP 2015) 1, 11.
736. CE, 24 November 1961, *Letisserand*. On this landmark decision, *see* in English Vernon V. Palmer, *The French Awakening in the Nineteenth Century*, in *The Recovery of Non-Pecuniary Loss in European Contract Law* (Vernon V. Palmer ed., CUP 2015) 58, 75–76.
737. *See,* for example, Muriel Fabre-Magnan, *Le dommage existentiel*, D 2010, 2376; Jonas Knetsch, *La désintégration du préjudice moral*, D 2015, 443.
738. For a detailed presentation, *see* paras 313, 324–339 below.
739. Jean-Pierre Dintilhac, *Rapport du groupe de travail chargé d'élaborer une nomenclature des préjudices corporels* (2005). The report is available on the website of the French Ministry of Justice: http://www.ladocumentationfrancaise.fr/rapports-publics/064000217-rapport-du-groupe-de-travail-charge-d-elaborer-une-nomenclature-des-prejudices.
740. *See* Benoît Mornet, *L'indemnisation des préjudices en cas de blessures ou de décès* (2020). There is no official source of publication for this handbook. It can be found on various websites of law firms specialized in personal injury cases and local bar councils (*ordres des avocats*). *See* e.g. https://barreau-montpellier.com/lindemnisation-des-prejudices-en-cas-de-blessures-ou-de-deces/.

293. Along with personal injury cases, the violation of personality rights is another important field for the application of non-pecuniary loss. Monetary compensation of *préjudice moral* is provided for in numerous cases: invasion of privacy; impersonation fraud and identity theft; injury to the right of image, honour and reputation; infringement of the presumption of innocence; and sequestration or arbitrary detention. However, unlike in personal injury cases, the courts do not divide the non-pecuniary loss into different items, and the monetary assessment of damages is subject to a highly casuistic approach.

294. Finally, there is a strong trend towards the compensation of non-pecuniary losses in cases in which the claimant did not suffer any infringement to personality rights or bodily integrity. In the famous *Lunus* case of 1962, the Court of Cassation decided that 'the death of an animal may, for its owner, be the cause of subjective and affective damage which may entail entitlement to redress'.[741] Despite the tough criticism raised by influential scholars, such as René Rodière and Paul Esmein,[742] the Court of Cassation has maintained its position and even expanded it to cases of damage to property with no market value but with a certain value of affection (*préjudice d'affection*) to its owner.[743] In the most recent case law, there was even a tendency towards the award of damages for *préjudice moral* in cases of mere contractual non-performance[744] on the grounds that worries, anxiety and hassles due to the litigation need to be compensated.[745]

§5. Pure Economic Loss

295. Although extensively studied in comparative law,[746] the concept of pure economic loss (*préjudice économique pur*) is almost completely unknown to French

741. Civ, 16 January 1962, D 1962, jur 199 (according to the Court, 'the court of appeal rightly considered that the harm suffered by [the owner] in respect of the death of his horse was not limited to the sum necessary to buy another animal having the same qualities, and that it was also necessary to bring into account, in calculating the damages, compensation intended to cover the harm suffered through loss of an animal to which he was attached'). The translation is provided by Vernon V. Palmer, *Immaterial Damages, the Protection of Personality Interests and the Relevance of Contract Law*, in *Liability in the Third Millennium: Liber Amicorum Gert Brüggemeier* (Nomos 2009) 215, 222. On this case, *see* also Borghetti, *France*, *supra* n. 720, at 729–730.
742. *See* the case notes by René Rodière, D 1962, jur 199 and Paul Esmein, JCP G 1962, no. 12557).
743. Civ 1, 25 January 1989, no. 87-13640 (loss of a photographic film roll). For other examples, *see* Viney, Jourdain & Carval, *Conditions*, *supra* n. 129, at para. 268.
744. On this issue, *see* in English Katarzyna Kryla-Cudna, *Breach of Contract and Damages for Non-Pecuniary Loss*, 26 ERPL 515 (2018); Vernon V. Palmer (ed.), *The Recovery of Non-Pecuniary Loss in European Contract Law* (CUP 2015).
745. Le Tourneau (ed.), *Droit de la responsabilité*, *supra* n. 54, at para. 2125.74 (with further references). In those cases, the compensation of non-pecuniary loss also tends to complete the rules on fee allocation under the Civil Procedure Code, which does not always allow the winning party to be reimbursed in full. *See* paras 305–306 below.
746. *See*, e.g., Vernon V. Palmer & Mauro Bussani (eds), *Pure Economic Loss: New Horizons in Comparative Law* (Routledge 2008); Mauro Bussani & Vernon V. Palmer (eds), *Pure Economic Loss in Europe* (CUP 2003); Willem H. van Boom, Helmut Koziol & Christian A. Witting (eds), *Pure Economic Loss* (Springer 2004). *See* also D. Marshall, *Liability for Pure Economic Loss Negligently Caused: French and English Law Compared*, 24 ICLQ 748 (1975).

tort lawyers. This is not surprising since Article 1240 Civil Code provides that anyone who causes a damage to another by his fault is obliged to compensate it but fails to provide any further explanation. The Civil Code does not make a distinction between economic loss due to material harm (personal injury or damage to property), also known as consequential economic loss, and economic loss without any physical injury. As has been said, French courts have not chosen to fill the gaps left by the legislator in a restrictive way. Any type of harm is deemed recoverable and the Court of Cassation apparently concluded that there was no legal basis to exclude pure economic loss from the scope of compensation or to treat it differently under tort law.

296. As a result, foreign lawyers might be surprised to discover that in so-called cable cases, the Court of Cassation did not see any particular objection to the compensation of the economic loss caused by a negligent power cut without any material harm to the factory.[747] Even more surprisingly, the Court of Cassation awarded compensation to a private bus company which suffered economic loss from a traffic congestion caused by an individual.[748] It should, however, be noted that those two cases date back to the 1960s and 1970s and that they cannot be qualified as landmark decisions. It actually seems that both decisions provoked greater interest among foreign tort lawyers than within French legal scholarship.[749]

297. The fact that pure economic loss is not an issue in French law does not mean that any kind of economic loss caused by a tortious act will lead to compensation in tort. The causation test is often used by courts to dismiss claims that are considered inappropriate. In a recent case in which the misconduct of a football player caused an economic loss to a sports bettor, the Court of Cassation decided that the invoked loss was not recoverable.[750] Even though some authors have pointed out the fact that the bettor's claim was for compensation of pure economic loss and that the case could be seen as a first step towards a more restrictive approach to this type of damage,[751] it is unlikely that the general position of French tort law has changed (or will change in the near future). It is more plausible that the dismissal of the compensation claim was due to the remoteness or indirectness of the claimant's loss, although the Court of Cassation did not mention considerations of causality in this decision.

747. Civ 2, 8 May 1970, no. 69-11446. *See* also CE, 2 June 1972, no. 79597.
748. Civ 2, 28 April 1965, no. 63-13624.
749. *See,* for example, Van Gerven, Larouche & Lever, *supra* n. 526, at 197; Willem H. van Boom, *Pure Economic Loss: A Comparative Perspective*, in *Pure Economic Loss* (Willem H. van Boom, Helmut Koziol & Christian A. Witting eds, Springer 2004) 1, para. 18; Thomas Kadner Graziano, *Comparative Tort Law. Cases, Materials and Exercises* (Routledge 2018) 98–99.
750. Civ 1, 14 June 2018, no. 17-20046, commented in Knetsch, *ETL 2018 (2019)*, *supra* n. 136, at paras 10–17.
751. Jean-Sébastien Borghetti, *Le parieur, le hors-jeu et la relativité de la faute civile*, D 2018, 1784; Marie Dugué, *Subordination de l'indemnisation du parieur déçu à la commission d'une faute intentionnelle du sportif*, Revue Lamy Droit civil 2018, no. 165, 35.

298. The 2017 Reform Draft confirms this wide approach under French tort law and refuses to exclude or even limit compensation for pure economic loss.[752] What is more, in a recent work on this issue, a tort law scholar of the younger generation argued that, for policy considerations, it would not be desirable to align the French model with the more restrictive solutions adopted in other jurisdictions.[753] Even if that standpoint may be questioned, it seems to reflect the current position of the legal doctrine in France.

§6. ACTUAL AND FUTURE DAMAGE; THEORY OF 'LOSS OF CHANCE' (*PERTE DE CHANCE*)

299. According to Article 11 of the Civil Code, the scope of compensation embraces both suffered loss (*perte subie*) and deprived profits (*gain manqué*). Although this provision is contained in the chapter on contractual damages, there is widespread acknowledgement that this rule also applies to compensation in tort.[754] The compound term *dommages-intérêts* (or *dommages et intérêts*) which is generally used to designate damages actually refers to both types of recoverable loss.[755] However, the importance of the distinction between *damnum emergens* and *lucrum cessans* should not be overstated since both categories of loss are primarily distinguished for educational reasons and are not separately treated in legislation or case law.[756]

300. Although not enshrined in the current Civil Code provisions, the concept of future damage (*préjudice futur*) is particularly important in practice. According to case law, future loss is recoverable provided it is a 'certain and direct extension of a current situation'.[757] In personal injury cases, a specific category is set out for permanent losses (*préjudices permanents*) which embrace *inter alia* future loss of income, medical expenses and the cost of the services of a caregiver (*assistance par tierce personne*). Over the past 10 years, civil courts have agreed on a set of guidelines intended to harmonize the assessment of future losses subsequent to bodily harm.[758] In contrast, the assessment of future loss is much less regulated outside the

752. According to Art. 1235 of the Draft, 'any certain loss is reparable where it results from harm and consists of an injury to a lawful interest, whether patrimonial or extra-patrimonial'. As no specification was made as to a list of 'lawful interests', it must be assumed that pure economic loss is a reparable loss under tort law.

753. Julie Traullé, *La réparation du préjudice économique 'pur' en question*, RTD civ 2018, 285. But *see* also the more restrictive approach suggested by Mathilde Cayot, *Le préjudice économique pur* (LGDJ 2017) paras 403–744.

754. *See*, for example, Brun, *Responsabilité*, *supra* n. 147, at para. 212.

755. On the etymology of the terms *dommages-intérêts* and *dommages et intérêts*, *see* Omid Saedi, *Dommages-intérêts ou dommages et intérêts. Celle-ci ou celle-là; ou bien les deux?*, Petites Affiches 7 June 2005, 6.

756. *See* also Borghetti, *France*, *supra* n. 720, at 301 ('only a descriptive … distinction').

757. Crim, 1 June 1932, Sirey 1933, 1, 49 and, more recently, Com, 7 July 2020, no. 18-20934. The 2017 Draft Reform suggests that this judge-made definition be implemented in the Civil Code (Art. 1236).

758. For more details, *see* para. 315 below.

field of personal injury, for example, in cases of harm to property or pure economic loss. When damages for future loss are requested by the claimant, the courts generally rely on actuary evidence brought by the parties to calculate the consequential loss (tax reports, accounting records, estimates, etc.).

301. In detail, the distinction between future loss (*préjudice futur),* which is a recoverable item of loss, and hypothetical loss (*préjudice éventuel*), which is not, is quite unclear. Courts do not hesitate to exclude a loss from the scope of compensation on the grounds that the degree of certainty is not high enough to consider it as a 'certain' future loss. To give an illustration of the narrow line between future and hypothetical loss, one can refer to cases in which the parents of an only child who was killed in an accident claimed damages for the loss of maintenance (*perte de secours alimentaire*) which may arise in their old age, given their economic and financial situation. Even though this claim sounds plausible, courts have been reluctant to award compensation on this ground, considering that this loss is a potential one and does not present a sufficient degree of certitude.[759]

302. The conceptual framework becomes even more complex when adding the 'loss of a chance' (*perte d'une chance*) doctrine to the distinction between future and hypothetical loss. This theory can be described as the compensation of the 'loss of a favourable eventuality' (*perte d'une éventualité favorable*) or, in other words, the loss of an opportunity either to realize a benefit or to avoid a loss.[760] It is widely used in several fields of tort law and, as has already been mentioned,[761] is also employed to bypass the uncertainty striking the causal link, especially in medical liability cases, thereby allowing courts to practice proportional liability without saying so.[762] Indeed, the amount of compensation for loss of chance is only a fraction of the value of the lost opportunity and is calculated according to the degree of likelihood that the chance would have occurred.[763] Based exclusively on case law (both civil and administrative courts), the *perte de chance* doctrine will be enshrined in the Civil Code if the 2017 Reform Draft becomes law.[764]

303. Three fields of application of the 'loss of a chance' doctrine can be identified. The first one concerns the liability of legal professionals for malpractice. As

759. Crim, 12 February 1979; Crim, 25 October 2000. *See* Brun, *Responsabilité, supra* n. 147, at para. 181.

760. *See* in English Khoury, *Uncertain Causation, supra* n. 588, at 110–114; Fairgrieve & G'sell-Macrez, *supra* n. 562, at 124. For a recent work in French, *see* Laura Vitale, *La perte de chances en droit privé* (LGDJ 2020).

761. *See* para. 253 above.

762. *See,* in particular, in English Pinto Oliveira, *supra* n. 117, at 256–257. On this 'shift from causation to damage', *see* also Moréteau, *Basic Questions, supra* n. 51, at paras 1/131–1/140 and, more extensively, Moréteau, *Causal Uncertainty, supra* n. 623, at 141.

763. In arithmetical terms, it could be said that damages for loss of chance = degree of likelihood x value of lost opportunity.

764. According to Art. 1238 of the Draft, 'a loss of a chance is reparable only where it is the present and certain disappearance of a favourable eventuality'; it 'must be calculated by reference to the chance lost and cannot be equal to the advantage which this chance would have procured if it had been realised'.

early as 1889, the Court of Cassation recognized damages for loss of a chance to the client of a *huissier de justice* for having delivered an irregular appeal;[765] compensation was also awarded in cases in which lawyers (*avocats, notaires*) or certified accountants (*experts-comptables*) made professional mistakes and deprived their clients of an opportunity to win a case.[766] The second category of application concerns so-called competition cases in which the claimant could not take part in a sports or business competition.[767] The third one is about the loss of educational or professional opportunities, for example, in cases in which a personal injury prevented the claimant from applying to a *concours* (French examination for public service) or for a higher job level.[768]

304. Over the past 30 years, the loss of chance doctrine has been expanded to medical liability cases and has become a major legal concept in this field. As the assessment of causal link can be difficult because of scientific uncertainty, the courts have recognized that a loss of chance could be awarded in cases in which the claimant could not establish that the doctor's fault was the cause of the aggravation of the patient's health condition or of his death but instead had caused the loss of a chance of recovery or survival (*perte d'une chance de guérison ou de survie*).[769] The courts have also used the concept of *perte de chance* in cases of unlawful non-disclosure of risks to the patient. In 1990, the Court of Cassation decided for the first time that in such cases the patient could claim damages for the loss of a chance to refuse the disputed medical act and to choose an available alternative therapy.[770] To put it in the words of Lara Khoury, 'loss of chance remains the French judiciary's preferred tool for dealing with causative difficulties caused by scientific uncertainty in medical malpractice'.[771]

305. Despite the massive expansion of the scope of the loss of chance theory, French courts have not yet taken a clear stance on its boundaries. Over the past 10 years, the case law of the Court of Cassation has proved remarkably unstable on this crucial question. For a long time, it was taken for granted that the lost chance had to be 'real and serious' (*réelle et sérieuse*), which meant that a certain threshold of probability had to be met.[772] In 2013, the First Civil Chamber of the Court of Cassation decided, however, that the 'certain loss of even a slight chance (*chance même faible*) was recoverable'.[773] A year later, the initial solution seemed to be re-established since the same chamber required the claimant to prove the loss of a

765. Req, 17 July 1889, Recueil Sirey 1891, 1, 399.
766. *See* le Tourneau (ed.), *Droit de la responsabilité*, *supra* n. 54, at para. 2123.92 (with further references).
767. *See*, for example, CA Montpellier, 17 May 1934, Sirey 1934, 2, 188. For further references, *see* le Tourneau (ed.), *Droit de la responsabilité*, *supra* n. 54, at para. 2123.92.
768. *See*, for example, Crim, 9 November 1983, no. 82-12427.
769. Civ, 18 March 1969, RTD civ 1969, 798. For other references, *see* le Tourneau (ed.), *Droit de la responsabilité*, *supra* n. 54, at para. 2123.131.
770. Civ 1, 7 February 1990, no. 88-14797.
771. Khoury, *Uncertain Causation*, *supra* n. 588, at 113.
772. For a comprehensive survey of the case law developments, *see* le Tourneau (ed.), *Droit de la responsabilité*, *supra* n. 54, at para. 2123.131.
773. Civ 1, 16 January 2013, no. 12-14439.

'reasonable chance' *(chance raisonnable)*.[774] Notwithstanding the positive feedback from tort law scholars who had commended the return to a more restrictive approach,[775] the Court of Cassation reaffirmed in a 2016 case on legal malpractice that 'every loss of chance gives rise to compensation', even if the probability is 'insignificant' (*minime*).[776] Surprisingly, the 2017 Reform Draft does not resolve this issue, merely asserting that 'a loss of a chance is reparable only where it is the present and certain disappearance of a favourable eventuality'.

§7. Other Costs

306. The assessment of the claimant's loss is generally prepared beforehand by an expert whose mission is to describe as exactly as possible the harm suffered by the claimant. Under French civil procedure, the claimant is free to appoint a 'private expert' (*expert amiable*) whose findings may help to build up the case with regard to civil proceedings or an out-of-court settlement. The expert's fees are to be paid by the claimant or, in case there is one, by the legal expenses insurer. If the claim is brought to court and the claimant is successful, the expert's fees (as well as travel and lodging expenses) will be taken into account by the court when assessing the amount of non-reimbursable expenses (*frais irrépétibles*) awarded under Article 700 Civil Procedure Code.[777] The honoraria of an expert appointed by the court (*expert judiciaire*)[778] are borne by the losing party. However, the claimant has to advance the expenses by depositing a specified amount with the court registry.[779]

307. In France, there are no charges payable to the state for acts of civil proceedings except for cases brought before commercial courts. However, there are certain expenses which are qualified as procedural expenses (*dépens*) and are subject to reimbursement, for example, translation costs or the fees of a *huissier de justice* whose intervention is necessary when the trial is to be introduced by a summons

774. Civ 1, 30 April 2014, nos 13-16380 and 12-22567, commented in Séjean & Knetsch, *ETL 2014 (2015)*, *supra* n. 180, at paras 27–34.

775. *See* e.g. Jean-Sébastien Borghetti, *Réparation de la perte de chance: la Cour de cassation pose l'exigence du caractère raisonnable de la chance perdue*, JCP G 2014, no. 28, 1381.

776. Civ 1, 12 October 2016, no. 15-23230, commented in Knetsch & Jacquemin, *ETL 2016 (2017)*, *supra* n. 45, at paras 31–37. On the whole case law development, *see* the comprehensive survey by Vitale, *supra* n. 760, at paras 492–573.

777. In recent personal injury cases, the Court of Cassation has decided that private expert fees could also be a recoverable loss under the item 'various charges' (*frais divers*) of the *nomenclature Dintilhac*. *See,* for example, Crim, 15 January 2019, no. 17-86254.

778. Courts may appoint an independent expert, either at the request of a party or on their own initiative.

779. For more details, *see* Isabelle Tinel, *Annex 32: Country Report France*, in *Study on the Transparency of Costs of Civil Judicial Proceedings in the European Union* (European Commission ed., 2008) 63–71. Claimants in financial need (who are awarded free legal aid [*aide juridictionnelle*]) do not have to advance those expenses. According to Art. 40 of the Law of 10 July 1991, 'the expenses for measures of investigation are advanced by the State'. On the French legal aid system, *see* Audrey Guinchard & Simon Wesley, *The French Approach to Justice*, in *Access to Justice: Beyond the Policies and Politics of Austerity* (Ellie Palmer, Tom Cornford, Audrey Guinchard & Yseult Marique eds, Bloomsbury 2016) 259, 270–279.

served on the defendant.[780] Honoraria of lawyers are freely negotiated and, in principle, to be set in a written agreement on fees (*convention d'honoraires*).[781] This agreement can fix the fees as a lump sum or an hourly rate. Contingency fees are very common in personal injury cases, but statutory provisions only allow them as a supplement to an hourly rate fee or a lump sum.[782] One of the peculiar features of the French system is that the winning party will not be entitled to full reimbursement of honoraria paid to his counsel. Instead, according to Article 700 of the Civil Procedure Code, the court will fix a lump sum which is deemed to compensate all non-reimbursable expenses (*frais irrépétibles*), including lawyer fees.[783] In practice, it is very common that the amount under Article 700 CPC does not even approximatively cover the expenses of the claimant.[784]

§8. Mitigation of Damages

308. Under current French tort law, there is no formal duty for claimants to mitigate their losses. The rejection of such a duty is based on the principle of full compensation (*réparation intégrale*), which is traditionally seen by French tort lawyers as a non-derogable dogma with even constitutional significance. However, the courts have not always been entirely reluctant to take into account the claimant's failure to mitigate. In the past, the Court of Cassation has decided on several occasions that the right to seek compensation could be restricted if the claimant's attitude could be qualified as contributory fault (*faute contributive*). In other cases, the courts have reduced compensation on the grounds that the claimant's passivity towards accruing losses was seen as a break in the causal chain. In 2003, however, the Second Civil Chamber of the Court of Cassation issued two landmark decisions in which it upheld the principle of *réparation intégrale*, awarding full compensation to a car accident victim who refused to undergo psychological treatment which could have improved her condition and to the manager of a bakery who, during his recovery, refused to instal a temporary manager.[785]

---

780. Whether a summons is necessary or not depends on the value of the case. Up to EUR 5,000, the trial can also be commenced upon a request (*requête*) filed to the registry of the court. On 1 January 2020, a comprehensive reform on civil and commercial litigation procedures entered into force. On this reform, *see* in English Tim Portwood, *France*, in *Dispute Resolution Review* (Dennis Taylor ed., The Law Reviews 12th ed. 2020) 130, 131–139.
781. Art. 10(3) of the Act of 31 December 1971. A written agreement is not mandatory in emergency or force majeure situations.
782. In practice, it is very common that personal injury lawyers are entitled to an additional fee of 10 to 20%, calculated on the damages awarded to the claimant.
783. For more details, *see* in English Yvon Desdevises & Anne-Laure Villedieu, *France*, in *The Costs and Funding of Civil Litigation: A Comparative Perspective* (Christopher Hodges, Stefan Vogenauer & Magdalena Tulbiacka eds, Hart 2010), 327, 342–344. *See* also Werner Pfennigstorf, *The European Experience with Attorney Fee Shifting*, 47 Law and Contemporary Problems 37, 56–57 (1984).
784. This might explain why the compensation of non-pecuniary loss has massively expanded over the last thirty years, even in commercial cases. *See* para. 294 above.
785. Civ 2, 19 June 2003, nos 00-22302 and 01-13289. *See* also Civ 1, 2 July 2014, no. 13-17599, commented in Séjean & Knetsch, *ETL 2014 (2015)*, *supra* n. 180, at paras 35–39.

309. This strong stand of the French courts raises concerns among tort law scholars and practitioners. More and more voices are calling for a statutory implementation of a duty to mitigate losses, arguing that the French solution is unique in Europe and that there are economic, moral and social justifications for embracing a duty to mitigate.[786] Accordingly, the 2017 Reform Draft suggests to put an end to this *exception française*, as Article 1263 provides that 'except in the case of personal injuries, damages are reduced where the victim did not take safe and reasonable measures, notably having regard to his ability to pay, appropriate to avoid the worsening of his own loss'.

786. *See,* for example, Stephan Reifegerste, *Pour une obligation de minimiser le dommage* (PUAM 2002); Dominique Gency-Tandonnet, *L'obligation de modérer le dommage dans la responsabilité extracontractuelle*, Gaz Pal 2004, 1485 and, more recently, Jean-Baptiste Racine, *L'obligation de minimiser le préjudice subi : propos sur une norme modèle*, in *Mélanges en l'honneur du professeur Claude Witz* (LexisNexis 2018) 725.

Chapter 3. Assessment and Compensation of Damages

§1. Objective/Abstract Versus Subjective/Concrete

310. Under French tort law, damage has to be assessed individually according to the principle of full compensation, which means that the compensation awarded has to recover in total the particular loss invoked by the claimant. It is unusual to present the methods of assessing damage in terms of an objective/subjective or abstract/concrete approach, even though some tort law scholars refer to the doctrine of *appréciation in concreto* as an important rule derived from the principle of full compensation.[787] The Court of Cassation regularly reminds the lower courts that a loss has to be assessed 'in a concrete way',[788] which means that it has to be done 'on the basis of the circumstances of the case'.[789] However, as in other jurisdictions, the methods of assessment are in fact a combination of objective and subjective aspects which are difficult to differentiate in practice. Both pecuniary and non-pecuniary losses are estimated according to abstract and concrete elements, and the relative weight of both categories largely depends on the nature of the harm.

311. The distinction between objective/abstract and subjective/concrete methods of assessment is particularly important in cases of damage to property (*dommage matériel*). As will be seen, the case law is dominated by an objective approach because destruction or damage to property gives rise to monetary compensation calculated in such a way as to repair the damage or to replace the property with an equivalent item.[790] This method could be qualified as an objective one since the courts have to determine the cost of replacement regardless of personal elements related to the claimant. The same objective approach is applied when it comes to the assessment of the lost use of property (*préjudice de jouissance*), especially in cases of damage to vehicles or to real estate. In spite of this being a non-pecuniary loss, the courts will make a calculation using standard rates, for example, the market rental values of comparable items. Only in exceptional circumstances will French courts take into account the personal, subjective value of property, for example, in cases in which a damaged and irreplaceable item had a specific sentimental value for the claimant.[791]

312. In cases of personal injury and infringement of other personality rights, the assessment of damages can be qualified as a more subjective one. The principle of full compensation is often understood as imposing on judges the duty to personalize the amount of damages and to take into account the actual and future implications of the harm. However, courts and insurance companies will rely on the reports of medical experts for the calculation of damages for pecuniary loss who often tend

787. *See,* in particular, the reference work of Dejean de la Bâtie, *supra* n. 137, at paras 337–413. *See* also Philippe Casson, *Dommages et intérêts*, in *Répertoire de droit civil* (Dalloz 2017) para. 16.
788. Com, 9 July 1996, no. 94-16829.
789. Civ 3, 23 October 2002, no. 00-22112.
790. *See* paras 341–344 below.
791. *See* para. 294 above.

to translate the different aspects of impairment in standard terms, sometimes indicating the seriousness of bodily injury on a numeric scale. The assessment of damages for non-pecuniary losses leaves more room for a personalized approach, in particular in cases of the infringement of personality rights, such as the right to privacy. However, the widespread use of ranges (*fourchettes*) indicated by the handbook on monetary assessment (*référentiel d'indemnisation*) introduces more and more objective and abstract elements into this field.[792]

§2. METHODS OF ASSESSING DAMAGES

313. Generally speaking, the assessment of damages is based upon actuary evidence brought by the claimant because the general principles of civil procedure place the burden of proof on the claimant. Traditionally, there were no specific guidelines applicable to the process of assessing damages and the lower courts enjoyed broad discretion (*appréciation souveraine des juges du fond*) to choose the adequate means of redress and, in the case of monetary compensation, to calculate the amount of damages. The role of the Court of Cassation was only to review the grounds (*motivation*) given by the trial courts to justify their assessment.[793]

314. Despite the doctrine of 'sovereign appreciation' recognized by the lower courts, the assessment of damages over the past 25 years has undergone fundamental changes towards greater transparency and equality of treatment, especially in the field of personal injury litigation. In 2006, an important reform of the rules on the deductibility of collateral benefits (*imputation des prestations des tiers payeurs*) imposed on the trial courts the duty to breakdown the general amount of damages for pecuniary loss by different items of loss. This reform entrenched the use of the *nomenclature Dintilhac*, a list of recoverable losses elaborated by a working group led by then Court of Cassation judge Jean-Pierre Dintilhac.[794] Although this tool does not yet have any official legal status,[795] it is now widely used by judicial and administrative courts, insurance companies and compensation funds.

792. *See* paras 334–336, 338, 340 below.

793. On the doctrine of *appréciation souveraine* and the role of the Court of Cassation, *see*, e.g., le Tourneau (ed.), *Droit de la responsabilité*, *supra* n. 54, at paras 2321.10–2321.72. More specifically on the review of the grounds given by trial courts, *see* Viney, Jourdain & Carval, *Effets*, *supra* n. 129, at paras 129–130.

794. Jean-Pierre Dintilhac, *Rapport du groupe de travail chargé d'élaborer une nomenclature des préjudices corporels* (2005). The report is available on the website of the French Ministry of Justice: http://www.ladocumentationfrancaise.fr/rapports-publics/064000217-rapport-du-groupe-de-travail-charge-d-elaborer-une-nomenclature-des-prejudices. *See* also Denise Amram, *Identifying and Calculating Personal Injury Damages in Ireland, Italy, France and Belgium: Recent Debates between Scholars, Judges and Practitioners*, in *Damages and Compensation Culture: Comparative Perspectives* (Eoin Quill & Raymond J. Friel eds, Hart 2016) 113, 114–116.

795. The 2017 Draft Reform suggests to officialise the *nomenclature* and the principle of an assessment 'item by item' (*poste par poste*). Art. 1269 of the Draft provides that 'patrimonial and extrapatrimonial losses resulting from personal injury shall be determined item by item following a non-exclusive terminology of items of loss fixed by decree'. On this point, *see* Leczykiewicz, *supra* n. 701, at 200.

315. In addition, the courts of appeal have elaborated a comprehensive handbook on the monetary assessment of damages in personal injury cases. This *référentiel d'indemnisation*, updated on a biannual basis, offers practical guidance for the assessment of all compensable items of loss, both pecuniary and non-pecuniary. Along with specific advice on the calculation of loss of income (*pertes de revenus professionnels*), medical expenses (*dépenses de santé*) and nursing costs (*assistance par tierce personne*), the handbook provides guidance brackets for the determination of non-pecuniary loss. As for now, the *référentiel* is used on an informal basis as it was elaborated without any official letter of assignment. As for the *nomenclature*, the 2017 Draft Reform calls for a formalization of this 'compensation index',[796] which has greatly contributed to the harmonization of assessment practices throughout France.

316. Even though they are still at very initial stages, similar harmonization efforts are being made for the assessment of economic and environmental loss.[797] In 2017, the Paris Court of Appeal published a series of practical worksheets (*fiches méthodologiques*) on the assessment of different kinds of economic losses, for example, in cases of anti-competitive practices, unfair competition or abrupt termination of a long-standing business relationship (*rupture abusive des relations commerciales établies*), subject to specific liability provisions in the Commercial Code.[798] These worksheets are intended to rationalize court practices through concrete calculation methods which possibly prefigure future *nomenclature* and *référentiel* in the field of commercial litigation.[799]

317. As for the assessment of environmental loss (*préjudice écologique*), an academic initiative has to be mentioned. In 2012, a working group of French tort and environmental law experts presented a *nomenclature des préjudices environnementaux* which was designed to accompany the emerging case law on the compensation

796. Art. 1271 of the Draft provides that 'a decree ... shall set the items of extrapatrimonial losses which can be assessed according to an indicative compensation index, whose manner of elaboration and publication it shall decide. This index shall be revalued every three years as a function of developments in the average of compensation awards made by the courts'.

797. On the *nomenclature* technique, *see*, in particular, the recent work by Émeline Augier-Francia, *Les nomenclatures de préjudices en droit de la responsabilité civile* (thesis Lyon 3, 2020).

798. As for the abrupt termination of a long-standing business relationship, Art. L 442-6, I of the Commercial Code provides that 'any producer, trader, manufacturer or person registered in the trades register shall be liable for, and obliged to compensate for the harm resulting from, any act which: ... 5. abruptly terminates an established business relationship wholly or in part without prior written notice that takes account of the duration of the business relationship and is in accordance with the minimum notice period as determined, with regard to standard commercial practices, by inter-industry agreements'.

799. Paris Court of Appeal, *Réparation du préjudice économique* (2017). The worksheets are available on the Internet: https://www.cours-appel.justice.fr/paris/la-reparation-du-prejudice-economique-octobre-2017.

of environmental harm.[800] In their book, the authors tried to identify a series of compensable items of loss based on the example of the *nomenclature* elaborated for personal injury cases. For now, this *nomenclature* has not been widely adopted by French courts[801] and is not referred to in the 2017 Draft Reform.[802]

318. On the contrary, damages for injury to personality rights (privacy, image, honour) are still widely assessed 'at large' (*tous chefs de préjudices confondus*) as a single lump sum for all non-pecuniary effects of the harm. Very little guidance is given to the courts other than to assess the harm on an individual basis, taking into account all circumstances of the case.

§3. Equitable Limitation of Damages

319. There is no specific provision in the Civil Code for equitable limitation of damages, and the Court of Cassation has always rejected the idea of reducing damages on the sole ground that they would lead to an unreasonable burden given the economic position of the tortfeasor.[803] The idea of an adjustment in monetary compensation due to 'budgetary constraints', expressed in the 1970s by Marie-Ève Roujou de Boubée,[804] did not gain acceptance among tort law scholars and civil or administrative courts.[805] It may be assumed that the generalization of health insurance coverage and the expansion of private liability insurance at a reasonable cost to society did not create a need to depart from the principle of full compensation and for the introduction of elements of equity into the law of damages.

320. However, there are some cases in which French courts seem to take into account the financial situation of the tortfeasor in order to reduce (or increase) the burden of compensation, despite not saying so. As has been said,[806] in cases of injuries to personality rights, the courts assess damages on the basis of several indices that are not necessarily linked to the claimant's harm, such as the gravity of fault, the profit made through the infringement and the economic situation of the defendant.[807]

321. Another illustration of an equitable limitation of liability can be identified in the field of recourse actions. In many tort law cases, the compensation of the

800. Laurent Neyret & Gilles Martin, *Nomenclature des préjudices environnementaux* (LGDJ 2012).
801. *See,* however, CA Nouméa, 25 February 2014, no. 11/00187. The limited success of this tool can be attributed to the fact that it was elaborated at too early a stage of environmental liability. *See* Augier-Francia, *supra* n. 797, at paras 194–195.
802. The legislator did not take up the proposal of a working group led by professor Yves Jégouzo. In its final report, the group suggested that 'for the purposes of establishing the various heads of damage …, reference shall be made to the nomenclature laid down by decree'. *See* Yves Jégouzo (ed.), *Pour la réparation du préjudice écologique* (2013) 18–19.
803. Civ 2, 21 July 1982, no. 81-15236.
804. Marie-Ève Roujou de Boubée, *Essai sur la notion de réparation* (LGDJ 1974) 399–417.
805. Viney, Jourdain & Carval, *Effets*, *supra* n. 129, at no. 118 (with further references).
806. *See* para. 47 above.
807. *See* the references cited by Lepage, *supra* n. 57, at paras 253–274.

claimant will imply so-called third party payers (*tiers payeurs*), for example, health insurance funds or private insurance companies, and it is only through recourse after subrogation that the tortfeasor will be held liable on the grounds of civil liability. However, it is an open secret that some *tiers payeurs* are reluctant to pursue the full recovery of damages in case the tortfeasor's financial situation is too fragile to bear the total burden of liability. In such cases, third-party payers tend to prefer out-of-court settlements to the extent of what is economically viable for the tortfeasor.[808]

§4. METHODS OF PAYMENT (LUMP SUM AND ANNUITIES)

322. It is often stated that the courts have the option of awarding a lump sum (*somme en capital*) or periodic payments (*rente*).[809] In practice, the wide discretion of the trial courts is limited to personal injury litigation and to cases in which the harmful consequences extend to the future, for example, in nuisance cases or for the compensation of environmental harm. In simple cases of harm to property, the award of a lump sum is the only viable solution as it would not occur to anyone to claim annuities for the loss of a destroyed vehicle or a collapsed building which needs to be rebuilt. It is common practice, however, that tort law damages are divided into a lump sum embracing all definitive losses and periodic payments for all continuing losses.

323. In cases in which the question of '*capital* v *rente*' arises, it has been reported that claimants tend to once-off lump sum awards despite the economic risk of misallocation.[810] Courts are not, however, bound by the claimant's choice and may decide to award a *rente* instead of a *capital* in light of the socio-economic situation of the claimant.[811] In this case, however, courts offer the claimant the possibility to turn the periodic payment into a lump sum through application of annuity tables (*barèmes de capitalisation*). In any case, Article 44 of the *loi Badinter* of 1985 provides for the right of any personal injury victim to convert due annuities into a lump sum 'if changes in his personal circumstances so justify'.

808. On the 'recourse policy' of health insurance funds, *see* Hélène Pélosse & Vincent Ruol, *Revue de dépenses. Le recours contre tiers des caisses de sécurité sociale* (La Documentation française 2017). The document is available on the Internet https://www.ladocumentationfrancaise.fr/var/storage/rapports-publics/174000833.pdf.

809. *See*, e.g., Brun, *Responsabilité*, *supra* n. 147, at para. 621; le Tourneau (ed.), *Droit de la responsabilité*, *supra* n. 54, at para. 2312.71. For a presentation of this issue in English, *see* Michel Cannarsa, *Personal Injury in France*, in *Personal Injury Compensation in Europe* (Marco Bona & Philip Mead eds, Kluwer International 2003) 169, 197–198.

810. *See* already Samuel A. Rea, *Lump-Sum Versus Periodic Damage Awards*, 10 Journal of Legal Studies 131 (1981). *See* also more recently Daniel Gardner, *La dilapidation des indemnités: plaidoyer pour une utilisation étendue de la rente*, in *Des spécificités de l'indemnisation du dommage corporel* (Philippe Brun, Laurence Clerc-Renaud & Christophe Quézel-Ambrunaz eds, Larcier 2017) 427 (with further references to surveys made in the US and Canada). One of the reasons why claimants (and their lawyers) prefer a lump sum is the fear of under-compensation due to underestimated growth in earnings.

811. Crim, 19 June 1996, no. 95-82631; 3 November 2009, no. 09-81321.

324. In detail, the range of judicial discretion and the methods used for the conversion of annuities into lump sums are highly controversial.[812] The 2017 Draft Reform suggests a proper legal framework by formalising an official annuity table and enacting the rule according to which damages for loss of income and nursing costs in personal injury cases are awarded, in principle, as periodic payments. According to Article 1272(2) of this draft, the claimant would be eligible for lump sum awards only for those items 'with the agreement of all parties' involved or 'by a specifically motivated decision' of the court.

812. In particular, the concurrent existence of different annuity tables is criticized. For a comparative survey, *see* Jean-Marc Houisse & François Blanchet, *Dommage corporel: De la pluralité des barèmes de capitalisation vers un barème officiel?*, RGDA 2020, no. 2, 7–12. *See* also for a comprehensive presentation, Viney, Jourdain & Carval, *Effets*, *supra* n. 129, at paras 139–140.

Chapter 4. Personal Injury and Death

325. As in other jurisdictions, the assessment of damages related to personal injury is preceded by a medical evaluation conducted by a medico-legal expert. This phase of ascertainment may take place upon the initiative of the victim's lawyer in order to 'build' the victim's case or at a preliminary stage of an out-of-court settlement.[813] The appointment of a medical expert can also be requested from a court, which is frequent in cases in which the parties could not reach an agreement. In principle, the court orders the claimant to advance the expenses by depositing a specified amount with the court registry.[814] Eventually, they are borne by the losing party.[815]

326. Whether conducted by a party-appointed or a judge-appointed expert,[816] the examination follows a 'letter of instruction' (*mission d'expertise*) chosen by the parties or by the judge[817] and leads to the drafting of the expert's report. In general, the report contains the following items: identity of the expert and the victim, reminder of the 'letter of instruction', description of the victim's statements (*dires de la victime*), findings of the medical examination, medical and forensic analysis and conclusions.[818]

327. Based upon the expert's report, the legal assessment of the damages subsequent to personal injury will be conducted by the court or, in case of an out-of-court settlement, by the involved parties and possibly an insurance company. Since 2006, the methods of assessment have been directly derived from the *nomenclature Dintilhac*,[819] which lists the recoverable items of loss by distinguishing between direct and indirect victims and pecuniary and non-pecuniary losses. Even though it

813. In this latter case, the medical examination is conducted by an expert appointed with the consent of all parties involved (claimant, insurer, tortfeasor). French tort lawyers speak of an *expertise amiable et contradictoire*.

814. Claimants in financial need who are awarded free legal aid (*aide juridictionnelle*) do not have to advance those expenses. According to Art. 40 of the Law of 10 July 1991, 'the expenses for measures of investigation are advanced by the State'. *See* para. 306 above.

815. *Ibid.*

816. Judge-appointed experts (*experts judiciaires*) have to meet standards of neutrality and independence. Before inclusion in the register of approved experts, they have to take an oath to fulfil their mission upon their honour and conscience. They are subject to disciplinary authority exercised by the court of appeal, according to Art. 6-2 of the Law no. 71-498 of 29 June 1971. *See* in English Romain Juston Morival & Jérôme Pélisse, *The Scalpel, the Calculator and the Judge in France: From Technical Perspective to Legal Evidence*, 16 International Journal of Law in Context 353 (2020).

817. There are different pre-drafted 'letters of instruction' used by courts, insurance companies and personal injury lawyers. The most widely used is the *mission d'expertise* drafted by the *Association pour l'étude de la réparation du dommage corporel* (https://www.aredoc.com/wp-content/uploads/2017/08/Preambule-et-mission.pdf).

818. For a comprehensive survey of this stage, *see* Lambert-Faivre & Porchy-Simon, *supra* n. 696, at paras 61–154. *See* also in English Eric Baccino & Jean-Sébastien Raul, *Methods of Ascertainment of Personal Damage in France*, in *Personal Injury and Damage Ascertainment under Civil Law* (Santo Davide Ferrara, Rafael Boscolo-Berto & Guido Viel eds, Springer 2016) 101, 103–109.

819. On the *nomenclature*, *see* para. 314 above.

still lacks an official status and notwithstanding some inconsistencies, the *nomenclature* has been an important factor in rationalising and harmonising the French law of damages.[820]

§1. Direct Victims

328. For both pecuniary and non-pecuniary losses of the direct victim, the typology of recoverable items arising from the *nomenclature Dintilhac* is based on the fundamental distinction between temporary and permanent losses. When assessing a compensation claim related to personal injury, a court (or the parties involved) have to draw a line between both categories according to the date of *consolidation*. The 'consolidation' of bodily injury refers to the moment when the claimant's physical condition does not evolve anymore, either because of a full recovery or because the after-effects of the injury are stabilized and no further medical treatment is needed other than to prevent aggravation.[821] Accordingly, personal injury cases always give rise to the compensation of temporary losses, whereas permanent losses are compensated only in cases in which a full recovery is not possible. Sometimes, *consolidation* will only take place several years after the initial injury, for example, in cases in which the direct victim is a young child, delaying the final settlement of the claim to early adulthood.[822] For chronic diseases which are progressive by their nature (such as Hepatitis or AIDS), the *nomenclature* provides for a specific item of non-pecuniary loss '*hors consolidation*'.[823]

I. Pecuniary Losses

329. Medical expenses (*dépenses de santé*) are one of the most important items of loss in personal injury cases. Given that every citizen living in France is given health insurance coverage, the assessment of this item is subject to the statement of expenses by the claimant's local health insurance fund (*caisse d'assurance maladie*).[824] As the French social security system does not cover all medical and paramedical expenses, the award for *dépenses de santé* is often split into three parts: the major part goes to the local health insurance fund, another part to a supplementary

820. For a comprehensive critical assessment of the *nomenclature Dintilhac*, *see* the recent work by Augier-Francia, *supra* n. 797, at paras 274–326.

821. On the concept of *consolidation*, *see* e.g. Lambert-Faivre & Porchy-Simon, *supra* n. 696, at paras 117–121.

822. It is very common that provisional damages are in the meantime awarded by courts or insurance companies.

823. On this controversial item, *see* e.g. Lambert-Faivre & Porchy-Simon, *supra* n. 696, at paras 222–230.

824. For a presentation of the French Social security system in English, *see* Victor G. Rodwin, *The Health Care System under French National Health Insurance: Lessons for Health Reform in the United States*, 93 American Journal of Public Health 31–37 (2003); Simone Sandier, Valérie Paris & Dominique Polton, *Health Care Systems in Transition: France* (WHO 2004).

health care insurer[825] and a final one to the victim for all expenses that are not covered by either the general health insurance fund or the supplementary health care insurer.

330. The calculation is more complicated for the assessment of loss of income (*pertes de gains professionnels*), especially for individuals with a permanent work incapacity, whether total or partial. In those cases, it has to take into account the likely evolution of the claimant's career. The calculation of the future loss of income of self-employed workers is based on a projection of their revenue, which is often purely hypothetical. As for unemployed claimants, the courts take into account re-employment prospects based on the average salary level that the claimant could expect from a new professional position.

331. Along with medical expenses and loss of income, nursing costs (*assistance par tierce personne*) for permanently impaired victims represent the most significant item of loss as they often reach more than a million euros, especially for children or young adults with severe bodily injury. Personal injury lawyers often ask the medical expert to perform an assessment of both individual medical and socio-professional needs.

332. It is well established in case law that the claimant can choose between the services of an employed caregiver or a contract with a caregiver agency. The calculation method will depend on the claimant's choice, as the hourly rate is not the same due to employer contributions and will also take into account regional discrepancies.[826] In addition to that, the Court of Cassation has decided that there shall not be any reduction in damages if one of the family members assumes the role of caregiver.[827] In that case, the loss of income of this family member is supposed to be compensated by the damages awarded under the *assistance par tierce personne* item.[828]

333. Several other items of pecuniary loss are listed in the *nomenclature*. The claimant is entitled to the compensation of expenses related to car and housing

825. Since January 2016, all private employers (irrespective of the size of their businesses) are required to offer private complementary health insurance to their employees. For a presentation in English, *see* Carine Franc & Aurélie Pierre, *Compulsory Private Complementary Health Insurance Offered by Employers in France: Implications and Current Debate*, 119 Health Policy 111–116 (2015).

826. For a calculation example, *see* Gisèle Mor & Laurence Clerc-Renaud, *Réparation du préjudice corporel* (Delmas 3d ed. 2020) para. 153.59.

827. *See* the recent decision Civ 2, 14 April 2016, no. 15-16697.

828. On this thorny issue, *see* Mireille Bacache, *Réparation des préjudices professionnels des proches : quels obstacles?*, Gaz. Pal. 27 Januar 2020, 34–37.

adjustments,[829] of work-related incidences of the injury other than the loss of income,[830] of a so-called schooling and academic prejudice[831] and of other 'various expenses' (*frais divers*).[832]

II. Non-pecuniary Losses

334. As has been said, the monetary compensation of non-pecuniary loss is of particular importance, as the French law of damages distinguishes a variety of heads of damages in personal injury cases.[833] Non-pecuniary loss is not understood as a single item of compensation but as a general term for a large number of categories in which the victim's suffering is split up. This trend of disaggregating *préjudice moral* has for long been the apanage of civil courts,[834] as the *Conseil d'État* refused to give up the broader concept of *troubles dans les conditions d'existence* ('disturbance of living conditions'), which was supposed to embrace any facet of the victim's suffering. However, over the past 10 years, administrative courts have begun to assess the non-pecuniary losses of the claimant according to the items laid out by the *nomenclature Dintilhac.*

335. As for pecuniary losses, the *nomenclature* distinguishes between temporary and permanent 'disturbances'. However, the typology is not entirely symmetric since some items which are distinct in the category of permanent losses are merged for the period before the consolidation of the claimant's health condition. Inversely, the item of 'pain and suffering' (*souffrances endurées*), which is a distinct loss on the side of temporary losses, is not on the list of permanent 'disturbances'. Over the last years, this asymmetry of the *nomenclature* has raised criticism among tort law experts as it impedes the detailed assessment of non-pecuniary losses for each of the two periods, that is, before and after consolidation.[835] One might argue, however, that the choices made by the *Dintilhac* working group are a significant (if not the last) bulwark against an excessively fragmented vision of non-pecuniary loss.

829. According to recent case law, it is perfectly possible for the claimant to argue that the purchase of a ground floor apartment or a detached house is necessary to guarantee decent living conditions, even though the claimant was a tenant of a modest apartment before the accident.
830. This includes the claimant's loss of value on the employment market, the loss of retirement income and even the loss of job satisfaction.
831. This item compensates the 'loss of time' (*perte de temps*) due to the repetition of a school or academic year as well as any difficulties the claimant might encounter to find the first job.
832. This includes, for example, travel expenses for medical examinations and temporary childcare expenses.
833. *See* paras 291–292 above.
834. For a critical assessment of this trend, *see* Knetsch, *Désintégration*, *supra* n. 737 and the response by Olivier Gout & Stéphanie Porchy-Simon, *Plaidoyer pour la défense des nomenclatures dans le droit du dommage corporel*, D 2015, 1499.
835. For a recent comprehensive survey, *see* Augier-Francia, *supra* n. 797, at paras 466–484. *See* also in English Amram, *supra* n. 794, at 115.

336. Along with the item of 'pain and suffering' (*souffrances endurées*), which is assessed according to a scale of severity from 0.5 to 7 and calculated on a standardized basis, the *nomenclature* also lists the following items:[836] 'functional impairment' (*déficit fonctionnel*),[837] 'loss of enjoyment of life' (*préjudice d'agrément*),[838] sexual impairment (*préjudice sexuel*),[839] 'aesthetic harm' (*préjudice esthétique*),[840] 'loss of the perspective of a family life' (*préjudice d'établissement*)[841] and so-called permanent exceptional losses (*préjudices permanents exceptionnels*).[842]

836. For a more detailed presentation in English, *see* Stathis Banakas, *Non-Pecuniary Loss in Personal Injury: Topography Architecture and Nomenclature in the European Landscape*, 10 Journal of Comparative Law 291, 323–328 (2015). *See* also in French Mor & Clerc-Renaud, *supra* n. 826, at Ch. 154–155 (with further references and detailed calculation examples).

837. The 'temporary functional impairment' (*déficit fonctionnel temporaire*) embraces the loss of enjoyment of life, sexual impairment and 'loss of enjoyment of life' during the period before consolidation. 'Permanent functional impairment' (*déficit fonctionnel permanent*) corresponds to the general impact of the sequalae on the victim's personal life. Both are assessed *au point*, with each point's value being proportionate to the degree of the impairment and the claimant's age. Damages for *déficit fonctionnel permanent* can reach EUR 90,000. For more details, *see*, e.g., Mor & Clerc-Renaud, *supra* n. 826, at paras 154.21–154.43 and 155.11–155.38.

838. This item is used in a very specific sense as *préjudice d'agrément* is only related to the loss of a specific leisure or sports activity. In the case of children, the impossibility of engaging in a specific activity is enough to claim damages for *préjudice d'agrément*. The limits of this item are still unclear as trial courts tend to award damages even in cases in which claimants invoke rather trivial leisure activities, such as shopping or going out with friends. According to case law, damages for this item can reach EUR 40,000.

839. According to the *nomenclature Dintilhac*, this item embraces three different dimensions of sexual impairment: the injury to the sexual organs (*préjudice sexuel morphologique*), the loss of enjoyment of sexual intercourse (*perte d'envie et de plaisir*) and the impossibility or difficulty to procreate (*préjudice lié à la procréation*). A recent statistical survey has shown that the courts tend to award higher damages to male claimants (EUR 12,000 in average) than to female claimants (EUR 8,500 in average). *See* Mor & Clerc-Renaud, *supra* n. 826, at para. 155.44.

840. Evaluated by medical experts on a scale from 1 to 7, *préjudice esthétique* is assessed on the basis of various elements specific to the claimant: sex, age, family situation, profession. The *référentiel d'indemnisation* suggests damages within a range from EUR 1,000 to more than EUR 80,000 (in cases with extreme disfiguration).

841. Even though there is a risk that this item overlaps with sexual impairment, the Court of Cassation agrees on awarding a specific amount for the loss of the inability to find a partner and to start a family life, especially in cases of children or young adults. Damages for this item range from EUR 5,000 to 50,000.

842. Designed as a residual item of non-pecuniary loss, 'permanent exceptional losses' have been recognized by the lower courts only in very few cases. The *nomenclature Dintilhac* gives the example of a Japanese person unable to perform the traditional bowing. The legal doctrine suggests that the different forms of 'prejudice of anxiety' (*préjudice d'anxiété* or *préjudice d'angoisse*) could be recognized under this category, as well as the specific psychological impact of mass accidents or terror attacks.

§2. INDIRECT VICTIMS (*VICTIMES PAR RICOCHET*)

I. In Case of Death

337. In case the direct victim dies, family members are entitled to damages for the losses of the deceased acquired by inheritance as well as for their own pecuniary losses. Along with funeral expenses (*frais d'obsèques*), this concerns mainly the loss of dependency (*pertes de revenus de proches*) for the spouse and children (if there are any). The monetary assessment of this item implies an exact calculation of the loss of income caused by the death of the direct victim. In practice, French courts compare the total income of the household before and after the tortious act and award compensation of the difference to the family members less a share corresponding to the expenses the deceased would have made for him or herself.[843]

338. As for non-pecuniary losses, the *nomenclature Dintilhac* lists damages for bereavement (*préjudice d'affection*) calculated on the basis of ranges for each family member[844] and the so-called *préjudice d'accompagnement* corresponding to the personal impact on family members of the end-of-life support.[845] It is notable that for the assessment of bereavement damages for the spouse, children and parents, courts do not require any proof of a close relationship with the deceased. However, for siblings, grandparents and grandchildren, the range is different depending on the proximity with the deceased.

II. In Case of Serious Personal Injury

339. In cases in which the direct victim survives, family members can only claim compensation if the injury had a personal impact on their situation, which mostly concerns cases of serious personal injury. If so, the *nomenclature Dintilhac* provides for compensation of loss of dependency (*perte de revenus de proches*), subject to the deduction of the direct victim's damages for loss of income. In case the impairment of the direct victim causes one of his relatives a professional incidence (e.g., a spouse giving up a job to assume the role of a caretaker), compensation can be awarded if, under the item of nursing costs (*assistance par tierce personne*), damages do not cover the caretaker's loss of income in total.[846] As for the non-pecuniary loss in case of death, the *nomenclature* lists a *préjudice d'affection* corresponding to the distress related to the sight of the suffering of the

843. According to the *référentiel d'indemnisation*, this share ranges from 15% for a couple with children up to 40% for a childless couple. *See* Benoît Mornet, *L'indemnisation des préjudices en cas de blessures ou de décès* (2020) 88–92. For a detailed calculation example, *see* Mor & Clerc-Renaud, *supra* n. 826, at para. 162.104.

844. For example, the range for bereavement damages awarded to the spouse of the deceased is from EUR 20,000 to 30,000. The same range applies to parents who lost their child.

845. Damages for this item range from EUR 300 to 500 per month. For more details, *see* Mor & Clerc-Renaud, *supra* n. 826, at paras 163.41–163.51.

846. *See* para. 331 above.

direct victim[847] and an 'exceptional non-pecuniary loss' (*préjudice extrapatrimonial exceptionnel*) which is recognized in cases in which the direct victim's health condition caused a significant disruption to the living conditions of family members.[848]

340. There is a trend in recent case law to award compensation for non-pecuniary loss even in cases of light personal injury to the direct victim and to duplicate the different items recognized under the *nomenclature* for direct victims. Accordingly, personal injury lawyers tend to claim compensation for an 'indirect sexual impairment' (*préjudice sexuel par ricochet*) or the loss of a specific leisure activity which a spouse or a child carried out with their disabled husband or father (*préjudice d'agrément par ricochet*).

847. There seems to be no specific calculation method for this item. *See* Mor & Clerc-Renaud, *supra* n. 826, at para. 163.26.
848. *See* Mor & Clerc-Renaud, *supra* n. 826, at paras 163.61–163.71.

Chapter 5. Various Damages (Property)

341. The calculation methods in case of damage to property (*atteinte aux biens* or *dommage matériel*) are exclusively judge-made and to some degree obscured by the wide discretion awarded to trial courts (*pouvoir souverain d'appréciation des juges du fond*). However, it is possible to formulate two series of assessment rules.

342. In case of destruction of property, it is well established that the claimant can obtain compensation for the replacement value (*valeur de remplacement*), that is, the cost of acquiring property of the same quality and the same price range.[849] The Court of Cassation has made it clear that no discount or factor of depreciation should be applied on the grounds of prior use (*coefficient de vétusté*),[850] which means that the claimant may end up with brand new property even though the destroyed one was dilapidated or obsolete. This apparent infringement of the principle of full compensation is recognized by the legal doctrine in so far as compensation of the replacement cost new (*valeur à neuf*) is regarded as the only solution to repair the harm. Especially in cases of damage to buildings or apartments, the application of a depreciation factor would prevent the claimant from recovering the use of the property.[851] However, in some exceptional cases, the Court of Cassation has found that a former lack of maintenance (*défaut d'entretien*) should be taken into account.[852]

343. In case the property is only deteriorated, the claimant can choose between the cost of replacement and the cost of repair (*coût de reparation*), but the compensation is capped by the lower of the two sums.[853] As for the destruction of property, the assessment does not take into account any depreciation because of prior use nor any possible increase of value due to the replacement or repair.

344. Under French tort law, the claimant can also be awarded damages for the lost use of the property (*préjudice de jouissance*) during its repair or replacement. In case the property was not used for profit (e.g., a private car or a family residence), the courts award damages on the basis of the rental value of a similar property.[854] For property used for profit, damages also embrace the operating loss (*perte d'exploitation*).[855]

---

849. This solution is confirmed in Art. 1278(2) of the 2017 Reform Draft.

850. Civ 2, 23 January 2003, no. 01-00200.

851. For a comprehensive survey of this issue, *see* Viney, Jourdain & Carval, *Effets*, *supra* n. 129, at para. 175. *See* also more recently Yohann Quistrebert, *Les méthodes d'évaluation de l'indemnité allouée en cas de dommages aux biens... trente ans plus tard*, Resp civ assur 2019, dossier 7.

852. Civ 2, 31 May 1989, no. 88-13567. On this solution, *see* Quistrebert, *supra* n. 851, at para. 12.

853. Civ 2, 31 March 1993, no. 91-18691; Crim, 22 September 2009, no. 08-88181. *See* also Art. 1278(1) of the 2017 Reform Draft. The rationale of this solution is 'to avoid wasting financial resources dedicated to the compensation of harm' (Viney, Jourdain & Carval, *Effets*, *supra* n. 129, at para. 170).

854. Le Tourneau (ed.), *Droit de la responsabilité*, *supra* n. 54, at para. 2321.132 (with further references).

855. Viney, Jourdain & Carval, *Effets*, *supra* n. 129, at para. 178.

Chapter 6. Deductibility of Collateral Benefits

§1. General Approach

345. There is no general doctrine of collateral benefits under French law[856] and the Latin phrase *compensatio lucri cum damno* is widely unknown among tort law scholars. The deductibility of (some) collateral benefits is a result of personal subrogation (*subrogation personnelle*). For example, an insurance company will have the insured sign a so-called subrogative receipt when paying a compensatory benefit for damaged property.[857] If so, according to Article 1346-4 Civil Code,[858] the insurer will be entitled to exercise the insured's right to compensation to the extent of the payment. For the victim, subrogation will therefore lead to a reduction or even a total loss of the right to compensation, depending on whether the benefit fully or partially compensates for the harm suffered.

346. The deduction of collateral benefits is much more complicated in personal injury cases in which the issue of interplay between private insurance, social security and tort law is raised.[859] Due to the comprehensive system of social security (*sécurité sociale*) and the generalization of both liability insurance (*assurance de responsabilité*) and supplementary health care insurance (*assurance complémentaire santé*), it is almost certain that the settlement of a personal injury case does not only involve the tortfeasor and the victim but also the local health insurance fund and different insurance companies. In order to straighten out a legal framework that had become unclear and victim-unfriendly over the years,[860] the legislator in 2006 revised the rules on the deduction of collateral benefits.

347. According to the (current) Article 31(1) of the *loi Badinter* (applicable to recourse actions whatever the cause of the personal injury), the subrogation of health insurance funds and insurance companies operates *poste par poste* ('item by item'), which means that third-party payers are allocated only specific parts of the victim's compensation claim and only for compensatory benefits.[861] This is to ensure that the victim can still obtain damages for those losses which were not compensated by social security, such as non-pecuniary loss. Although this restrictive and

856. For an attempt, *see* Jonas Knetsch, *La déduction des avantages nés d'un fait dommageable (*compensatio lucri cum damno*). Esquisse d'une théorie*, in *Mélanges en l'honneur de Suzanne Carval* (IRJS éditions 2021) forthcoming.

857. Even without a subrogative receipt, the insurer is subrogated to the rights of the insured victim according to the general provision of Art. 1346 of the Civil Code and to the more specific Art. L 121-12 of the Insurance Code.

858. This text provides that 'subrogation transfers to its beneficiary, up to the limit of the satisfaction which he has rendered, the right arising from the obligation and its ancillary rights, apart from rights which belong exclusively to the creditor personally'.

859. For a recent collective work on this issue, *see* Jonas Knetsch (ed.), *Quelle prise en charge des dommages corporels au XXIe siècle* (EN3S/Université Jean Monnet Saint-Étienne 2020).

860. For a brief presentation in English of the legal developments before 2006, *see* Leczykiewicz, *supra* n. 701, at 194–196. *See* also Suzanne Carval, *France*, in *The Impact of Social Security Law on Tort Law* (Ulrich Magnus ed., Springer 2003) 74; Cannarsa, *supra* n. 809, at 199–201.

861. For more details, *see* in English Leczykiewicz, *supra* n. 701, at 196–198.

fragmented approach to subrogation is complex and still raises many questions, the 2006 reform had the effect of improving the victim's position before the courts. While social security funds could benefit from the lack of harmonization between tort law and social security law and recover damages on a larger base, the victim is now entitled to a so-called preferential right which allows the victim to take precedence over concurring third-party payers for specific items of loss.[862]

348. It is to be noted that in the field of traffic accidents, a specific agreement was signed in 1983 by the health insurance funds and private insurance companies. According to this so-called *Protocole Bergeras*, the recoupment of healthcare expenses and the costs of other benefits is simplified and operates automatically on a transactional basis.[863] Even though this agreement has accelerated the settlement of personal injury claims, recourse litigation has not been completely ousted since some of the health insurance funds refused to sign the *Protocole,* and in case the involved parties do not agree on the allocation, a specific arbitration panel will settle the dispute.

§2. Different Types of Collateral Benefits

349. Private insurance benefits are only deductible if they are of compensatory nature (*nature indemnitaire*), which is the case when the benefits arise from an insurance contract governed by the indemnity principle.[864] This limitation results from Article L 121-12 Insurance Code which provides that 'the insurer who paid the insurance benefit (*indemnité d'assurance*) shall be subrogated within the limit of such compensation in the insured's rights and actions against the third parties who, by their acts, caused the damage that gave rise to the insurer's liability'. This provision applies to all kinds of property insurance (*assurance de choses*) and will lead to the reduction or the loss of the victim's right to compensation after payment of the benefit. However, the deductibility of insurance benefits is not restricted to property insurance, and French insurance companies have developed over the past 30 years insurance policies with so-called life accident guarantees (*garanties contre les accidents de la vie [GAV]*). Unlike traditional life or health insurance contracts, such policies are subject to the indemnity principle since the insurer shall compensate a victim of personal injury according to the general tort law rules up to a specified limit.[865] Benefits arising from such a hybrid insurance contract are also deductible on the basis of the insurer's subrogation to the insured rights against the tortfeasor.

---

862. Art. 31(2) *loi Badinter*. For more details, *see* Julien Bourdoiseau, *Le droit de la préférence de la victime : entre état des lieux et état des vœux*, Gaz Pal 2017, 734.

863. For a comprehensive survey, *see* Henri Margeat & James Landel, *Le protocole assureurs-organismes sociaux*, Droit social 1984, special issue no. 4 and, more recently, Lambert-Faivre & Porchy-Simon, *supra* n. 696, at para. 350.

864. *See* Lambert-Faivre & Porchy-Simon, *supra* n. 696, at para. 346; Yvonne Lambert-Faivre & Laurent Leveneur, *Droit des assurances* (Dalloz 14th ed. 2017) paras 655–656.

865. On these insurance policies, *see* Sabine Abravanel-Jolly, *Une garantie essentielle dans la prise en charge du dommage corporel : La GAV (Garantie des Accidents de la Vie privée)*, in *Quelle prise*

350. As for benefits under social security law, Article 29 of the *loi Badinter* lists the kind of payments which give rise to a recourse action based on subrogation: benefits paid by all compulsory health insurance funds and by the State and other public bodies (for some civil servants), salary continuance paid by the employer, daily subsistence allowances and disability benefits paid by (mutual or commercial) insurance companies.[866] All of these benefits have to be deducted 'item by item' from the victim's right to compensation. In practice, the allocation of social security benefits to specific items of loss is not always simple, as some benefits are hybrid and embrace more than one item of loss. This is the case, for example, with disability pensions paid under the work accident scheme which compensates the victim's loss of income, the 'professional impact' (*incidence professionnelle*) of his injury and his 'functional impairment' (*déficit fonctionnel*). For the Court of Cassation, these pensions are to be deducted from all three items, while the *Conseil d'État* limits the subrogation to the first two items, leaving untouched the victim's damages for non-pecuniary loss.[867]

351. The situation is even more complex for benefits paid by compensation funds, such as FIVA, ONIAM or FGTI. It is acknowledged that those benefits are not immune to deduction as most compensation funds pay compensation under the indemnity principle. However, until now, there has been no general framework governing the subrogation of compensation funds and the deductibility of benefits. For each compensation scheme, the legislator provides for a specific legal basis of subrogation which is not always identical to the rules governing insurance companies and health insurance funds.[868]

---

en charge des dommages corporels au XXIe siècle (Jonas Knetsch ed., EN3S/Université Jean Monnet Saint-Étienne 2020) 117. *See* also Henri Margeat, *La subrogation en assurances de personnes à caractère indemnitaire*, RGAT 1993, 251.

866. For more details, *see* Viney, Jourdain & Carval, *Effets*, *supra* n. 129, at paras 253–259. *See* also Patrice Jourdain, *Retour sur la pertinence de l'équation subrogation = imputation*, Gaz Pal 2017, 721.

867. Civ. 2, 16 July 2020, no. 19-16042; CE, 8 mars 2013, no. 361273. *See* Lambert-Faivre & Porchy-Simon, *supra* n. 696, at paras 376–378.

868. For a critical assessment, *see* Lambert-Faivre & Porchy-Simon, *supra* n. 696, at para. 329; Viney, Jourdain & Carval, *Effets*, *supra* n. 129, at para. 262.

Chapter 7. Other Remedies

§1. Restitution (for Unjust Enrichment)

352. In the French law of obligations, unjust enrichment (*enrichissement injustifié*) is recognized as an autonomous branch, distinct from civil liability and enclosed within the category of quasi-contracts.[869] The French Civil Code distinguishes three types of quasi-contracts: *negotiorum gestio* referring to the benevolent intervention in another person's affairs (*gestion d'affaires*), recovery of undue payments (*restitution de l'indu*) and unjust enrichment as a subsidiary 'catch-all' provision.[870] A claim for restitution of an *enrichissement injustifié* will thus be outside of the framework of civil liability, even though tort law concepts of *dommage* and *préjudice* are sufficiently wide to integrate some of the cases which are today considered as classical quasi-contractual cases. During the preparation of the 2016 reform of the law of obligations and the future reform of tort law, too little time and energy was devoted to address the inconsistencies of the law of quasi-contracts. To quote an author, 'despite the silence of the *Projet de réforme*, interactions between unjustified enrichment and civil liability are numerous and complex'.[871] It will be up to the legal doctrine to fill this void in research in order to restore a coherent link between civil liability and unjust enrichment.

353. Given this context, the issue of disgorgement of illicit profits may provide the beginnings of an answer in that respect. Even though there is no general legal framework which enables the award of restitutory damages (*dommages-intérêts restitutoires*), this remedy is not completely unknown to French tort lawyers.[872] In the field of intellectual property, several provisions of the Intellectual Property Code allow the courts to include the 'profits' (*bénéfices*) made by the counterfactor in the calculation of damages awarded to the claimant.[873] In counterfeit cases, the court may also order the confiscation of all items realized or manufactured in breach of

869. For a recent comparative survey, *see* James Gordley, *Unjust Enrichment: a Comparative Perspective and a Critique*, in *Research Handbook on Unjust Enrichment and Restitution* (Elise Bant, Kit Barker & Simone Degeling eds, Edward Elgar 2020) 41; D Visser, *Unjustified Enrichment in Comparative Perspective*, in *The Oxford Handbook of Comparative Law* (Matthias Reimann & Reinhard Zimmermann eds, OUP 2d ed. 2019) 961.

870. For a recent presentation in English, *see* Mélodie Combot, *Unjustified Enrichment and Civil Liability*, in *French Civil Liability in Comparative Perspective* (J.-S. Borghetti & S. Whittaker eds, Hart 2019) 353, 356–358. *See* also the magisterial historical survey by Eric Descheemaeker, *Quasi-contrats et enrichissement injustifié en droit français*, RTD civ 2013, 1.

871. Combot, *supra* n. 870, at 374.

872. For a presentation in English, *see* Michel Séjean, *The Disgorgement of Illicit Profits in French Law*, in *Disgorgement of Profits* (Ewoud Hondius & André Janssen eds, Springer 2015) 121. *See* also in French Rodolphe Mésa, *L'opportune consécration d'un principe de restitution intégrale des profits illicites comme sanction des fautes lucratives*, D 2012, 2754.

873. Art. L 521-7, L 615-7, L 623-28, L 716-14 and L 722-6 Intellectual Property Code. On the assessment method applicable to intellectual property cases, *see* Guillaume Henry, *Les nouvelles méthodes d'évaluation du préjudice en matière de contrefaçon*, Contrats Concurrence Consommation 2009, étude 2; Camille Maréchal, *L'évaluation des dommages-intérêts en matière de contrefaçon*, RTD com 2012, 245.

the intellectual property rights and to their delivery to the claimant.[874] Other illustrations of a disgorgement of illicit profits can be found in press and media litigation. As noted,[875] it is common that French trial courts assess non-pecuniary loss for the infringement of personality rights (privacy, honour, etc.) by taking into account the profits made by the media operator.

354. Even though there is no shortage of examples, the concept of 'restitutionary damages' (*dommages-intérêts restitutoires*) has not been extensively investigated in French legal doctrine and, what is more, is often confused with the more controversial issue of punitive damages.[876]

§2. Injunctive Relief

355. As noted in the general introduction of this monograph,[877] one of the most disputed issues in the debate on tort law reform is the link between tort law and prohibitory injunctions (*actions en cessation de l'illicite*). Civil procedure rules already allow a claimant to request injunctive relief (*mesures conservatoires*) before the president of a *tribunal judiciaire* or a *tribunal de commerce* according to Articles 809(1) and 873(2) of the Civil Procedure Code.[878] There are numerous examples in various fields, such as neighbourhood disputes, unfair competition, labour law and environmental litigation.[879] Even though the request for injunctive relief is designed as an interlocutory procedure (*procédure de référé*), it is not necessary to establish any emergency nor is it subject to the absence of a serious challenge (*absence de contestation sérieuse*) of the claim. It comes, therefore, as no surprise that a certain 'substantialization trend' has been observed in this matter.[880]

356. Under these circumstances, some scholars have argued that the reform of civil liability rules should be an opportunity to integrate a legal framework on injunctive relief.[881] According to them, the functions of tort law are not restricted to the compensation of a harm that has already occurred but should also address situations in which an individual is facing a risk of imminent harm. In those cases, the

874. Art. L 331-1-3 Intellectual Property Code.
875. *See* paras 47, 320 above. *See* also Séjean, *Disgorgement*, *supra* n. 872, at 128–129.
876. On the resemblances between both concepts, *see* Philippe Pierre, *Les dommages et intérêts punitifs ou restitutoires (en droit français et européen)*, Revue juridique de l'Ouest 2014, 23. An author has suggested that the possibility of awarding restitutionary damages for breach of contract should be extended. *See* Jacquemin, *Payer*, *supra* n. 78, at paras 430–452.
877. *See* para. 47 above.
878. According to Art. 809(1) of the Civil Procedure Code, 'the president (of a *tribunal judiciaire*) may always, even where confronted with a serious challenge, order in a summary procedure such protective measures or measures to restore the parties to their previous state as required, either to avoid an imminent damage or to stop a manifestly unlawful nuisance'. On this provision, *see* in English Cumming, Spitz & Janal, *supra* n. 60, at 212–215.
879. For a list of examples, Bloch, *supra* n. 59, at paras 180–190.
880. Bloch, *supra* n. 59, at paras 196–206.
881. *See*, in particular, Bloch, *supra* n. 59. *See* also Cyril Sintez, *La sanction préventive en droit de la responsabilité civile* (Dalloz 2011).

2017 Reform Draft contains a suggestion to transform the existing interlocutory procedure (*procédure de référé*) into a tort law-related procedure available to all individuals confronted with the risk of imminent harm or exposed to unlawful nuisance (*trouble illicite*) which does not give rise to a tortious loss.[882] It is debatable to what extent this proposal would really make a difference and would lead to greater clarity and legal certainty.

§3. Punitive Damages

357. According to the principle of full compensation (*réparation intégrale*), which has already been mentioned,[883] French tort law does not recognize punitive damages. It is a well-established principle that damages in tort are intended 'to re-establish as exactly as possible the balance disturbed by the harm and to replace the victim in the situation in which he would have been if the harm had not occurred'.[884] An overcompensation of the claimant would be a derogation of the indemnity principle (*principe indemnitaire*) which is at the core of the French law of damages. Despite the strong attachment to the traditional vision of damages and a widespread fear of the excesses which would result from an Americanization of the French tort law system,[885] the idea of adapting damages to the gravity of fault is no longer a taboo subject. A thorough assessment of the case law reveals that there is already a disguised practice of punitive damages within the context of wilful violations of personality rights (e.g., through press, television or Internet). The Court of Cassation does not hesitate to confirm assessment methods used by the lower courts, taking into account the deliberate character of fault and the position of the tortfeasor.[886]

358. Nevertheless, over the past three decades, voices have been raised to criticize the general inability of French tort law to adequately respond to deliberate harmful conduct, considering that the gravity of fault should have an effect on the

882. Art. 1266 of the 2017 Draft provides that 'in extra-contractual matters, independently of any reparation of loss which may have been suffered, a court may prescribe reasonable measures appropriate to prevent harm or to see that an unlawful nuisance to which a claimant is exposed is stopped'. On this proposal, *see* Giliker, *Injunctions*, *supra* n. 680, at 377. *See* also van Boom, *supra* n. 61.
883. *See* paras 279–280 above.
884. *See,* for example, Cass Com, 10 January 2012, no. 10-26837. The formula is borrowed from Savatier, *supra* n. 46, at para. 601.
885. *See,* for example, Loïc Cadiet, *Le spectre de la société contentieuse*, in *Droit civil: procédure, linguistique, juridique. Mélanges écrits en hommage à Gérard Cornu* (PUF 1994) 29; François Terré, *L'américanisme et le droit français*, Philosophie politique 1995, no. 7, 137. *See* also Lambert-Faivre & Porchy-Simon, *supra* n. 696, at para. 35 (for the authors, 'the American example of punitive damages are one of the causes of the *dérive* of its tort law system').
886. *See* the examples cited by Lepage, *supra* n. 57, at paras 255–257.

assessment of damages. This is particularly discussed for so-called *fautes lucratives*, that is, deliberately committed fault for the purpose of making a gain or saving money. For some authors, the courts or legislator should put a more punitive spin on the rules of civil liability in order to strengthen the dissuasive dimension of the tort law system.[887]

359. A first step towards the recognition of punitive damages was taken when the Court of Cassation decided in 2010 to allow the enforcement of foreign punitive damage awards in France. In a landmark decision, the First Civil Chamber decided that 'an award of punitive damages is not, by itself, contrary to public policy' and that the enforcement of foreign judgments could only be denied 'when the amount awarded is disproportionate to the harm actually suffered and the breach of the debtor's contractual obligations'.[888] For most commentators, this new solution shows a growing acceptance of the foreign concept of 'over-compensatory damages',[889] even though the outcome of the proportionality test is difficult to predict and seems to resurrect the *révision au fond* doctrine that the Court of Cassation abandoned in 1964.[890]

360. Given this context, it came as no surprise when the 2017 Draft of the civil liability reform suggested the recognition of a so-called civil penalty (*amende civile*). According to Article 1266-1 of this text, 'in extra-contractual matters, where the author of the harm has deliberately committed a fault with the view to making a gain or to saving money, a court may, at the request of the victim or the *ministère public* and by specially justified decision, condemn him to the payment of a civil penalty'.[891] Although the principle of a civil penalty has met with approval of several legal scholars, it is fair to say that Article 1266-1 is probably the provision that raised the most serious reservations from a legal policy standpoint. In particular, the industry and insurance lobby is opposed to a measure seen as expensive and unpredictable. Tort law scholars have raised the concern that the text might even be

887. For an overview, *see* Viney, *Introduction*, *supra* n. 55, at paras 114–117. *See* also the reference work Galand-Carval, *supra* n. 56.
888. Civ 1, 1 December 2010, no. 09-13303 (*Fountaine Pajot* case).
889. For a survey on this case in English, *see* Benjamin Janke & François-Xavier Licari, *Enforcing Punitive Damage Awards in France after Fountaine Pajot*, 60 American Journal of Comparative Law 775 (2012); Cedric Vanleenhove, *The Current European Perspective on the Exequatur of U.S. Punitive Damages: Opening the Gate but Keeping a Guard*, 35 Polish Yearbook of International Law 235, 254–257 (2015) and *A Normative Framework for the Enforcement of U.S. Punitive Damages in the European Union: Transforming the Traditional '¡No Pasarán!'*, 41 Vermont Law Review 347, 365–369 (2016); Michel Cannarsa, *French Perspective on Punitive Damages*, 26 ERPL 661 (2018).
890. On the issue, *see* also Jonas Knetsch, *La réparation du dommage extracontractuel en droit international privé*, in *Mélanges en l'honneur du Professeur Bertrand Ancel* (LGDJ/Iprolex 2018) 979.
891. On this proposal, *see* the detailed presentation in English Capeletti, *supra* n. 58, at 343–349. *See* also Knetsch & Jacquemin, *ETL 2016 (2017)*, *supra* n. 45, at para. 19; *ETL 2017 (2018)*, *supra* n. 45, at para. 8. On previous proposals (*projet Terré*, *avant-projet Catala*), *see* Matthew Parker, *Changing Tides: The Introduction of Punitive Damages Into the French Legal System*, 41 Georgia Journal of International and Comparative Law 389 (2013); Solène Rowan, *Comparative Observations on the Introduction of Punitive Damages in French Law*, in *Reforming the French Law of Obligations* (John Cartwright, Stefan Vogenauer & Simon Whittaker eds, Hart 2009) 325.

unconstitutional as the principle of *ne bis in idem* could be infringed by the mere possibility of awarding a civil penalty along with a criminal sanction.[892]

892. *See,* for example, Nicolas Rias, *L'amende civile: une fausse bonne idée?*, D 2016, 2072; Emmanuel Dreyer, *L'amende civile concurrente de l'amende pénale?*, JCP E 2017, no. 25, 1344; Johan Prorok, *L'amende civile dans la réforme de la responsabilité civile*, RTD civ 2018, 327; F Graziani, *La généralisation de l'amende civile: entre progrès et confusions*, D 2018, 428.

Selected Bibliography

General Works on French Law (in English language)

Contemporary Works

John Bell, *French Legal Cultures* (CUP 2001, reprint 2008).

John Bell, Sophie Boyron & Simon Whittaker (eds), *Principles on French Law* (OUP 2d ed. 2008).

George A. Bermann & Étienne Picard (eds), *Introduction to French Law* (Wolters Kluwer 2008).

Catherine Elliott, Catherine Vernon & Éric Jeanpierre, *French Legal System* (Pearson Longman 2d ed. 2006).

Eva Steiner, *French Law: A Comparative Approach* (OUP 2d ed. 2018).

Older Works

Maurice Amos & Frederick Walton, *An Introduction to French Law* (Clarendon Press 3d ed. 1967 by F. H. Lawson, A. E. Anton & L. Neville Brown) [chapter on tort law 199–238].

Walter Cairns & Robert McKeon, *Introduction to French Law* (Cavendish 1995).

Christian Dadomo & Susan Farran, *The French Legal System* (Sweet & Maxwell 2d ed. 1996).

René David, *French Law. Its Structure, Sources, and Methodology* (Louisiana State University Press 1972).

René David & Henry P. de Vries, *The French Legal System: An Introduction to Civil Law System* (Oceana Publications 1958).

Brice Dickson, *Introduction to French Law* (Pitman 1994) [chapter on tort law 154–165].

Otto Kahn-Freund, Claudine Lévy & Bernard Rudden, *A Source-Book on French Law. Public Law: Constitutional and Administrative Law. Private Law: Structure, Contract* (Clarendon Press 3d ed. 1991).

David Pollard, *Sourcebook on French Law* (Cavendish 2d ed. 1998).

Andrew West, Yvon Desdevises, Alain Fenet, Dominique Faurier, Marie-Clet Heussaff & Bruno Lévy, *The French Legal System* (Butterworths 2d ed. 1998).

Martin Weston, *An English Reader's Guide to the French Legal System* (Berg 1996).

Selected Bibliography

French Legal Sources on the Internet

Non-commercial Sites

Légifrance (official website of the French government for legal publication; English translations partly available)
http://www.legifrance.gouv.fr
Court of Cassation (official website)
http://www.courdecassation.fr

Commercial Sites

Dalloz (online service of the legal editor Dalloz)
http://www.dalloz.fr/
Doctrinal Plus (bibliographical database of more than 550 000 doctrinal references)
http://www.doctrinalplus.fr/
Lamyline (online service of the legal editor Lamy)
http://www.lamyline.fr/
Lexis360 (online service of the legal editor LexisNexis France)
http://www.lexis360.fr/
Lextenso (online service of the legal editor LGDJ)
http://www.labase-lextenso.fr

General Works on French Tort Law

In English Language

Richard Azarnia, *Tort Law in France: A Cultural and Comparative Overview*, 13 Wisconsin International Law Journal 471–492 (1994).

Jean-Sébastien Borghetti, *The Culture of Tort Law in France*, 3 JETL 158–182 (2013).

Jean-Sébastien Borghetti & Simon Whittaker (eds), *French Civil Liability in Comparative Perspective* (Hart 2019).

Philippe Brun & Christophe Quézel-Ambrunaz, *French Tort Law Facing Reform*, 4 JETL 78–94 (2013).

John Cartwright, Stefan Vogenauer & Simon Whittaker (eds), *Reforming the Law of Obligations* (Hart 2009) [four contributions on tort law 271–344].

Pierre Catala & John Anthony Weir, *Delict and Torts: A Study in Parallel (Parts I to IV)*, 37 Tulane Law Review 574–620 (1963); 38 Tulane Law Review 221–278, 664–716 (1964); 39 Tulane Law Review 701–783 (1965).

Chantal Mahé, *Re-codification Attempts of French Tort Law: Traditional and Comparative Arguments in the Terré Tort Draft*, in *Tradition, Codification and Unification: Historical-Comparative Essays* 207–231 (J. Michael Milo, Jan H.A. Lokin & Jan M. Smits eds, Intersentia 2013).

Olivier Moréteau, *The Draft Reforms of French Tort Law in the Light of European Harmonization*, in *Festschrift für Ulrich Magnus* 77–92 (Peter Mankowski & Wolfgang Wurmnest eds, Verlag Otto Schmidt 2012).

Olivier Moréteau, *French Tort Law in the Light of European Harmonization*, 6 Journal of Civil Law Studies 759–801 (2013).

Olivier Moréteau, *Basic Questions of Tort Law from a French Perspective*, in *Basic Questions of Tort Law from a Comparative Perspective* 3–95 (Helmut Koziol ed., Jan Sramek Verlag 2015).

Eva Steiner, *French Law: A Comparative Approach* (OUP 2d ed. 2018) 250–280.

André Tunc, *A Codified Law of Tort – The French Experience*, 39 Louisiana Law Review 1051–1075 (1979).

Simon Whittaker, *The Law of Delict*, in *Principles on French Law* 360–417 (John Bell, Sophie Boyron & Simon Whittaker eds, OUP 2d ed. 2008).

Contributions on French law in *European Tort Law Yearbook* (Springer, 2001–2009; de Gruyter 2010–).

In French Language (Treatises and Standard Textbooks)

Mireille Bacache-Gibeili, *Les obligations: La responsabilité civile extracontractuelle* (Economica 3d ed. 2016).

Philippe Brun, *La responsabilité civile extracontractuelle* (LexisNexis 5th ed. 2018).

Muriel Fabre-Magnan, *Droit des obligations*, vol 2 *Responsabilité civile et quasi contrat* (PUF 5th ed. 2021).

Jacques Flour, Jean-Louis Aubert & Éric Savaux, *Droit civil : Les obligations*, vol 2 *Le fait juridique* (Sirey 14th ed. 2011).

Yvonne Lambert-Faivre & Stéphanie Porchy-Simon, *Droit du dommage corporel : Systèmes d'indemnisation* (Dalloz 8th ed. 2015).

Philippe le Tourneau (ed.), *Droit de la responsabilité et des contrats : Régimes d'indemnisation 2018–2019* (Dalloz 12th ed. 2020).

Philippe Malaurie, Laurent Aynès & Philippe Stoffel-Munck, *Droit civil. Les obligations* 21–192 (LGDJ 11th ed. 2020).

François Terré, Philippe Simler, Yves Lequette & François Chénedé, *Droit civil: Les obligations* 969–1328 (Dalloz 12th ed. 2018).

Geneviève Viney, *Introduction à la responsabilité* (LGDJ 4th ed. 2019).

Geneviève Viney, Patrice Jourdain & Suzanne Carval, *Les conditions de la responsabilité* (LGDJ 4th ed. 2013).

Geneviève Viney, Patrice Jourdain & Suzanne Carval, *Les régimes spéciaux et l'assurance de responsabilité* (LGDJ 4th ed. 2017).

Geneviève Viney, Patrice Jourdain & Suzanne Carval, *Les effets de la responsabilité* (LGDJ 4th ed. 2017).

Part I

Bernadette Auzary-Schmaltz, *Liability in Tort in France before the Code Civil: The Origins of Art. 1382 ff. Code Civil*, in *Negligence: The Comparative Legal History of the Law of Torts* 309–340 (Eltjo J.H. Schrage ed., Duncker & Humblot 2001).

John Bell, *The Reform of Delict in the Civil Code and Liability in Administrative Law*, in *French Civil Liability in Comparative Perspective* 425–443 (Jean-Sébastien Borghetti & Simon Whittaker eds, Hart 2019).

Jean-Sébastien Borghetti, *The Definition of* la faute *in the* Avant-projet de réforme, in *Reforming the French Law of Obligations* 271–288 (John Cartwright, Stefan Vogenauer & Simon Whittaker eds, Hart 2009).

Selected Bibliography

Jean-Sébastien Borghetti, *The Effects of Contracts and Third Parties*, in *The Code Napoléon Rewritten: French Contract Law after the 2016 Reforms* 227–253 (Jean-Sébastien Borghetti & Simon Whittaker eds, Hart 2017).

Marie Dugué, *The Definition of Civil Fault*, in *French Civil Liability in Comparative Perspective* 79–97 (Jean-Sébastien Borghetti & Simon Whittaker eds, Hart 2019).

Duncan Fairgrieve & François Lichère, *France*, in *The Liability of Public Authorities in Comparative Perspective* 155–175 (Ken Oliphant ed., Intersentia 2017).

Paula Giliker, *The Role of* la faute *in the* Avant-projet de réforme, in *Reforming the French Law of Obligations* 289–302 (John Cartwright, Stefan Vogenauer & Simon Whittaker eds, Hart 2009).

Jonas Knetsch, *Compensation Funds in France and Germany*, in *Compensation Funds in Comparative Perspective* 45–65 (Thierry Vansweevelt & Britt Weyts eds, Intersentia 2020).

Cristina Mauro, *France*, in *Directors' Personal Liability for Corporate Fault: A Comparative Analysis* 139–158 (Helen Anderson ed., Wolters Kluwer 2008).

Vernon V. Palmer, *A Comparative Study (from a Common Law Perspective) of the French Action for Wrongful Interference with Contract*, 40 American Journal of Comparative Law 297–342 (1992).

Christophe Quézel-Ambrunaz, *Fault, Damage and the Equivalence Principle in French Law*, 3 JETL 21–43 (2012).

Simon Taylor, *Medical Accident Liability and Redress in English and French Law* (CUP 2015).

André Tunc, *The French Concept of* abus de droit, in *The Cambridge Lectures 1981* 151–160 (Nancy E. Eastman & Boris Krivy eds, Butterworths 1981).

Part II

Laurence Francoz-Terminal, Fabien Lafay, Olivier Moréteau & Caroline Pellerin-Rugliano, *Children as Tortfeasors under French Law*, in *Children in Tort Law vol 1* 169–215 (Miquel Martín-Casals ed., Springer 2006).

Paula Giliker, *Vicarious Liability in Tort: A Comparative Perspective* (CUP 2010).

Birke Häcker, Fait d'autrui *in Comparative Perspective*, in *French Civil Liability in Comparative Perspective* 143–177 (Jean-Sébastien Borghetti & Simon Whittaker eds, Hart 2019).

Part III

Jean-Sébastien Borghetti, *Causation in Hepatitis B Vaccination Litigation in France: Breaking through Scientific Uncertainty?*, 91 Chicago-Kent Law Review 543–566 (2016).

Jean-Sébastien Borghetti, *Product Liability in France*, in *European Product Liability* 205–236 (Piotr Machnikowski ed., Intersentia 2016).

Jean-Sébastien Borghetti, *Extra-Strict Liability for Traffic Accidents in France*, 53 Wake Forrest Law Review 265–292 (2018).

Jean-Sébastien Borghetti, *Liability for False Information in French Law: The Limits of Civil Law*, in *Tatsachenmitteilungen und Werturteile: Freiheit und Verantwortung* 133–145 (Helmut Koziol ed., Jan Sramek Verlag 2018).

Duncan Fairgrieve, L'exception française? *The French Law of Product Liability*, in *Product Liability in Comparative Perspective* 84–99 (Duncan Fairgrieve ed., CUP 2005).

Julie Foulon, *Recent Developments in French Environmental Law: Recognition and Implementation of Ecological Damage in French Tort Law*, 21 Environmental Law Review 309–317 (2019).

Ciara Kennefick, *Nuisance and Coming to the Nuisance. The Porous Boundary between Torts and Servitudes in England and France*, in *French Civil Liability in Comparative Perspective* 223–244 (Jean-Sébastien Borghetti & Simon Whittaker eds, Hart 2019)

Jonas Knetsch, *The Role of Liability Without Fault*, in *French Civil Liability in Comparative Perspective* 123–142 (Jean-Sébastien Borghetti & Simon Whittaker eds, Hart 2019).

Ruth Redmond-Cooper, *The Relevance of Fault in Determining Liability for Road Accidents: The French Experience*, 38 ICLQ 502–521 (1989).

Simon Taylor, *Harmonisation or Divergence? A Comparison of French and English Product Liability Rules*, in *Product Liability in Comparative Perspective* 221–243 (D. Fairgrieve ed., CUP 2005).

Simon Taylor, *Extending the Boundaries of Tort Law: Ecological Harm in the French Civil Code*, 9 JETL 81–103 (2018).

Simon Taylor, Duncan Fairgrieve & Véronique Wester-Ouisse, *Medical Accidents and Pharmaceutical Product Liability in France*, in *Regulating Risk through Private Law* 301–322 (Matthew Dyson ed., Intersentia 2018).

Edward A. Tomlinson, *Tort Liability in France for the Act of Things: A Study of Judicial Lawmaking*, 48 Louisiana Law Review 1299–1367 (1988).

André Tunc, *Traffic Accidents Compensation under Tort Law and under a Specific Law: The French Experience*, in *The Law of Obligations: Essays in Celebration of John Fleming* 363–376 (Peter Cane & Jane Stapleton eds, Clarendon Press 1998).

Simon Whittaker, *Liability for Products. English Law, French Law and European Harmonization* (OUP 2005).

Part IV

Jean-Sébastien Borghetti, *Prescription in Tort Law*, in *Prescription in Tort Law* 309–338 (Israel Gilead & Bjarte Askeland eds, Intersentia 2020).

Zoé Jacquemin, *Contracts Concerning Civil Liability*, in *French Civil Liability in Comparative Perspective* 309–326 (Jean-Sébastien Borghetti & Simon Whittaker eds, Hart 2019).

Sandy Steel, *Defences to Tortious and Contractual Liability in French Law*, in *French Civil Liability in Comparative Perspective* 285–307 (Jean-Sébastien Borghetti & Simon Whittaker eds, Hart 2019).

Robert Wintgen & John Cartwright, *Reforming the French Law of Prescription: A French Perspective and an English Perspective*, in *Reforming the French Law of Obligations* 347–380 (John Cartwright, Stefan Vogenauer & Simon Whittaker eds, Hart 2009).

Selected Bibliography

Part V

Duncan Fairgrieve & Florence G'sell-Macrez, *Causation in French Law: Pragmatism and Policy*, in *Perspectives on Causation* 111–129 (Richard Goldberg ed., Hart 2011).

Florence G'sell, *Alternative Causation under French Law*, 25 ERPL 1109–1116 (2018).

Lara Khoury, *Uncertain Causation in Medical Liability* (Hart 2006).

Carlos Gómez Ligüerre, *'Solidary' Liability and the Channelling of Liability*, in *French Civil Liability in Comparative Perspective* 263–282 (Jean-Sébastien Borghetti & Simon Whittaker eds, Hart 2019).

Olivier Moréteau, *Causal Uncertainty and Proportional Liability in France*, in *Proportional Liability: Analytical and Comparative Perspectives* 141–152 (Israel Gilead, Michael D. Green & Bernhard Koch eds, de Gruyter 2013).

Nuno Manuel Pinto Oliveira, *Liability for Alternative Causation and for the Loss of a Chance*, in *French Civil Liability in Comparative Perspective* 247–261 (Jean-Sébastien Borghetti & Simon Whittaker eds, Hart 2019).

Part VI

Maria José Azar-Baud & Alexandre Biard, *The Dawn of Collective Redress 3.0 in France?*, in *Class Actions in Europe: Holy Grail or a Wrong Trail?* (Alan Uzelac & Stefaan Voet eds, Springer 2021) forthcoming.

Michel Cannarsa, *Personal Injury in France*, in *Personal Injury Compensation in Europe* 169–206 (Marco Bona & Philip Mead eds, Kluwer International 2003).

Marco Capeletti, *Comparative Reflections on Punishment in Tort Law*, in *French Civil Liability in Comparative Perspective* 329–351 (Jean-Sébastien Borghetti & Simon Whittaker eds, Hart 2019).

Mélodie Combot, *Unjustified Enrichment and Civil Liability*, in *French Civil Liability in Comparative Perspective* 353–375 (Jean-Sébastien Borghetti & Simon Whittaker eds, Hart 2019).

Yvon Desdevises & Anne-Laure Villedieu, *France*, in *The Costs and Funding of Civil Litigation: A Comparative Perspective* 327–348 (Christopher Hodges, Stefan Vogenauer & Magdalena Tulbiacka eds, Hart 2010).

Paula Giliker, *Injunctions Requiring the Cessation of Unlawful Action*, in *French Civil Liability in Comparative Perspective* 377–394 (Jean-Sébastien Borghetti & Simon Whittaker eds, Hart 2019).

Dorota Leczykiewicz, *Loss and Its Compensation in the Proposed New French Regime of Extra-contractual Liability*, in *French Civil Liability in Comparative Perspective* 181–204 (Jean-Sébastien Borghetti & Simon Whittaker eds, Hart 2019).

Vernon V. Palmer, *The French Awakening in the Nineteenth Century*, in *The Recovery of Non-Pecuniary Loss in European Contract Law* 58–76 (Vernon V. Palmer ed., CUP 2015).

Solène Rowan, *Comparative Observations on the Introduction of Punitive Damages in French Law*, in *Reforming the French Law of Obligations* 325–344 (John Cartwright, Stefan Vogenauer & Simon Whittaker eds, Hart 2009).

Michel Séjean, *The Disgorgement of Illicit Profits in French Law*, in *Disgorgement of Profits* 121–137 (Ewoud Hondius & André Janssen eds, Springer 2015).

Pietro Sirena, *The Concepts of 'Harm' in the French and Italian Laws of Civil Liability*, in *French Civil Liability in Comparative Perspective* 205–221 (Jean-Sébastien Borghetti & Simon Whittaker eds, Hart 2019).

Selected Bibliography

Index

The numbers here refer to paragraph numbers.

Index

Index

Index

www.ingramcontent.com/pod-product-compliance
Lightning Source LLC
Chambersburg PA
CBHW071445230926
51846CB00001B/343
9789403535746